Checks and Balances

The Three Branches of the American Government

volume **3**

Checks and Balances

judicial

The Three Branches of
the American Government

Daniel E. Brannen Jr.

Lawrence W. Baker, *Project Editor*

U·X·L
*An imprint of Thomson Gale,
a part of The Thomson Corporation*

THOMSON

GALE

Detroit • New York • San Francisco • San Diego • New Haven, Conn. • Waterville, Maine • London • Munich

Checks and Balances:
The Three Branches of the American Government

Daniel E. Brannen Jr.

Project Editor
Lawrence W. Baker

Editorial
Michael Lesniak

Rights Acquisition and Management
Jacqueline Key, Ronald Montgomery,
Sheila Spencer

Imaging and Multimedia
Randy Bassett, Lezlie Light, Denay
Wilding

Product Design
Kate Scheible

Composition and Electronic Prepress
Evi Seoud

Manufacturing
Rita Wimberley

LIBRARY OF CONGRESS CATALOGING-IN-PUBLICATION DATA

Brannen, Daniel E., 1968–
  Checks and balances : the three branches of the American government / Daniel E. Brannen, Jr. ; Lawrence W. Baker, project editor.
    p. cm.
  Includes bibliographical references and index.
  ISBN 0-7876-5409-4 (set hardcover : alk. paper) — ISBN 0-7876-5410-8 (v. 1) — ISBN 0-7876-5411-6 (v. 2) — ISBN 0-7876-5412-4 (v. 3)
    1. United States—Politics and government. I. Baker, Lawrence W. II. Title.
  JK271.B6496 2005
  320.473—dc22
                                                                              2005009975

This title is also available as an e-book.
ISBN 1-4144-0468-9
Contact your Thomson Gale sales representative for ordering information.

Printed in the United States of America
10 9 8 7 6 5 4 3 2 1

Contents

Reader's Guide **vii**

Timeline of Events **ix**

Words to Know **xxvii**

volume 1 **executive branch**

1: American Government: An Overview **1**

2: Historic Roots of the Executive Branch **19**

3: Constitutional Role of the Executive Branch **37**

4: Changes in the Executive Branch **61**

5: Key Positions in the Executive Branch **89**

6: Daily Operations of the Executive Branch **113**

7: Executive-Legislative Checks and Balances **131**

8: Executive-Judicial Checks and Balances **159**

volume 2 **legislative branch**

1: American Government: An Overview **179**

2: Historic Roots of the Legislative Branch **197**

3: Constitutional Role of the Legislative Branch **217**

4: Changes in the Legislative Branch **239**

5: Key Positions in the Legislative Branch **265**

6: Daily Operations of the Legislative Branch **283**

7: Legislative-Executive Checks and Balances **309**

8: Legislative-Judicial Checks and Balances **337**

volume 3 judicial branch

1: American Government: An Overview **359**

2: Historic Roots of the Judicial Branch **379**

3: Constitutional Role of the Judicial Branch **395**

4: Changes in the Judicial Branch **415**

5: Key Positions in the Judicial Branch **435**

6: Daily Operations of the Judicial Branch **455**

7: Judicial-Executive Checks and Balances **473**

8: Judicial-Legislative Checks and Balances **493**

Appendix: Constitution of the United States of America; Constitutional Amendments **xxxvii**

Where to Learn More **lxi**

Index **lxv**

Reader's Guide

Checks and Balances: The Three Branches of the American Government offers relevant, easy-to-understand information on the inner workings of the American federal government, from its earliest beginnings to its current structure. The eight chapters of each volume focus on the American government and a particular branch: Volume 1, executive; Volume 2, legislative; and Volume 3, judicial. The first chapter of each volume begins with an identical overview of the American government. The other seven chapters focus on the following aspects of the specific branch:

★ Historic roots

★ Constitutional role

★ Changes through the years

★ Key positions

★ Daily operations

★ Checks and balances with each of the other two branches (two chapters)

Each of the "checks and balances" chapters appears twice in the set. For instance, the "Executive-Legislative Checks and Balances" chapter in the executive branch volume is duplicated as the "Legislative-Executive Checks and Balances" chapter in the legislative branch volume. Illustrations and sidebars vary in those chapters, however.

All chapters include "Words to Know" boxes that provide definitions of important words and concepts within the text. Other sidebars highlight significant facts and describe other related governmental information. A timeline of events, a general glossary, reprints of the U.S. Constitution and the Constitutional Amendments, a general bibliography, and a cumulative index are included in each volume. Approximately 150 black-and-white photos help illustrate *Checks and Balances*.

Acknowledgments

Many thanks go to copyeditor Rebecca Valentine, proofreader Amy Marcaccio Keyzer, indexer Dan Brannen, and the folks at Integra Software Services for their fine work.

Comments and suggestions

We welcome your comments on *Checks and Balances* and suggestions for other topics to consider. Please write: Editors, *Checks and Balances,* UXL, 27500 Drake Rd., Farmington Hills, Michigan 48331-3535; call toll free: 800-877-4253; fax to 248-699-8097; or send e-mail via http://www.gale.com.

Timeline of
Events

6th century • Emperor Justinian I of the Byzantine Empire oversees the compilation of the *Corpus Juris Civilis,* or Body of Civil Law. This enormous collection and organization of the laws and legal opinions from emperors and jurists of the Roman Empire affects the development of legal systems in Europe after the Dark Ages (476–1000), and eventually affects the development of American legal systems.

1100s–1200s • England establishes three permanent courts to hear cases that affect the interests of the monarch. The courts, called superior common law courts, influence the development of law in America.

June 1215 • King John of England signs the Magna Carta, a document that proclaims and protects the political and civil liberties of English citizens.

1300s • Political philosopher Niccolò Machiavelli writes *Discourses on the First Ten Books of Titus Livius.* Machiavelli champions the Roman Republic system of government, which influences the convention delegates in Philadelphia, Pennsylvania, nearly five hundred years later.

1648 • British Parliament member Clement Walker writes of a British government that divides its power into three branches.

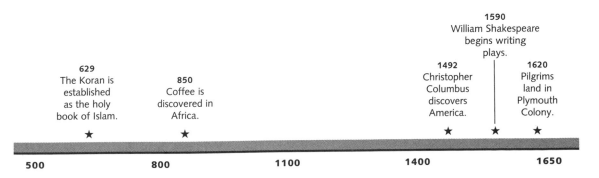

				1590 William Shakespeare begins writing plays.	
	629 The Koran is established as the holy book of Islam.	850 Coffee is discovered in Africa.		1492 Christopher Columbus discovers America.	1620 Pilgrims land in Plymouth Colony.
500	800	1100	1400		1650

1689 • British Parliament adopts the English Bill of Rights, strengthening Parliament's power in the constitutional monarchy.

1689 • English philosopher John Locke publishes *Two Treatises of Government.* In it, he argues that the legislative branch of government should be separate from the executive branch.

1696 • British Parliament establishes the Board of Trade to oversee Great Britain's commercial interests worldwide. The Board of Trade has the power to review and strike down colonial laws that violate British law. In this way, the Board of Trade resembles the U.S. Supreme Court.

1748 • French philosopher Charles Montesquieu publishes *The Spirit of Laws,* influencing the authors of the U.S. Constitution four decades later.

1765–69 • English legal scholar Sir William Blackstone publishes *Commentaries on the Laws of England,* a thorough description of English law at the time. In it, he celebrates the checks and balances of the British system. Most of the men who write the U.S. Constitution two decades later were familiar with Blackstone's work.

1773 • American colonists express their displeasure over taxes by dumping tea into the harbor during the famous Boston Tea Party.

1774 • The thirteen American colonies first send delegates to the Continental Congress.

1775 • The American Revolutionary War begins.

1776 • Revolutionary figure Thomas Paine criticizes the British system of checks and balances in his pamphlet *Common Sense.*

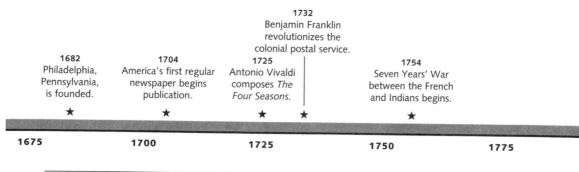

1732
Benjamin Franklin
revolutionizes the
colonial postal service.

1682
Philadelphia,
Pennsylvania,
is founded.

1704
America's first regular
newspaper begins
publication.

1725
Antonio Vivaldi
composes *The
Four Seasons.*

1754
Seven Years' War
between the French
and Indians begins.

★   ★   ★   ★   ★

1675   1700   1725   1750   1775

July 1776 • The United States of America is born when representatives from the thirteen American colonies join together to break from English rule by signing the Declaration of Independence.

1777 • Delegates serving in the Continental Congress write the Articles of Confederation, one year after America declared independence from Great Britain.

1777 • Pennsylvania physician and political leader Benjamin Rush publishes *Observations on the Government of Pennsylvania*, in which he alludes to a checks and balances form of government. He supports men of moderate wealth having representation in one chamber and men of great wealth having representation in another chamber.

1781 • The states adopt a new form of government with the Articles of Confederation. The articles provide for only a Congress, with no president or judiciary.

1783 • The American Revolutionary War ends.

1786 • Farmers protest debtor laws in Massachusetts in Shays's Rebellion.

1787 • Fifty-five state delegates meet at the Constitutional Convention to frame a Constitution for a federal government.

1787 • In the draft of the Constitution, delegates James Madison and Elbridge Gerry suggest changing Congress's power to "make war" to "declare war."

1787 • The Constitution is presented to the states for approval.

May–June 1787 • Virginia delegate Edmund Randolph proposes that the free men of the states elect members to the

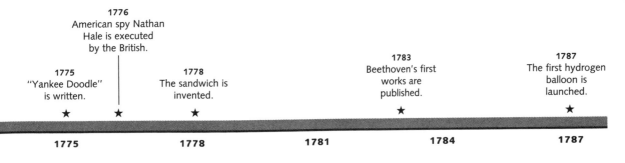

1776
American spy Nathan
Hale is executed
by the British.

1775
"Yankee Doodle"
is written.

1778
The sandwich is
invented.

1783
Beethoven's first
works are
published.

1787
The first hydrogen
balloon is
launched.

★   ★   ★   ★   ★

1775   **1778**   **1781**   **1784**   **1787**

House of Representatives. In turn, members of the House would choose the members of the Senate from nominations made by the state legislatures. Most of the large states, however, want free men to control elections to Congress. They also want state population to be the basis for determining how many members each state would have in each chamber. Most of the small states want at least one chamber of Congress to be elected by the states, and they want that chamber to provide equal representation to each state. A set of compromises leads to the delegates agreeing that free men will elect the members of the House and state legislatures will elect the members of the Senate; also, representation in the House will be based on population, while representation in the Senate will be equal for each state.

1787–88 • New York politician Alexander Hamilton and Secretary of Foreign Affairs John Jay write a series of essays called "The Federalist," an attempt to convince Americans to adopt the U.S. Constitution.

1788 • Virginia delegate and future U.S. president James Monroe writes *Observations upon the Proposed Plan of Federal Government*, in which he states that a preamble would be an important part of the Constitution.

June 1788 • The Constitution becomes law in the United States following ratification.

1789 • The new federal government begins to operate under the Constitution, with George Washington as the country's first president.

1789 • The Judiciary Act of 1789 creates a federal judiciary with trial courts (district and circuit courts) and appellate courts to serve under the Supreme Court, as well as the position of attorney general, who is the lead attorney for the United States, and U.S. attorneys to assist the attorney general with the government's caseload. Congress sets the number of

1787
The dollar currency is introduced in the United States.
★

1788
New York City becomes the temporary U.S. capital.
★

1789
The U.S. Army is established.
★

1787   **1788**   **1789**

Supreme Court justices at six, a number that is raised and lowered seven times until 1869, when it settles on nine justices.

1789 • Congress creates four departments to oversee certain aspects of the government: State, Treasury, War, and Navy.

1789 • President George Washington signs the first appropriations law for the United States. He approves of $568,000 to fund the Departments of War and Treasury, as well as to fund government salaries and pensions.

January 1790 • President George Washington delivers the nation's first annual message, as required by the Constitution.

1790 • Maryland donates land to the U.S. government to be used as the location for the federal capital. The new city is called Washington, D.C., or the District of Columbia.

1791 • The states approve the first ten constitutional amendments, often called the Bill of Rights.

1794 • President George Washington helps end the Whiskey Rebellion by granting a full pardon to rebels involved in the skirmish. The rebellion was a protest by grain farmers against a tax on whiskey.

1797 • The House of Representatives impeaches U.S. senator William Blount of Tennessee, the only time in U.S. history a member of Congress has been impeached. Blount is accused of conspiring to conduct military activities for the king of England; the Senate opts not to conduct an impeachment trial, reasoning that it does not have power under the Constitution to conduct an impeachment trial of a senator.

1798 • Congress passes and President John Adams signs into law the Sedition Act. The new law makes it a crime to say or write anything "false, scandalous and malicious" against the government.

1792	1794	1796
Farmer's Almanac is first published.	The cotton gin is patented.	Edward Jenner introduces the smallpox vaccination.
★	★	★

1789	1792	1794	1796	1798

1798 • The Eleventh Amendment is officially declared part of the Constitution, nearly three years after it was ratified. The amendment decrees that a citizen of one state (or foreign country) may not use the federal court system to sue the government of another state.

1800 • Congress creates the Library of Congress; one year later, it receives its first collection of materials.

1800 • Vice President Thomas Jefferson and New York politician Aaron Burr receive the same number of electoral votes in the presidential election, forcing the House of Representatives to break the tie vote, as required by the Constitution (even though the electors clearly intended Jefferson to be president and Burr to be vice president). Jefferson wins on the thirty-sixth ballot.

1801 • President Thomas Jefferson begins the tradition of delivering his messages to Congress in written form. This form of communication between president and Congress continues for 112 years.

1801 • President Thomas Jefferson repeals the Sedition Act.

1801 • The Federalist-controlled Congress lowers the number of Supreme Court seats from six to five so that the new president, Democratic-Republican Thomas Jefferson, would be unable to appoint a replacement if Justice William Cushing, who was ill at the time, died.

1802 • The Democratic-Republican Party gains control of Congress, and raises the number of justices back to six.

1802 • Congress assigns one Supreme Court justice to travel to each circuit to hear trials.

1803 • In *Marbury v. Madison,* the U.S. Supreme Court rules that a federal law giving the Supreme Court the power to hear cases for compelling government action is unconstitutional.

1799 The Rosetta Stone is found in Egypt.	1800 John Adams is the first president to live in the White House.	1803 The United States nearly doubles, following the Louisiana Purchase.
★	★	★

1798	1799	1800	1801	1803

Under the Constitution, such cases must begin in a lower federal court, with the Supreme Court permitted to review them only on appeal.

1803 • Federal district court judge John Pickering is the first judge to be impeached. He is convicted of drunkenness and removed from office.

1803 • Judicial review becomes a permanent part of the federal judiciary after the U.S. Supreme Court announces its power to strike down congressional laws that violate the U.S. Constitution.

1804 • The House of Representatives impeaches Supreme Court justice Samuel Chase; the Senate, however, votes not to convict him.

1804 • The Twelfth Amendment to the Constitution is adopted, requiring that electors label their two votes: one for president and the other for vice president. Previously, electors voted for their top two choices, with the leading vote-getter becoming president and the runner-up being elected vice president. In 1800, this flawed system resulted in a tie vote between two members of the same party.

1812 • Congress uses its constitutional right by declaring war (the War of 1812).

1824 • None of the presidential candidates receives a majority of electoral votes, forcing the U.S. House of Representatives to choose between the leading three vote-getters. Secretary of State John Quincy Adams wins the election after the candidate who was no longer eligible, Speaker of the House Henry Clay, convinces the states that had voted for him to support Adams. Later, Clay becomes Adams's secretary of state, leading many to believe that Adams had promised Clay the position in exchange for his votes.

1804 Napoléon Bonaparte is crowned emperor of France.	1806 Webster's Dictionary is first published.	1814 Francis Scott Key writes the "Star Spangled Banner."	1825 The New York Stock Exchange opens.	1834 The Braille system for the blind is invented.
★	★	★	★	★
1803	1810	1817	1824	1837

April 1841 • President William Henry Harrison dies after only a month in office. His vice president, John Tyler, insists that the Constitution allows him to fill the office of the presidency for the remainder of Harrison's term. Evidence to the contrary does not exist, so Tyler stays on as president, establishing a line-of-succession tradition.

1846 • Congress uses its constitutional right by declaring war (the Mexican War).

1857 • In *Scott v. Sandford*, the U.S. Supreme Court rules that former slave Dred Scott is not a citizen of the United States because African Americans could not be citizens under the U.S. Constitution.

1860 • Congress creates the Government Printing Office, which serves as a printer for Congress and collects and publishes information about the federal government for all three of its branches.

1861 • The American Civil War begins.

1862 • U.S. district judge West H. Humphreys of Tennessee is impeached by the U.S. House of Representatives and removed by the Senate, on charges of joining the Confederacy without resigning his judgeship.

1862 • President Abraham Lincoln creates the U.S. Department of Agriculture.

1863 • Congress raises the number of justices on the U.S. Supreme Court to ten. This allows President Abraham Lincoln to appoint a new justice at a time when he is stretching his constitutional powers to conduct the American Civil War.

1865 • The Thirteenth Amendment bans slavery.

1865 • The American Civil War ends.

1844 Samuel F. B. Morse transmits the first telegraph message.	1852 The Otis safety elevator is invented.	1856 Neanderthal man fossils are found.	1862 Jefferson Davis becomes president of the Confederacy.	1865 President Abraham Lincoln is assassinated.
★	★	★	★	★

1841	1847	1853	1859	1865

1866 • Congress reduces the number of U.S. Supreme Court seats from ten to seven. Congress fears that President Andrew Johnson, who is against many of Congress's Reconstruction Acts for rebuilding the country after the American Civil War, will appoint justices who will strike down the acts as unconstitutional.

1868 • The states adopt the Fourteenth Amendment, which declares that all people born or naturalized in the United States are citizens of the country and of the state in which they live.

1868 • Andrew Johnson is the first U.S. president to be impeached. He escapes removal from office by a single vote in the U.S. Senate.

1869 • Congress raises the number of Supreme Court seats from seven to nine, shortly after the inauguration of Ulysses S. Grant. The number has been fixed there ever since.

1870 • The Fifteenth Amendment makes it illegal to deny a person the right to vote based on race or color.

1870 • The attorney general becomes head of the U.S. Department of Justice.

1873 • England combines common law and equity courts into one court. U.S. federal courts would later do the same thing.

1875 • Congress passes the Civil Rights Act of 1875, making discrimination illegal in places of public accommodation, such as inns and theaters.

1875 • Congress reorganizes the judiciary by passing the Judiciary Act of 1875. It shifts some kinds of trials from the circuit courts to the district courts and gives the circuit courts more responsibility for hearing appeals.

1866 The first U.S. oil pipeline is completed.	1868 Louisa May Alcott publishes *Little Women*.	1870 The first African American congressmen take office.	1874 The first American zoo opens in Philadelphia.	1876 Alexander Graham Bell invents the telephone.
★	★	★	★	★

| 1866 | 1869 | 1872 | 1875 | 1878 |

1883 • The U.S. Supreme Court strikes down the Civil Rights Act of 1875, saying the Fourteenth Amendment only made discrimination by states illegal, not by private persons in their businesses.

1891 • Congress passes the Circuit Courts of Appeals Act, finishing the judicial branch reorganization that began in 1875. The act transfers most federal trials to the district courts, creates nine new circuit courts of appeals, and requires the Supreme Court to hear only certain kinds of appeals from the district and circuit courts and from the circuit courts of appeals.

1896 • The U.S. Supreme Court decides in *Plessy v. Ferguson* that the Fourteenth Amendment does not prevent states from requiring whites and blacks to use separate railway cars. The Court rules that "separate but equal" facilities satisfy the "equal protection" requirements of the Fourteenth Amendment.

1898 • Congress uses its constitutional right by declaring war (the Spanish-American War).

1899 • The U.S. House of Representatives names its first official whip.

1912 • The number of members of the U.S. House of Representatives reaches 435, a total that has not changed in subsequent years.

1913 • President Woodrow Wilson revives the practice of delivering his annual address to Congress orally.

February 1913 • The Sixteenth Amendment is ratified, giving Congress the power to collect an income tax.

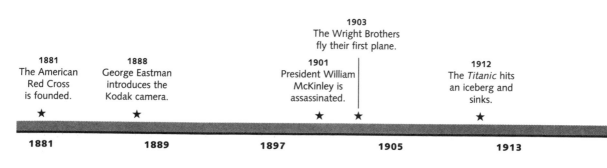

1903
The Wright Brothers
fly their first plane.

1881
The American
Red Cross
is founded.

1888
George Eastman
introduces the
Kodak camera.

1901
President William
McKinley is
assassinated.

1912
The *Titanic* hits
an iceberg and
sinks.

1881   1889   1897   1905   1913

May 1913 • The Seventeenth Amendment is ratified, which changes the way U.S. senators are elected to office. Instead of state legislatures electing them, citizens vote them in.

1917 • Congress uses its constitutional right by declaring war (World War I).

January 1919 • The Eighteenth Amendment is ratified, making the manufacture, sale, and transportation of alcoholic beverages illegal.

1920s • U.S. senators of both the Republican and Democratic parties began to elect official majority and minority leaders.

August 1920 • The Nineteenth Amendment is ratified, giving women the right to vote.

1921 • Congress passes the Budgeting and Accounting Act. The act gives the president the job of preparing an initial budget plan each year, and also creates the Bureau of the Budget (later renamed the Office of Management and Budget), a governmental office for helping the president prepare the budget.

1923 • President Calvin Coolidge is the first president to broadcast his annual address to Congress on the radio.

1933 • The Twentieth Amendment is ratified, changing the dates the president, vice president, and members of Congress take office, following the November election. The amendment also states that the vice president–elect becomes president in the event of the death of the president-elect.

1933 • The Twenty-first Amendment is ratified, ending nationwide prohibition by repealing the Eighteenth Amendment.

1937 • President Franklin D. Roosevelt tries to change the philosophical makeup of the Supreme Court by asking Congress to increase the number of seats on the Supreme Court from nine to fifteen and allow Roosevelt to fill the new seats

1913 The first Charlie Chaplin silent movie is released.	1920 Joan of Arc is canonized a saint.	1923 Edwin Hubble identifies galaxies beyond the Milky Way.	1929 The Great Depression begins.	1933 German Nazis build the first concentration camps.
★	★	★	★	★
1913	1919	1925	1931	1937

whenever a justice over seventy years of age does not resign. (Four justices who regularly voted against Roosevelt's New Deal program were already over seventy, and the president wanted to appoint new justices who would support his New Deal.) The plan is controversial, and is proved to be unnecessary; the Court winds up approving much of Roosevelt's New Deal legislation and the president names five replacement justices through 1940 as a result of three retirements and two deaths. Congress does not approve of Roosevelt's "court-packing."

1939 • President Franklin D. Roosevelt creates the Executive Office of the President to help the president manage the executive branch. Four of the most important positions in the department are the chief of staff, director of the Office of Management and Budget, director of the National Economic Council, and national security advisor.

1940 • President Franklin D. Roosevelt tells Democratic Party officials he will not run for a third term unless they select Secretary of Agriculture Henry A. Wallace as his vice presidential running mate. The party grants Roosevelt's wish, thus beginning the tradition of presidential candidates choosing their running mates.

1941 • Congress uses its constitutional right by declaring war (World War II).

1947 • President Harry S. Truman is the first president to broadcast his annual address to Congress on television.

1947 • The War Department, Navy Department, and Department of the Air Force combine to form the Department of Defense.

1947 • The National Security Council is created to advise the president on national security affairs.

1939	1942	1945	1948
The Baseball Hall of Fame is established.	Humphrey Bogart stars in *Casablanca*.	The United States drops two atomic bombs on Japan.	Jews in Palestine form the State of Israel.
★	★	★	★

1937	1940	1943	1946	1949

1949 • Congress passes a law making the vice president an official member of the National Security Council.

March 1951 • The Twenty-second Amendment is ratified, limiting presidents to a maximum of two terms, or two terms and two years if the president was finishing no more than half of his predecessor's term.

1954 • The U.S. Supreme Court unanimously decides in *Brown v. Board of Education of Topeka* that separate public services are not equal under the Fourteenth Amendment. This is an example of an amendment not changing but the Supreme Court's *interpretation* of it changing.

1961 • The Twenty-third Amendment is ratified, allowing Washington, D.C., to select a number of electors equal to the number of senators and representatives it would have if it were a state, but no more than the number of electors allowed for the least populous state. This gives electors from Washington, D.C., the chance to vote in a presidential election.

January 1964 • The Twenty-fourth Amendment is ratified, making it illegal for the United States or any state to charge a poll tax for participating in presidential and congressional elections.

July 1964 • President Lyndon B. Johnson signs into law the Civil Rights Act, making discrimination illegal in public places, such as motels and restaurants. Congress says it passed the act using its power under the Interstate Commerce Clause. Later, in *Heart of Atlanta Motel v. United States* and *Katzenbach v. McClung,* the U.S. Supreme Court rules that the Civil Rights Act is lawful under the Constitution because Congress can outlaw private discrimination under its power to regulate interstate commerce, but not under the equal rights provisions of the Fourteenth Amendment.

1951	1954	1955	1959	1963
Color television is introduced in the United States.	Elvis Presley makes his first commercial recording.	Jonas Salk invents the polio vaccine.	Fidel Castro becomes premier of Cuba.	President John F. Kennedy is assassinated.
★	★	★	★	★

| 1949 | 1953 | 1957 | 1961 | 1965 |

1967 • The Twenty-fifth Amendment is ratified, officially providing for the vice president to become president "in case of the removal of the president from office or his death or resignation." Prior to the adoption of this amendment, the vice president's swearing-in to office—which had happened seven times before—was by tradition only.

1967 • The Department of Transportation is established.

1968 • Congress passes the Federal Magistrates Act, giving district courts the power to appoint magistrate judges to help district court judges do their jobs.

July 1971 • The Twenty-sixth Amendment is ratified, lowering the voting age to eighteen.

1972 • The U.S. Supreme Court rules in *Roe v. Wade* that states cannot ban abortions completely because women have a constitutional right to have abortions in some cases. After that decision, some states rewrite their abortion laws to ban abortions in situations allowed under the Supreme Court's ruling. This is an example of a legislative check on judicial power.

1973 • Congress passes the War Powers Resolution to try to strengthen the constitutional separation of military powers. President Richard Nixon vetoes the bill, but both chambers of Congress vote to override the veto. The resolution says presidents should commit troops only with congressional consultation and authorization.

1973 • President Richard Nixon tries to use executive privilege to hide information about the Watergate scandal from Senate investigators.

October 1973 • Spiro T. Agnew resigns as vice president after it is divulged that he failed to report almost $30,000 on his federal income tax return in 1967 while he was governor of

1967	1969	1970	1972	1973
The first human heart transplant takes place.	Neil Armstrong is the first astronaut to walk on the moon.	Four Vietnam War protesters are killed at Kent State University.	The United States reestablishes relations with the People's Republic of China.	U.S. troops pull out of Vietnam.
★	★	★	★	★
1967	1969	1970	1972	1973

Maryland. He is also accused of taking bribes while serving as a county official in Maryland.

December 1973 • The Twenty-fifth Amendment is invoked for the first time when U.S. representative Gerald Ford is approved by Congress as the new vice president.

1974 • Congress passes the Budget and Impoundment Control Act, which creates the Congressional Budget Office and standing budget committees in both chambers of Congress.

August 1974 • President Richard M. Nixon resigns from office, the first president in history to do so. The House was almost certainly about to impeach him for his role in covering up a 1972 burglary of the offices of the Democratic National Committee by members of the Republican Party, a scandal known as Watergate. Gerald Ford succeeds him, becoming the only person to serve as both president and vice president without being elected to either office.

September 1974 • President Gerald Ford pardons former president Richard Nixon for any involvement he had in the Watergate scandal. Ford reasons that a long trial involving Nixon would not allow the country to move beyond the scandal.

1980 • Congress creates the Department of Education.

1981 • Sandra Day O'Connor becomes the first female U.S. Supreme Court justice.

1983 • The U.S. Supreme Court decides in *INS v. Chadha* that the legislative veto violates the Constitution. The Constitution says the only way Congress can pass a bill or resolution is when both chambers approve it and present it to the president for executive veto consideration. Legislative vetoes violate this by giving either one or both chambers of

1974 Hank Aaron passes Babe Ruth as baseball's all-time home run hitter.	1976 The United States celebrates its bicentennial.	1978 John Paul II begins his reign as pope.		1982 The compact disc (CD) is introduced.
★	★	★		★
1973	**1976**	**1978**	**1981**	**1983**

Congress the power to take official action that the president cannot veto. Despite the Court's ruling, Congress continues to include the legislative veto power in the nation's laws.

1984 • U.S. congresswoman Geraldine Ferraro of New York becomes the first female vice presidential candidate on a major party ticket, running unsuccessfully with the Democratic presidential contender, former vice president Walter Mondale.

1992 • More than two hundred years after it was first proposed by Congress, the Twenty-seventh Amendment is ratified. It says that if Congress passes a law changing the salaries for senators or representatives, the law cannot take effect until after at least one House election passes. This prevents representatives from giving themselves pay raises while in office.

1993 • The National Economic Council is created to help the president develop and implement economic policies, both domestic and international.

1996 • Congress passes the Line Item Veto Act, allowing the president to strike specific dollar amounts and tax benefits from appropriations bills passed by Congress. Congress can override the line item veto only by passing another bill containing the portions the president has stricken.

1997 • Madeleine Albright becomes the first female secretary of state.

1998 • The U.S. Supreme Court strikes down the 1996 Line Item Veto Act. The Court rules that it violates the Constitution, which states that the president may use his veto power to veto only an *entire* bill.

1998 • President Bill Clinton becomes the second president to be impeached. He is charged with perjury and obstruction of justice relating to an Arkansas real estate deal, a sexual

1985
Microsoft introduces Windows to the market.
★

1989
The Berlin Wall is torn down.
★

1993
Toni Morrison becomes the first African American to win the Nobel Prize for literature.
★

1994
Nelson Mandela becomes the first black president of South Africa.
★

1999
The euro is accepted as legal tender in Europe.
★

| 1984 | 1988 | 1992 | 1996 | 2000 |

harassment case, and a relationship with a White House intern. The U.S. Senate vote leaves him in office, however.

2000 • In the extremely tight presidential election of 2000 between Texas governor George W. Bush and Vice President Al Gore, a narrow victory for Bush in Florida leads Gore to sue to have votes in certain counties recounted. Bush appeals one of the cases from the Florida Supreme Court to the U.S. Supreme Court. The U.S. Supreme Court issues a decision in December, stopping the recounts in Florida, giving Bush Florida's twenty-five electoral votes and, therefore, making him the presidential victor.

September 2001 • President George W. Bush delivers a special message to Congress following the terrorist attacks of September 11, 2001. Aside from their annual addresses to Congress, it is rare for presidents to speak to the complete Congress.

October 2001 • The Office of Homeland Security is created following the terrorist attacks of September 11, 2001. A year later, it becomes a full department in the executive branch.

2001	2002	2003	2004	2005
Terrorists attack the World Trade Center and the Pentagon.	Washington, D.C., snipers kill ten, wound others.	The United States declares war on Iraq.	A powerful tsunami in the Indian Ocean kills hundreds of thousands.	George W. Bush begins his second term as president.
★	★	★	★	★
2001	**2002**	**2003**	**2004**	**2005**

Words to Know

appropriations bill: A bill, or law, that assigns money to a government department or agency.

Articles of Confederation: The document that established the federal government for the United States of America from 1781 to 1789.

bicameralism: The practice of dividing the legislative, or law-making, power of government into two chambers.

Bill of Rights: The first ten amendments to the U.S. Constitution, proposed in 1789 and adopted in 1791. The Bill of Rights contains some of the rights of citizens of the United States of America.

cabinet: A group of executive officials who advise the president on important policy matters and decisions. By law, the cabinet includes the heads of the executive departments. Presidents can also include other important executive officials in their cabinets, such as the vice president.

casework: Work that a member of Congress does to help a voter with a personal governmental problem.

checks and balances: The specific powers in one branch of government that allow it to limit the powers of the other branches.

circuit court of appeals: A court in the federal judicial system that handles appeals from the trial courts, called federal district courts. The United States is divided into twelve geographic areas called circuits, and each circuit has one court of appeals that handles appeals from the federal district courts in its circuit. A party who loses in a circuit court of appeals may ask the Supreme Court to review the case.

civil case: A case that involves a dispute between private parties or a noncriminal dispute between a private party and a government.

cloture rule: A rule that allows senators to end a filibuster, or prolonged speech, by a vote of three-fifths of the Senate.

common law: A law developed by judges in England and America on a case-by-case basis for governing relationships between private parties. Examples of common law include contract law and tort law.

Congress: The legislative, or lawmaking, branch of the federal government. Congress has two chambers, the Senate and the House of Representatives.

constituents: The voters who are in a representative's district or a senator's state.

Constitution of the United States of America: The document written in 1787 that established the federal government under which the United States of America has operated since 1789. Article I covers the legislative branch, Article II covers the executive branch, and Article III covers the judicial branch.

Constitutional Convention of 1787: Convention held in Philadelphia, Pennsylvania, from May to September 1787, during which delegates from twelve of the thirteen American states wrote a new Constitution for the United States.

Continental Congress: The main body of American government from 1774 until 1779.

courts of appeals: Federal appellate courts that review district court trials to correct serious errors made by judges and juries.

criminal case: A case in which a person is charged with violating a criminal law.

district courts: The courts in the federal judicial system that handle trials in civil and criminal cases. Each state is divided into one or more federal judicial districts, and each district has one or more federal district courts. A party who loses in a federal district court may appeal to have the case reviewed by a circuit court of appeals.

executive branch: The branch of the federal government that enforces the nation's laws. The executive branch includes the president, the vice president, and many executive departments, agencies, and offices.

executive departments: Departments in the executive branch responsible for large areas of the federal government. As of 2005, there are fifteen departments: Agriculture, Commerce, Defense, Education, Energy, Health and Human Services, Homeland Security, Housing and Urban Development, Interior, Justice, Labor, State, Transportation, Treasury, and Veterans Affairs. The heads of the departments, called secretaries, make up the president's cabinet.

executive privilege: A privilege that allows the president to keep information secret, even if Congress, federal investigators, the Supreme Court, or the people want the president to release the information. The privilege is designed to protect information related to national security, or public safety.

federalism: A principle of government under which independent states join to form a central government to serve their collective needs.

filibuster: A tactic used by one or more senators who speak for a prolonged period of time so that the time for considering a bill runs out before a vote can be taken on the Senate floor.

Founding Fathers: General term for the men who founded the United States of America and designed its government. The term includes the men who signed the Declaration of Independence in 1776 and the Constitution of the United States in 1787.

impoundment: The presidential practice of refusing to spend money that Congress appropriates for an executive department, agency, or program.

income tax: A tax on the money and property that a person earns during the year.

Interstate Commerce Clause: The clause in Article I, Section 8, of the Constitution that gives Congress the power "to regulate commerce ... among the several states."

iron triangle: The three-way relationship between congressional committees, executive agencies, and private interest groups that all specialize in the same area of government.

judge: A public official who presides over a court and who often decides questions brought before him or her.

judicial interpretation: The process by which federal courts interpret the meaning of laws passed by Congress.

judicial review: The process by which federal courts review laws to determine whether they violate the U.S. Constitution. If a court finds that a law violates the Constitution, it declares the law unconstitutional, which means the executive branch is not supposed to enforce it anymore. Congress can correct such a defect by passing a new law that does not violate the Constitution.

judiciary: The branch of the federal government that decides cases that arise under the nation's law. The federal judiciary includes the Supreme Court of the United States, circuit courts of appeals, and federal district courts.

justice: One of nine jurists who serve on the U.S. Supreme Court. The chief justice serves as the head of the Supreme Court; the other eight are called associate justices.

legislative courts: Courts created by Congress to handle some of its lawmaking powers under Article I of the U.S. Constitution.

lobbying: Meeting with members of Congress to convince them to pass laws that will benefit businesses, citizen's groups, or other organizations.

monarchy: A government under which power is held by a monarch, such as a king or queen, who inherits power by birth or takes it by force.

natural law: The idea that human laws must conform to a higher law—one of nature, often believed to come from God.

Necessary and Proper Clause: The clause in Article I, Section 8, of the Constitution that gives Congress the power "to make all laws which shall be necessary and proper" for exercising the other powers of the federal government.

personnel floor: A congressional minimum on the number of employees a governmental department, agency, or program must employ.

plutocracy: A government under which power is held by the wealthy class of society.

president: The highest officer in the executive branch of the federal government, with primary responsibility for enforcing the nation's laws.

quorum: The number of members of Congress who must be present for Congress to conduct business, such as voting on bills. The U.S. Constitution says a chamber has a quorum when a simple majority of its members is present.

ratification: The process of formally approving something, such as a treaty, constitution, or constitutional amendment.

reception provisions: Laws passed by some of the new American states around 1776 to define which parts of the common law, English statutes, and colonial statutes continued to apply in the states after they separated from Great Britain.

reprogramming: The practice of using money that Congress appropriates to one governmental program for a different program.

republicanism: Theory of government under which power is held by the people, who elect public servants to represent them in the bodies of government.

separation of powers: Division of the powers of government into different branches to prevent one branch from having too much power.

suffrage: The right to vote.

Supreme Court: The highest court in the federal judiciary. The judiciary is the branch of government responsible for resolving legal disputes and interpreting laws on a case-by-case basis.

unicameralism: The practice of placing the legislative, or law-making, power of government in one chamber.

veto: Rejection of a bill, or proposed law, by the president of the United States. If the president vetoes a bill, it does not become law unless two-thirds of both chambers of Congress vote to override the veto.

vice president: The second highest officer in the executive branch of the federal government. The vice president replaces the president if the president dies or becomes unable to serve. The vice president also serves as president of the Senate, with power to break tie votes when the whole Senate is equally divided on an issue.

Checks
and
Balances

**The Three Branches of
the American Government**

American Government: An Overview

The Constitution is the framework for the federal government of the United States of America. Written in 1787 and adopted in 1788, it carves the federal government into three branches. Generally, the legislative branch makes America's laws, the executive branch enforces the laws, and the judicial branch decides cases under the laws. The Constitution also gives the three branches duties outside the realm of the nation's laws.

The division of government into branches is what political scientists call the separation of powers. The separation of powers prevents the same person or branch of government from having full power to make, enforce, and interpret the nation's laws. The separation set up by the Constitution, however, is not absolute. Each branch has powers that allow it to affect the affairs of the other branches. These checks and balances prevent the branches of government from being completely separate. Indeed, some observers believe the checks and balances make the federal government one of shared powers, not separate powers.

The legislative branch: Congress

The Constitution contains six parts called articles and, as of 2005, twenty-seven parts called amendments. Amendments are changes made since the original six articles were adopted in 1788. The first three articles cover the three branches of government, and the very first article covers the legislative branch. It begins, "All legislative Powers herein granted shall be vested in a Congress of the United States, which shall consist of a Senate and House of Representatives."

Words to Know

checks and balances: The specific powers in one branch of government that allow it to limit the powers of the other branches.

Congress: The legislative, or lawmaking, branch of the federal government. Congress has two chambers, the Senate and the House of Representatives.

judicial interpretation: The process by which federal courts interpret the meaning of laws passed by Congress.

judicial review: The process by which federal courts review laws to determine whether they violate the U.S. Constitution. If a court finds that a law violates the Constitution, it declares the law unconstitutional, which means the executive branch is not supposed to enforce it anymore. Congress can correct such a defect by passing a new law that does not violate the Constitution.

president: The highest officer in the executive branch of the federal government, with primary responsibility for enforcing the nation's laws.

separation of powers: Division of the powers of government into different branches to prevent one branch from having too much power.

Supreme Court: The highest court in the federal judiciary. The judiciary is the branch of government responsible for resolving legal disputes and interpreting laws on a case-by-case basis.

The powers of Congress The legislative power is the power to make laws, so Congress is the nation's main lawmaker. Article I, Section 8, lists Congress's lawmaking power, including the power to:

★ collect taxes and other money for paying the nation's debts and providing for its common defense and general welfare

★ regulate commerce, or business, that crosses the boundaries of states, Indian lands, and foreign nations

★ establish rules for naturalization, which is the process by which people from other countries can become citizens of the United States

★ create money and punish counterfeiters (people who make fake money to be used as real money)

★ raise and support armies and navies and provide rules for regulating them

In the Constitution, this list ends with a general clause that says Congress has the power "to make all Laws which shall be necessary and proper for carrying into Execution the foregoing Powers, and all other Powers vested by this Constitution in the

Government of the United States, or in any Department or Officer thereof." In other words, Congress has the general power to make all laws the government needs to exercise its specific powers.

The chambers of Congress The very same section of the Constitution that makes Congress the lawmaker divides it into two chambers, the Senate and the House of Representatives. The Senate contains two senators from each state of the United States, for a total of one hundred as of 2005. Delegates from small states, such as New Jersey and New Hampshire, insisted on this arrangement when they met to write the Constitution in steamy Philadelphia, Pennsylvania, in the summer of 1787. The delegates from small states feared that the large states would control the federal government without a legislative chamber that gave each state equal representation. Two senators from each state—regardless of geographic size or population—means each state has equal power in the Senate.

As of 2005, the House of Representatives contains 435 members, a total that has not changed since 1912. This number comes from a law passed by Congress, not from the Constitution. The Constitution only says that each state must have at least one member in the House, and may have no more than one member for every thirty thousand people in the state.

Under the Constitution, the total number of members in the House must be divided among the states once every ten years based on the population of each state. Roughly speaking, then, each state has control in the House in proportion to the size of its population. States then divide themselves into districts, with one House member representing each district. Redistricting is the process of dividing the total number of House members for a state among its districts based on the population census taken every ten years. The most recent redistricting happened after publication of the 2000 federal census.

The Senate and the House of Representatives share most of the powers of Congress equally. Both chambers can propose changes to the Constitution, called amendments, although three-fourths of the states must approve an amendment before it becomes law. Action by both chambers is necessary to admit new states to the United States, a topic that occasionally arises concerning the District of Columbia and Puerto Rico, which are not states as of 2005. Congress as a whole shares the power to

Birth of a Government

The U.S. Constitution, written in 1787, created a federal government that has lasted into the twenty-first century. The Constitution was signed by representatives, then called delegates, from twelve of the thirteen states that made up the United States in 1787: Connecticut, Delaware, Georgia, Maryland, Massachusetts, New Hampshire, New Jersey, New York, North Carolina, Pennsylvania, South Carolina, and Virginia. (Rhode Island sent no delegates to the Constitutional Convention of 1787. Its population of mostly farmers rejected the Convention's goal of creating a strong central government, which would be hard for the people to control from their communities, far away from the capital.)

The Constitution became law in the United States in June 1788 after ten of the thirteen states ratified, or approved, it. The new federal government began to operate under the Constitution in 1789.

The Constitution, however, did not create the United States of America, and was not the blueprint for its first government. The country was born on July 4, 1776, when representatives from the thirteen American colonies joined together to break from English rule by signing the Declaration of Independence.

At the time of independence in 1776, the new American states operated together as a nation in the Continental Congress. In 1781, the states adopted a new form of government with the Articles of Confederation. American government under the Articles of Confederation had only a Congress, with no president or judiciary. The weakness of this government led the men who wanted a powerful federal government to call for writing the U.S. Constitution in 1787.

George Washington holds a copy of the U.S. Constitution as he addresses his fellow Founding Fathers. © Bettmann/Corbis.

make rules and regulations for territories of the United States, which are lands that the United States controls without making them states. Examples of territories are Puerto Rico and the U.S. Virgin Islands in the Caribbean Sea, and Guam and the Northern Mariana Islands in the Pacific Ocean.

Each chamber of Congress must pass a bill for the bill to become law. Both chambers can pass bills for raising money, such as through taxes, but such bills must start in the House. If the president vetoes, or rejects, a bill, the bill dies unless two-thirds of the members of each chamber of Congress vote to override the veto. In this case, the bill becomes law despite the president's veto.

Only the House can impeach the president, vice president, and other civil officers of the United States, including judges. Impeachment is a formal accusation that someone has committed treason, bribery, or other high crimes or misdemeanors. The Constitution defines treason as levying war against America or giving aid and comfort to its enemies. Bribery is an illegal payment to influence official action. U.S. district judge West H. Humphreys (1806–1882) of Tennessee was impeached in 1862, and removed by the Senate, on charges of joining the Confederacy without resigning his judgeship, but nobody has been impeached specifically for treason. Additionally, nobody has been impeached for bribery, but six of the seventeen impeachments in history to date have involved accusations that an official used his office for improper personal gain. The Constitution does not define "high crimes" or "misdemeanors." The House has interpreted the phrase loosely to mean any conduct that makes a person unfit to continue in office. The two highest-profile impeachments were presidents: Andrew Johnson (1808–1875; served 1865–69) in 1868 and Bill Clinton (1946–; served 1993–2001) in 1998.

Once accused by impeachment in the House, a civil officer stands trial in the Senate. The Senate alone can convict the officer. To convict an impeached officer, two-thirds of the senators at an impeachment trial must vote for conviction. Following their impeachment, neither President Johnson nor President Clinton were voted out of office, though Johnson missed conviction by only a single vote.

In addition to conducting impeachment trials, the Senate has two other powers that the House does not. If the president makes a treaty, or formal agreement, with another country, the treaty becomes law in America only if two-thirds of the senators present approve it. Similarly, a simple majority of senators must approve the president's selection of Supreme Court justices, ambassadors, and other important government officers, including the heads of the departments in the executive branch, such as the Justice Department.

Limits on congressional power The Constitution limits the powers given to Congress. Section 9 of Article I says Congress may not eliminate the writ of habeas corpus. A writ is a judicial order, and habeas corpus is a Latin term meaning "to have the body." The writ of habeas corpus is a procedure that prisoners can use to get released if they are being held in violation of the law. The writ requires a jailer to bring the prisoner before a court, where a judge can set the prisoner free if he or she is being held in violation of constitutional rights.

The Constitution also says Congress may not pass bills of attainder or ex post facto laws. A bill of attainder is a law that convicts a person of treason or other serious crime without a trial. An ex post facto law is one that punishes a person for doing something that was not illegal when done.

Amendments adopted since 1789, when the federal government began to operate under the Constitution, also limit the power of Congress. The states approved the first ten of these amendments, often called the Bill of Rights, in 1791. The Bill of Rights limits but does not eliminate Congress's power to restrict the freedoms of religion, speech, and assembly (First Amendment) and the right to bear arms (Second Amendment). The Eighth Amendment prevents Congress from passing a law that would impose cruel and unusual punishment on convicted criminals.

In addition to limits imposed by the Constitution, the system of checks and balances limits congressional power, too. As chief executive of the United States, the president enforces the laws made by Congress. A president who thinks a particular law is unwise or unimportant can ignore it by devoting people and money to enforcing other laws. As commander in chief of the U.S. Army and Navy, the president controls the military that Congress establishes.

The judiciary also checks the power of Congress. The primary judicial check is judicial review, which is the power to review congressional laws to determine if they violate any of the limitations in the Constitution. Judicial review is a controversial part of the system of checks and balances, because the Constitution does not specifically say the judiciary has this power. Many of the men who wrote the Constitution, however, presumed the judiciary would exercise this power. The Supreme Court confirmed this presumption in the 1803 case of *Marbury v. Madison*. In that case, the Supreme Court decided that a federal law giving the Supreme Court the power to hear cases for compelling government action was unconstitutional. Under the Constitution, such cases must begin in a lower federal court. The Supreme Court may only review them on appeal.

The executive branch: the president

The second Article of the Constitution begins, "The executive power shall be vested in a President of the United States of America." The executive power is the power to enforce the laws made by Congress.

The president's duties Only four paragraphs in the Constitution say what the president's duties are. The power to enforce the nation's laws comes from the clause that says, "he shall take care that the laws be faithfully executed."

Making sure the laws are enforced would be impossible for one person, even in 1789. The Constitution says the president "may require the Opinion, in writing, of the principal Officer in each of the Executive Departments." This clause is a seed that has grown to give the executive branch fifteen major departments plus many more agencies. As of 2005, the fifteen departments are: Agriculture, Commerce, Defense, Education, Energy, Health and Human Services, Homeland Security, Housing and Urban Development, Interior, Justice, Labor, State, Transportation, Treasury, and Veterans Affairs. Some of the agencies are the Central Intelligence Agency (CIA), the Environmental Protection Agency (EPA), the National Aeronautics and Space Administration (NASA), the Peace Corps, and the U.S. Postal Service.

Many of the departments and agencies make and enforce laws, called regulations, that relate to their area of service. For example, under power given to it by Congress, the EPA makes rules concerning the nation's air, land, and water. Executive departments and agencies also administer government programs. The Department of Agriculture, for instance, gives money to industrial farming operations that qualify for financial help under congressional laws.

The head of each of the fifteen executive departments is called the secretary (except for the head of the Department of Justice, who is called the attorney general). The fifteen department heads make up the core of the president's cabinet. Presidents also may include other officials in their cabinet, such as the vice president, the chief of staff (the person who manages the president's staff), and important directors from executive agencies, such as the Central Intelligence Agency or the Office of Management and Budget. Presidents rely on their cabinet not only to run the departments, but also to give the president information and advice for making important decisions.

Besides enforcing the nation's laws, the president is commander in chief of the U.S. Army and Navy. This means the

President Abraham Lincoln (third from left) and members of his cabinet. Cabinet members are the president's top advisors. Library of Congress.

military is ultimately controlled by a civilian, a person who is not part of the military. Putting a civilian in control of the military is supposed to prevent the military from using its power against civilians.

The Constitution requires the president to give Congress "information of the State of the Union" and to recommend "such Measures as he shall judge necessary and expedient [proper]." President George Washington (1732–1799; served 1789–97) delivered the nation's first annual message on January 8, 1790. Washington read his written speech to Congress. President Thomas Jefferson (1743–1826; served 1801–9) thought this practice was too formal, so he simply delivered a written copy of his messages to Congress. President Woodrow Wilson (1856–1924; served 1913–21) revived the practice of delivering the address orally in person in 1913. President Calvin Coolidge's (1872–1933; served 1923–29) message of 1923 was the first to be broadcast by radio, and President Harry S. Truman's (1884–1972; served 1945–53) 1947 speech was the first to be televised.

President Harry S. Truman speaks before a joint session of Congress on March 12, 1947, during which he urged aid for Greece and Turkey. AP/Wide World Photos.

Each year in January, the president delivers a televised State of the Union address to both chambers of Congress, with Supreme Court justices attending, too. The address gives Congress the president's view on how the country is doing, what is working, and what needs to be changed. On rare occasions, presidents appear before Congress to deliver special messages, such as when President George W. Bush (1946–) addressed Congress to explain his plan for responding to the terrorist attacks of September 11, 2001.

The president recommends "Measures" by proposing an annual budget for the federal government, which outlines how the government plans to raise and spend money. The president also recommends new laws, or changes to old laws, for Congress to consider. Because the president can veto, or reject, a law passed by Congress, Congress pays close attention to the president's

President Richard Nixon delivers his State of the Union address to a joint session of Congress on January 22, 1971. Vice President Spiro Agnew (left) and Speaker of the House Carl Albert applaud behind the president. © Corbis.

recommendations. It is not, however, required to do what the president wants.

Another major role for the president under the Constitution is receiving "ambassadors and other public ministers." This makes the president the head of America's relations with foreign nations.

Limits on presidential power One of the major limitations on the power of the executive branch is Congress's power to override a presidential veto by a two-thirds vote. Without this congressional power, the president would have full control over what bills become law. For example, in 1995, Congress passed a bill called the Private Securities Litigation Reform Act. The bill made it more difficult to sue private companies for misleading their investors, the people who invest money in a company. President Bill Clinton vetoed the bill in December 1995. Both chambers of Congress voted to override the veto, making the bill law.

The president can make treaties with other nations only when two-thirds of the senators approve. On May 24, 2002, for example, President George W. Bush and President Vladimir Putin (1952–) of Russia signed the Moscow Treaty on Strategic Offensive Reductions. The Moscow Treaty was an agreement to reduce the number of strategic nuclear warhead arsenals in America and Russia to between 1,700 and 2,200 each by December 2012. The U.S. Senate ratified the treaty unanimously in March 2003.

The Senate also must approve the president's selection of federal judges, ambassadors to other countries, executive department heads, and other important officers. This approval, however, need only be by a simple majority.

Both chambers of Congress check the president by playing a role in impeachment and conviction for treason, bribery, and other high crimes and misdemeanors. The House has the power to impeach, or formally accuse, a president of such misconduct. The Senate then has the power to try (put on trial) and convict a president accused of impeachable offenses.

The federal judiciary also checks the president's power, mostly by hearing and deciding cases under the nation's criminal laws. In these cases, federal courts determine whether an accused person is guilty of breaking the law. Many of these

Russian president Vladimir Putin (left) and U.S. president George W. Bush share a laugh on May 24, 2002. Behind Putin are his wife, Lyumilla, and first lady Laura Bush. President Bush was in Russia to sign the Moscow Treaty on Strategic Offensive Reductions. © Reuters/Corbis.

cases also involve questions of whether the executive branch has violated the accused person's constitutional rights.

The judicial branch: the Supreme Court and lower federal courts

Article III of the Constitution says, "The judicial power of the United States, shall be vested in one supreme Court, and in such inferior Courts as the Congress may from time to time ordain and establish." This means the Supreme Court is the only federal court created by the Constitution. Congress has sole authority to create federal courts underneath the Supreme Court.

Congress has used that power to create a vast federal judicial system. At the lowest level are federal district courts, the courts that hold trials. Criminal trials deal with people and businesses accused of violating the nation's criminal laws. A criminal law is a law that makes it unlawful to do something that is harmful to society, such as making illegal drugs or committing murder. Civil trials typically involve people or businesses that have private disputes to resolve, such as when one person breaks a contract, or agreement, that he or she has with another person.

As of 2005, the United States has ninety-four federal district courts. The districts cover either a portion of a state or an entire state, the District of Columbia, the Commonwealth of Puerto Rico, and the territories of the U.S. Virgin Islands, Guam, and the Northern Mariana Islands.

The next level of the federal judiciary is the circuit courts of appeals. There are twelve circuit courts of appeals, each of which covers a geographic region containing federal district courts. When a party loses a trial in federal district court, the party usually can appeal to the court of appeals in that district's circuit. The job of the courts of appeals is to review cases from the federal district courts to make sure the judges and juries there have not made significant errors.

If a party loses in the circuit court of appeals, the last place to go is to the Supreme Court of the United States, often called the court of last resort. As with the courts of appeals, the Supreme Court's job is to make sure the courts below did not make any major errors in a case.

The U.S. Supreme Court does not only hear appeals from the federal courts. It also hears appeals from the state judicial systems. Generally speaking, each state has trial courts similar to the federal district courts, courts of appeals similar to the federal circuit courts, and supreme courts similar to the U.S. Supreme Court. If a case that reaches a state supreme court involves federal laws or rights, the losing party can ask the U.S. Supreme Court to review the decision of the state supreme court. In the tight presidential election of 2000 between Texas governor George W. Bush and Vice President Al Gore (1948–), for example, an extremely narrow victory for Bush in Florida led Gore to sue to have votes in certain counties recounted. Bush appealed one of the cases from the Florida Supreme Court to the U.S. Supreme

The U.S. Supreme Court in 1982. Front row (left to right): Thurgood Marshall, William J. Brennan Jr., Chief Justice Warren Burger, Byron R. White, and Harry A. Blackmun. Back row (left to right): John Paul Stevens, Lewis Powell Jr., William H. Rehnquist, and Sandra Day O'Connor. UPI/Corbis-Bettmann.

Court. The U.S. Supreme Court issued a decision in December 2000, stopping the recounts in Florida, giving Bush the victory. Florida's twenty-five electoral votes put Bush over the top and made him the presidential victor.

There is a limited amount of work the Supreme Court can do in one year, so it has a procedure for deciding which cases to review. The losing party in a federal circuit court of appeals or in a state supreme court can begin the process by filing a document called a petition for a writ of certiorari. (A writ is a court order, and *certiorari* is a Latin word that means "to certify a court case for review.") In the petition, the party asks the Supreme Court to review the case, explaining why the case is important enough to deserve the Supreme Court's attention. If four of the nine Supreme Court justices agree to review the case, the Supreme Court issues a writ of certiorari, which allows the losing party to present its appeal to the Supreme Court. Out of the tens of thousands of petitions that the Supreme Court receives each year, it agrees to hear only around one hundred of them.

Cases and controversies: the lifeblood of the courts The federal judiciary at all levels (district courts, circuit courts of appeals, and Supreme Court) only has power to hear cases and controversies listed in the Constitution:

- ★ cases arising under the Constitution, laws, and treaties of the United States
- ★ cases affecting ambassadors and other public ministers
- ★ cases concerning the use of navigable waters
- ★ controversies in which the United States is a party
- ★ controversies between two or more states, between citizens of different states, and between citizens of the same state claiming lands under grants from different states
- ★ controversies between a state (or its citizens) and a foreign state or nation (or its citizens or subjects)

Most of the time, a case or controversy that falls into one of these categories must be brought in a federal court. State courts cannot handle these cases. One exception is cases between citizens of different states. If their dispute does not involve a federal law, they may resolve it in a state court, or they may choose to go to federal court anyway if their dispute involves an amount of money that exceeds (as of 2005) $75,000.

In cases involving ambassadors or in which a state is a party, the Supreme Court acts like a trial court and hears the case originally. In all other federal cases, the Supreme Court has appellate jurisdiction. This means the trial must first be handled by a federal district court and then might be appealed to the circuit court of appeals and, finally, to the Supreme Court by petition for certiorari.

Judicial interpretation and judicial review The plain language of Article III of the Constitution says the judiciary hears "cases and controversies." Some scholars and citizens believe that the sole power of the federal judiciary is to decide cases—that is, determine guilt or innocence in a criminal trial, and resolve a legal disagreement in a civil trial. Criminal and civil cases can both require the courts to interpret what a congressional law means, because the meaning is not always clear from the way Congress writes the laws. Such interpretation is one of the most important duties of the courts.

Federal courts, however, also exercise a power called judicial review. This is the power to review congressional and state laws that are involved in a case to decide whether the laws violate the U.S. Constitution. Some people think judicial review is necessary to prevent Congress and the president (who approves Congress's laws) from being too powerful. In other words, judicial review is part of the system of checks and balances set up by the Constitution. Others think that because the Constitution does not mention the power of judicial review, the federal judiciary should not exercise that power.

Judicial review, for example, was an important part of the case of *Elk Grove Unified School District v. Newdow*. In that case, a father named Michael Newdow sued the school district where his daughter attended public school. Newdow wanted the school to stop saying the Pledge of Allegiance because the Pledge says America is a nation "under God." Newdow, who is an atheist (a person who does not believe in God), argued that the pledge is a religious prayer that violates the First Amendment, which prevents government from favoring one religion over others. The Ninth Circuit Court of Appeals agreed with Newdow, banning public schools in western states from using the Pledge. On Flag Day in June 2004, the U.S. Supreme Court reversed the ruling on a technicality. It said Newdow, who was never married to his daughter's mother and did not have custody of the child, had no power to file the lawsuit. The case, however, illustrated the controversy that arises when the Supreme Court is asked to use judicial review to strike down a widely accepted government practice based on an important constitutional right.

Because of judicial review, the federal judiciary is perhaps the branch most responsible for protecting civil liberties. These are rights that people have to be free from unreasonable governmental power. Civil liberties come primarily from the Constitution. As previously noted, the First Amendment in the Bill of Rights protects the freedoms of speech, religion, and assembly. The Fourth Amendment says the federal government may not search or arrest a person in an unreasonable fashion. The Sixth Amendment says accused criminals have a right to trial by jury and to face the witnesses against them with assistance from counsel, or a lawyer. The Eighth Amendment prevents cruel and unusual punishment. Criminal cases often require the courts to decide whether the government has violated a defendant's civil liberties.

Limiting judicial power Just as with Congress and the president, the Supreme Court and lower courts have checks on their power. One of these comes not from the Constitution, but from the makeup of the Supreme Court. Under federal law, the Supreme Court contains up to nine justices. (Nine is the accepted total, but the Court continues to function with less than nine in the event of a justice's retirement or death.) Four out of the nine must vote to hear a case by issuing a writ of certiorari in order to review it. When the justices vote on how to decide a case, five must agree in order to change the result from the courts below. This means that, in theory, one justice alone has little power, and so not much ability to abuse it.

The biggest check on judicial power is the power of Congress. If senators and representatives disagree with how the Supreme Court is interpreting a law, they can amend, or change, the law to clarify it so the Court can alter its interpretation. Congress can also pass a new law to correct a constitutional defect when the Supreme Court strikes a law down as unconstitutional. For example, in *Roe v. Wade* in 1972, the Supreme Court ruled that states cannot ban abortions completely because women have a constitutional right to have abortions in some cases. After that decision, states rewrote their abortion laws to ban abortions in situations allowed under the Supreme Court's ruling. For example, most states ban abortions during the last three months of pregnancy unless the abortion is necessary for the health of the mother. In addition to its lawmaking power, Congress has the power to propose constitutional amendments, which change the Constitution if approved by the legislatures or conventions in three-fourths of the states.

As for the president, when a Supreme Court justice or lower court judge retires or dies, the president gets to appoint a replacement, and the Senate confirms or rejects the president's selection. Presidents use these opportunities to fill the courts with justices and judges who agree with the president on the proper role of government and its three branches. If a majority of senators are from the same political party as the president, these appointments easily receive Senate approval. If the president and a majority of the Senate are from different political parties, the appointments can result in political battles, especially for appointments to the Supreme Court. As of 2005, presidents have nominated 148 people to the Supreme Court. The Senate has rejected twelve. The most recent rejections were during the Reagan administration with Robert H. Bork (1927–) in 1987, and twice in the Nixon administration with Clement Haynsworth Jr. (1912–1989) in 1969 and G. Harrold Carswell (1919–1992) in 1970. The Senate also has taken no action on five, and postponed voting on three, leading to unofficial rejection of these nominees.

The final significant check on the power of the judiciary is the power to remove judges from office. All officers of the federal government, including the president, vice president, and judges of the Supreme Court and lower courts, can be impeached and removed if convicted of treason, bribery, or other high crimes and misdemeanors. The House of Representatives has the sole power to impeach, or accuse, a judge of such crimes, and the Senate has the sole power to try, convict, and remove the judge from office.

As of 2005, only seven judges in the nation's history have been removed from office as a result of impeachment. The very first was John Pickering (c. 1738–1805), a federal district court judge who was impeached, convicted, and removed from office in March 1803 for drunkenness. The Pickering impeachment was a test run for Congress's real target, Supreme Court justice Samuel Chase (1741–1811), who was making speeches critical of the presidential administration of Thomas Jefferson. The House of Representatives impeached Chase in 1804. The Senate, however, voted not to convict, so Chase remained on the bench. As of 2005, he is the only Supreme Court justice to have been impeached.

For More Information

BOOKS

Beard, Charles A. *American Government and Politics*. 10th ed. New York: Macmillan Co., 1949.

Kelly, Alfred H., and Winfred A. Harbison. *The American Constitution: Its Origins and Development*. 5th ed. New York: W. W. Norton & Co., 1976.

McClenaghan, William A. *Magruder's American Government 2003.* Needham, MA: Prentice Hall School Group, 2002.

Roelofs, H. Mark. *The Poverty of American Politics.* 2nd ed. Philadelphia: Temple University Press, 1998.

Shelley, Mack C., II. *American Government and Politics Today.* 2004–2005 ed. Belmont, CA: Wadsworth Publishing, 2003.

Volkomer, Walter E. *American Government.* 8th ed. Upper Saddle River, NJ: Prentice Hall, 1998.

Woll, Peter. *American Government: Readings and Cases.* 15th ed. New York: Longman, 2003.

Zinn, Howard. *A People's History of the United States.* New York: HarperCollins, 2003.

Historic Roots of the Judicial Branch

The federal judiciary is the branch of government that holds trials and decides cases under the nation's laws. The main part of the federal judiciary has three kinds of courts: district courts, courts of appeals, and the U.S. Supreme Court.

Overview of the federal judiciary

Federal district courts are trial courts. Trial courts are where judges and juries hear and decide civil and criminal cases. A civil case is a dispute between private parties, or a noncriminal dispute between a private party and the government. Criminal cases involve violations of federal criminal law.

District court judges apply congressional laws and agency regulations in federal trials. In jury trials, the judge instructs the jury on the applicable law. After hearing all the evidence by listening to witnesses and seeing documents, the jury decides who wins the case based on the applicable law.

Sometimes judges decide cases without juries. These are called bench trials. In bench trials, the judge determines the facts after hearing the evidence and then decides who wins based on the applicable law. Judges and juries are supposed to apply the nation's laws fairly to all people.

Courts of appeals are one level above district courts in the federal system. If a party loses a case in district court, he or she can appeal the case to a court of appeals. The court of appeals reviews the case to make sure the judge or jury did not make a serious mistake. A court of appeals can either affirm, or agree

Words to Know

Articles of Confederation: The document that established the federal government for the United States of America from 1781 to 1789.

checks and balances: The specific powers in one branch of government that allow it to limit the powers of the other branches.

civil case: A case that involves a dispute between private parties or a noncriminal dispute between a private party and a government.

common law: A law developed by judges in England and America on a case-by-case basis for governing relationships between private parties. Examples of common law include contract law and tort law.

Continental Congress: The main body of American government from 1774 until 1779.

courts of appeals: Federal appellate courts that review district court trials to correct serious errors made by judges and juries.

criminal case: A case in which a person is charged with violating a criminal law.

district courts: The courts in the federal judicial system that handle trials in civil and criminal cases. Each state is divided into one or more federal judicial districts, and each district has one or more federal district courts. A party who loses in a federal district court may appeal to have the case reviewed by a circuit court of appeals.

judicial interpretation: The process by which federal courts interpret the meaning of laws passed by Congress.

judicial review: The process by which federal courts review laws to determine whether they violate the U.S. Constitution. If a court finds that a law violates the Constitution, it declares the law unconstitutional, which means the executive branch is not supposed to enforce it anymore. Congress can correct such a defect by passing a new law that does not violate the Constitution.

natural law: The idea that human laws must conform to a higher law—one of nature, often believed to come from God.

reception provisions: Laws passed by some of the new American states around 1776 to define which parts of the common law, English statutes, and colonial statutes continued to apply in the states after they separated from Great Britain.

separation of powers: Division of the powers of government into different branches to prevent one branch from having too much power.

Supreme Court: The highest court in the federal judiciary. The judiciary is the branch of government responsible for resolving legal disputes and interpreting laws on a case-by-case basis.

with, the result in the district court, or reverse it, sending the case back to the district court for further proceedings.

The U.S. Supreme Court is the highest court in the federal judicial system. Parties who lose in the courts of appeals can ask the U.S. Supreme Court to review their case. If it decides to review a case, the Supreme Court can either affirm or reverse the result in the circuit court of appeals. Just like the courts of

Multiple Appeals in Schiavo Case

A well-known recent case is a good example of the appeals process. In the late 1990s, there arose a dispute over whether to remove life-support from a Florida woman named Terri Schiavo (1963–2005). She collapsed in 1990 after her heart stopped beating temporarily due to a chemical imbalance in her body. This deprived her brain of blood, sending her into a coma. Some doctors believe Terri Schiavo lacked consciousness completely after the collapse. After she remained in the coma for several years, her husband, Michael Schiavo, sought to remove artificial life support, saying that his wife had told him that she would not want to remain alive in a vegetative state. After seven years of litigation—during which time Terri Schiavo's feeding tube was removed and reinserted twice—Michael Schiavo got an order from a state court to remove her life support in 2005. Her feeding tube was removed on March 18, 2005.

Terri Schiavo's parents, Robert and Mary Schindler, wanted their daughter to remain on life support. They said she laughed, cried, and tried to speak with them when they visited her in the hospice where she lived. After the case attracted national attention, Congress passed a bill specifically giving the Federal District Court for the Middle District of Florida power to review the state court's order. President George W. Bush (1946–; served 2001–) signed the bill into law just after 1:00 AM on Monday, March 21, 2005. That same day, the Schindlers filed a lawsuit in federal court. The first thing they asked was for the court to prevent the state court order from being used to remove life support until the federal court had time to hear and decide the whole case.

U.S. district judge James D. Whittemore (1952–) denied that request, so the Schindlers appealed to the U.S. Court of Appeals for the Eleventh Circuit. A three-judge panel denied the appeal in a 2–1 decision. The court said the parents could not get the temporary relief for two reasons. First, the law passed by Congress did not give the court power to issue such temporary relief. Second, under normal federal law, parties can only get temporary relief if they are likely to win the case in the end. The court said the parents were not likely to win in the end, so they could not get temporary relief.

On March 23, the parents asked the U.S. Supreme Court to review the case, but the next day the Court announced it would not. At that point, the Schindlers filed a second complaint with the federal district court, alleging that their daughter's Fourteenth Amendment right to life was violated. The following day, district judge Whittemore denied the Schindlers' second motion; an appeal to the Court of Appeals also failed. Additional state and federal appeals were unsuccessful. On March 31, 2005, Terri Schiavo died.

appeals, the Supreme Court's job is to make sure judges in the lower courts do not make serious mistakes.

The federal judiciary has roots in the Roman Republic and Empire, the British Empire, American colonial courts, British supervision of colonial law, and American state courts. It also has roots in the national courts under the Continental Congress and the Articles of Confederation, which were the frameworks for American government from 1775 to 1788.

Roman statesman, lawyer, and scholar Marcus Tillius Cicero was a proponent of natural law, which is the idea that human laws must conform to a higher law, presumably from God.

The Roman Republic and Empire

The Roman Republic and Empire were centered around the city of Rome from 509 BCE until the latter half of the fifth century CE. The Republic, which ended with the creation of the Empire in 27 BCE, had a government that was republican for the free men of society. In a republic, people control their government through elected leaders. Many legal systems and political structures of the Republic and Empire were forerunners of modern government.

Natural law Marcus Tullius Cicero (106 BCE–43 BCE) was a Roman statesman, lawyer, and scholar who lived during the waning days of the Republic. Cicero wrote about natural law, which is the idea that human laws must conform to a higher law—one of nature, often believed to come from God. As reprinted in *American Law and Politics,* Cicero said:

> There is in fact a true law—namely, right reason— which is in accordance with nature, applies to all men, and is unchangeable and eternal. By its commands this law summons men to the performance of their duties; by its prohibitions it restrains them from doing wrong. . . . It will not lay down one rule at Rome and another at Athens, nor will it be one rule to-day and another to-morrow. But there will be one law, eternal and unchangeable, binding at all times upon all peoples; and there will be, as it were, one common master and ruler of men, namely God, who is the author of this law, its interpreter, and its sponsor.

The notion that law should apply equally to all people affected the development of the federal judicial system. Federal judges take an oath to apply the law equally and fairly, without regard to the identity of the parties. Juries are supposed to do the same.

Roman codes The Roman Republic first recorded its laws around 450 BCE. According to tradition, common citizens, called plebeians, insisted that all citizens had a right to know the laws. Government officials organized and wrote the laws onto twelve tablets, probably made of bronze, called the Law of the Twelve Tables. The tablets hung in the Roman Forum, which

A court scene in Old Rome.
© Bettmann / Corbis.

was a place for public meetings, court proceedings, and other public events.

Nine hundred years later, Emperor Justinian I (483–565) of the Byzantine Empire had lawyers and scholars compile the *Corpus Juris Civilis,* or Body of Civil Law. It was an enormous collection and organization of the laws and legal opinions from emperors and jurists of the Roman Empire. Roman law from the *Corpus* affected the development of legal systems in Europe after the Dark Ages (476–1000), which eventually affected the development of American legal systems.

Roman courts Courts in the Roman period were not like courts in the American judiciary. There was no separate judicial branch of government. Instead, judicial duties were spread among various government officials. Praetors, for example, were Roman Republic officials who commanded armies and also had judicial duties in civil cases. Quaestors helped the leaders of the Republic with financial matters and also had criminal justice responsibilities.

During the Roman Republic, civil cases followed a formulary system. Under this system, parties to a case appeared before a praetor to get a "formula." A formula was a written definition of the legal dispute between the parties. Praetors drafted formulas after hearing what the legal dispute was about. Similarly, in the American judiciary, parties prepare pleadings, which are legal documents that define the nature of their dispute.

Once they had a formula, parties in the Roman Republic selected an arbitrator, called a judex. A judex was a private individual who heard the evidence and decided the case. In the American federal judiciary, judges and juries have that responsibility.

The British Empire

The thirteen colonies that formed the United States in 1776 were British colonies. Naturally, then, the American judicial system drew heavily from the British legal system for its structures and processes.

British courts Like the Roman Empire, England did not have a separate judicial system prior to the Middle Ages (500 CE–1350 CE). By the time of the Norman dynasty (1066–1154), England had a loose system of local courts, manorial courts, and royal courts. Local courts held trials in small political subdivisions, such as counties. Feudal lords who owned large pieces of land had manorial courts, which heard local cases involving people on those lands. Royal courts in Westminster, England, heard local disputes at the English seat of government.

During the Norman dynasty, English kings traveled around the country, hearing cases that affected the interests of the monarch, or ruler. In the twelfth and thirteenth centuries, England established three permanent courts in Westminster for serving this function. They were called superior common law courts because they had more power than the local and manorial courts.

One of the superior common law courts was the Court of Exchequer, which heard cases affecting England's revenues. Another was the Court of Common Pleas, which heard civil cases between private parties under the common law. (The common law is judicial rules governing relations between private parties.) The third superior common law court was the Court of Queen's

Bench (or King's Bench), which heard criminal cases plus civil cases that affected the interests of the monarch.

In addition to hearing criminal and civil cases, the Court of Queen's Bench had power to review cases from the local and manorial courts and from the Court of Exchequer and Court of Common Pleas. This made the Court of Queen's Bench a high appellate court similar to the U.S. Supreme Court.

British law The law applied by the superior common law courts influenced the development of law in America. It included common law, equity, criminal law, and statutory law.

Common law is a system of rules governing the relationships between private parties. For example, when two people make a contract to buy and sell goods or services, the common law of contracts provides rules for their relationship. If one person injures another, the common law of tort, or wrongful acts, provides rules for how the injured person can recover from the offender. Judges in England developed the common law on a case-by-case basis in the Middle Ages and modern times.

Equity was a special area of law that grew out of the common law. Under the common law, a person could not sue for a wrong unless it fit neatly into one of the categories of the common law. For example, if a person agreed to sell an item and then decided not to honor the contract, the common law awarded damages to the buyer but could not force the seller to part with the item.

Equity arose as a system for doing justice in private cases where the common law did not provide an adequate remedy. Equity cases in Great Britain were heard in courts of equity by people called chancellors. In 1873, England combined common law and equity courts into one court. Federal courts in America went through a similar period of handling common law and equity cases separately before combining them into one court.

Criminal law developed out of the common law during the Middle Ages. It was based on the notion that a person who did something harmful to the community had offended the monarch's peace. As a result, the crown of England gradually took on increased responsibility for enforcing criminal laws.

Statutory law is law enacted by a legislature. In England, the legislature is Parliament. In the United States, the federal courts apply statutory law enacted by Congress.

American colonial courts

American colonial governments had various forms, but they tended to include a governor, a council, and an assembly. British monarchs appointed governors to serve as the executive heads of the colonies. The council was a legislative body that represented the interests of Great Britain or of the British company that owned the colony. Assemblies were legislatures that the free men of the colonies elected for representing their interests in government.

Colonies did not have separate judicial systems. Instead, the governors and councils had judicial powers in addition to their executive and legislative functions. Initially, they sat as trial courts to hear and decide cases, and they sat as appellate courts to review decisions from lower courts.

Lower courts grew slowly in the colonies beginning in the seventeenth century. Justices of the peace heard minor criminal violations and disputes. Governors set up local courts to hear specific cases that arose in the colonies. Over time, legislatures established permanent local trial courts, often at the county level of government, to hear civil and criminal cases. The common law of England governed most civil cases. The legislatures also set up chancery courts to hear equity cases.

As permanent local courts grew, governors and councils held fewer trials and heard more appeals. Some colonies eventually set up permanent courts of appeals, relieving governors and councils of some of their appellate duties. The American judicial system follows this practice of holding trials in lower courts and hearing appeals in higher courts.

British supervision of colonial law

Great Britain tried to control the colonies through various laws, courts, and government offices. Legal cases in the colonies often ended with review by the governor and council sitting as a supreme court. If the result in these cases was against the law of England, parties could appeal to the Privy Council, a council that worked for the monarch in England. The Privy Council could modify the results in cases from the colonies. This made the Privy Council similar to the U.S. Supreme Court, which can review cases from the highest courts of the states.

In the latter half of the seventeenth century, Parliament passed a series of Navigation Acts. The acts made rules for the shipment and taxation of goods going to and coming from England and its colonies. To enforce the acts against the colonists, Great Britain set up a system of vice admiralty courts (relating to laws of the sea) in 1696. This system resembled the federal district courts that America would establish for enforcement of federal laws.

Colonial governments also faced review in the British Board of Trade. Parliament established the Board of Trade in 1696 to oversee Great Britain's commercial interests worldwide. The Board of Trade had power to review and strike down colonial laws that violated British law. In this way, the Board of Trade resembled the U.S. Supreme Court, which strikes down federal and state laws that violate the U.S. Constitution. Displeasure with the Board of Trade was one of the many things that led the colonists to declare independence from Great Britain in 1776.

American state laws and courts

Upon signing the Declaration of Independence in 1776, the thirteen colonies became states in a new country. Many states adopted constitutions to define the framework for their governments. Many also adopted declarations of rights, which defined citizens' rights. (See sidebar, "History of Religious Freedom.")

Prior to independence, the colonies operated under English and colonial laws. As new states, they had to decide what old laws would continue to apply. Beginning in May 1776, Virginia and ten other states passed reception provisions. A reception provision explained in general terms what parts of the common law, English statutes, and colonial statutes would continue to apply in a newly formed state. Reception provisions stated that old laws and statutes that violated a state's new constitution or declaration of rights could not continue to apply in the state.

State legislatures did not have the time to review all old laws and statutes to determine which violated their new constitutions and declarations. State courts ended up making these decisions on a case-by-case basis. A party to a case, for example, might ask the court to enforce a particular old law, and the other party might argue that the old law violated the new constitution or declaration of rights. The court could strike down the old law if it agreed that the law violated the state's reception provision.

Striking down old laws under reception provisions was an exercise of judicial review. Judicial review is the practice of nullifying, or invalidating, laws that violate a society's

History of Religious Freedom

Federal courts are an important place for protecting religious freedom in America. Religious freedom is the freedom to practice the religion of your choice or no religion at all. The First Amendment of the U.S. Constitution makes it illegal for Congress to pass laws "prohibiting the free exercise of religion." States must allow religious freedom, too, under the Fourteenth Amendment.

Religious freedom in America grew from a history of religious persecution and intolerance. In seventeenth-century England, people were required to worship in the Church of England. People who practiced a different kind of Christianity, such as Puritans and Quakers, faced punishment. Many of them left England for the American colonies to find religious freedom.

The American colonies, however, did not have religious freedom. The powerful Christian sects in the New World persecuted members of the weaker sects. In a letter in 1772 (as reprinted in *The Founders' Constitution*), Pennsylvania politician Benjamin Franklin (1706–1790) wrote about Christian persecution in New England:

> The primitive Christians thought persecution extremely wrong in the Pagans, but practised it on one another. The first Protestants of the Church of England, blamed persecution in the Roman church, but practised it against the Puritans: these found it wrong in the Bishops [of the Church of England], but fell into the same practice themselves both here and in New England.

In *Notes on the State of Virginia* (also reprinted in *The Founders' Constitution*), Thomas Jefferson (1743–1826) wrote of similar persecution in the Virginia colony:

> The poor Quakers were flying from persecution in England. They cast their eyes on these new countries as asylums [protectors] of civil and religious freedom; but they found them free only for the reigning sect. Several acts of the Virginia assembly of 1659, 1662, and 1693, had made it penal [worthy of punishment] in parents to refuse to have their children baptized; had prohibited the unlawful assembling of Quakers; had made it penal for any master of a vessel to bring a Quaker into the state; had ordered those already here, and such as should come thereafter, to be imprisoned till they should abjure [give up] the country; provided a milder punishment for their first and second return, but death for their third; had inhibited [prevented] all persons from suffering [allowing] their meetings in or near their houses, entertaining them individually, or disposing of [distributing] books which supported their tenets [beliefs].

Documents from the seventeenth century show how the colonists made religion part of their governments. On June 4, 1639, the free men of the colony of New Haven met to set up a government "as might be most pleasing unto God" (as reprinted in *The Founders' Constitution*). They agreed that the Old and New Testaments in the Christian Bible would be the basis for their laws.

Massachusetts colony had strict laws concerning Christianity in 1641. As reprinted in *The Founders'* fundamental laws, such as the constitution or declaration of rights. Judicial review was not too controversial when state courts struck down old English laws and statutes. It became very

Constitution, one law said, "If any man after legall conviction shall have or worship any other god, but the lord god, he shall be put to death." Another said, "If any person shall Blaspheme [disrespect] the name of god, the father, Sonne or Holie Ghost, with direct, expresse, presumptuous or high handed blasphemie, or shall curse god in the like manner, he shall be put to death."

The idea of religious tolerance slowly began to grow in the colonies by the middle of the eighteenth century. Tolerance means allowing people to pursue religion in their own way. In *Religious Tolerance,* published in 1766 (as reprinted in *The Founders' Constitution*), Virginia politician Patrick Henry (1736–1799) wrote, "A general toleration of Religion appears to me the best means of peopling our country. . . ." The Virginia Declaration of Rights of 1776 said all men were entitled to the free exercise of religion, though it added that all men had a duty "to practice Christian forbearance, love, and charity, toward each other."

Nine years later, Virginia adopted an Act for Establishing Religious Freedom. The law made it illegal to force someone to worship a particular way or to punish someone for his or her religion. In his *Autobiography* in 1821 (as reprinted in *The Founders' Constitution*), Jefferson wrote that the law was meant to extend religious freedom even beyond the bounds of Christianity:

> [A] singular proposition proved that its protection was meant to be universal. Where the preamble declares, that [religious] coercion is a departure from the plan of the holy author of our religion,

an amendment was proposed, by inserting the word "Jesus Christ," so that it should read, "a departure from the plan of Jesus Christ, the holy author of our religion;" the insertion was rejected by a great majority, in proof that they meant to comprehend, within the mantle of its protection, the Jew and the Gentile, the Christian and Mahometan [Muslim], the Hindoo [Hindu], and Infidel [nonbeliever] of every denomination.

Both Benjamin Franklin (left) and Thomas Jefferson wrote about Christian persecution. © Bettmann/Corbis.

controversial, however, when they began to strike down new laws passed by state legislatures.

Over time, however, judicial review became an accepted feature of American jurisprudence, or system of law. In 1803, judicial review became a permanent part of the federal judiciary. That year, the U.S. Supreme Court announced its power to strike down congressional laws that violate the U.S. Constitution.

Courts under the Continental Congress and the Articles of Confederation

In 1774, as relations between Great Britain and the American colonies approached the breaking point, the colonies sent delegates to the First Continental Congress. It was the first American government with power to try to resolve the conflict with Great Britain. When the American Revolution (1775–83) erupted, the Second Continental Congress managed the war effort for the colonies.

The Continental Congress continued as the government of America after the colonies declared independence in 1776. The following year, delegates from the American states drafted the Articles of Confederation. It was the blueprint for American government from 1781 until the adoption of the U.S. Constitution in 1788. Congress continued to be the primary body of American government until the Articles were composed.

There was no judicial branch of government under the Continental Congress or the Articles of Confederation. Congress, however, established a commission and a court of appeals that had judicial powers eventually held by the federal judiciary under the U.S. Constitution.

Commission for land claims In 1781, when the Articles of Confederation took effect, the land west of the thirteen states was considered the American frontier. Despite the presence of Native Americans on much of this land, American states claimed parts of the land as their own, and claims by two states sometimes overlapped.

The Articles of Confederation set up an elaborate procedure for settling such claims. If the two states could not agree on who should sit on a panel for deciding the case, Congress appointed three men from each of the thirteen states. The states with the dispute then took turns eliminating people from the panel of thirty-nine until thirteen remained. Finally, Congress drew seven to nine names from the remaining thirteen to serve on a commission to hear and decide the case.

Only one case got to trial before a commission under this procedure—a dispute between Pennsylvania and Connecticut. When America adopted the U.S. Constitution in 1788, the federal judiciary received power to resolve "controversies between two or more States" under Article III, Section 2.

The Court of Appeals in prize cases Prize cases were cases in which a private vessel captured a merchant ship from an enemy nation. Nations gave private vessels the power to do this by issuing written authority in documents called letters of marque. When a private vessel captured an enemy ship, it brought the ship into port, where a court of admiralty determined if the capture

The *Sloop Active*

One of the most famous prize cases during the American Revolution involved the *Sloop Active*. As told by Edward Dumbauld in "The Case of the Mutinous Mariner" on the Supreme Court Historical Society's Web site, the case began in 1778 when the British captured a Connecticut fisherman named Gideon Olmsted (1749–1845) and three of his crew members. In Jamaica, the British put Olmsted and his crew on the *Sloop Active,* a vessel bound for New York with supplies for the British army.

On the way to New York, Olmsted and his men mutinied, taking control of the vessel by locking the British below deck. When the vessel neared Little Egg Harbor at Cape May, New Jersey, a vessel owned by Pennsylvania captured the *Active*. The captain of the Pennsylvania vessel, Thomas Houston, took control away from Olmsted and brought the *Active* to Philadelphia.

In Philadelphia, Houston filed a case in admiralty court to claim the *Sloop Active* as a prize. Olmsted and his crew filed their own claim, arguing that the whole prize belonged to them because they had captured the vessel from the British before Houston arrived. A jury decided that Olmsted and his crew deserved only one-fourth of the prize.

Olmstead appealed the case to Congress's commission of appeals in prize cases. On December 15, 1778, the commission reversed the decision of the Pennsylvania court and awarded the whole prize to Olmsted and his men.

According to Erwin Surrency in *History of the Federal Courts,* Judge George Ross (1730–1779) of the Pennsylvania court of admiralty was furious with the commission's decision and refused to comply with it. Olmsted spent the next thirty years in lawsuits trying to recover what the commission of appeals said he deserved. He did not get his money until 1809.

General George Washington crosses the Delaware River with his troops during the Battle of Trenton. Getty Images.

was valid. If so, the ship was sold and the captors received a share of the proceeds.

In November 1775, General George Washington (1732–1799), who was leading the American army in the Revolutionary War, sent a letter to Congress from Massachusetts. Washington asked Congress to set up an admiralty court for deciding cases involving ships that received letters of marque from Congress. Congress decided state admiralty courts should hear such cases, but agreed to hear prize appeals from the state courts.

When Congress received its first prize appeal, it referred the case to a commission for decision. Commissions appointed by Congress heard all admiralty appeals until 1780. That year, Congress created a Court of Appeals, the first official American court. It decided eleven appeals over the next few years.

States sometimes refused to enforce the decisions of the Court of Appeals. The men who wrote the Constitution in 1787 kept this in mind. The Constitution gave Congress the power to grant letters of marque, gave the federal judiciary power to hear admiralty cases, and provided that "the judges in every state shall be bound" by the Constitution and laws of the United States.

For More Information

BOOKS

Goebel, Julius, Jr. *Antecedents and Beginnings to 1801.* Vol. I. New York: Macmillan, 1971.

Kelly, Alfred H., and Winfred A. Harbison. *The American Constitution: Its Origins and Development.* 5th ed. New York: W. W. Norton & Co., 1976.

Kurland, Philip B., and Ralph Lerner. *The Founders' Constitution.* 5 vols. Indianapolis: Liberty Fund, 1987.

McClenaghan, William A. *Magruder's American Government 2003.* Needham, MA: Prentice Hall School Group, 2002.

Shelley, Mack C., II. *American Government and Politics Today.* 2004–2005 ed. Belmont, CA: Wadsworth Publishing, 2003.

Surrency, Erwin C. *History of the Federal Courts.* 2nd ed. Dobbs Ferry, NY: Oceana Publications, 2002.

Volkomer, Walter E. *American Government.* 8th ed. Upper Saddle River, NJ: Prentice Hall, 1998.

Young, Roland. *American Law and Politics: The Creation of Public Order.* New York: Harper & Row, 1967.

WEB SITES

Dumbauld, Edward. "The Case of the Mutinous Mariner." *The Supreme Court Historical Society.* http://www.supremecourt history.org/04_library/subs_volumes/04_c02_h.html (accessed on March 23, 2005).

Hudson, David L., Jr. "Schiavo Law Prompts Constitutional Questions." *ABA Journal E-report.* http://www.abanet.org/journal/ereport/m25schiavo.html (accessed on March 28, 2005).

"Judge Nixes Delay in Coma Case." *CBSnews.com.* http://www.cbsnews.com/stories/2005/03/10/national/main679430.shtml (accessed on March 28, 2005).

"Key Events in the Case of Theresa Marie Schiavo." *University of Miami Ethics Programs.* http://www.miami.edu/ethics2/schiavo/timeline.htm (accessed on March 28, 2005).

Supreme Court of the United States. http://www.supremecourtus.gov (accessed on February 18, 2005).

U.S. Courts: The Federal Judiciary. http://www.uscourts.gov (accessed on March 23, 2005).

Constitutional Role of the Judicial Branch

The federal judiciary is the branch of government that holds trials and decides cases under the nation's laws. The powers of the federal judiciary appear in Article III of the U.S. Constitution. America adopted the Constitution in 1788. Before then, the country did not have a separate judiciary. Instead, a body called Congress exercised all the powers of the nation's government.

The thirteen American colonies first sent delegates to Congress in 1774. Beginning in 1781, Congress functioned under a document called the Articles of Confederation. The Articles gave Congress the power to make and enforce the nation's laws. It also gave Congress the power to establish courts to resolve particular kinds of disputes. There was no general judicial system to hear and decide cases under the nation's laws.

During the 1780s, some Americans became dissatisfied with the government under the Articles of Confederation. One main concern related to taxes. Congress could not collect taxes directly from the people. It had to collect tax money from the states instead. The states did not pay their shares reliably, and Congress could not force them to do so.

Another concern related to commerce, or business. Congress had the power to regulate commerce, but it could not stop the states from making their own commercial laws with foreign states. This prevented Congress from resolving trade problems with England, which was banning the importation, or bringing in, of certain manufactured goods from America.

Words to Know

Articles of Confederation: The document that established the federal government for the United States of America from 1781 to 1789.

checks and balances: The specific powers in one branch of government that allow it to limit the powers of the other branches.

civil case: A case that involves a dispute between private parties or a noncriminal dispute between a private party and a government.

Constitution of the United States of America: The document written in 1787 that established the federal government under which the United States of America has operated since 1789. Article III covers the judicial branch.

criminal case: A case in which a person is charged with violating a criminal law.

Founding Fathers: General term for the men who founded the United States of America and designed its government. The term includes the men who signed the Declaration of Independence in 1776 and the Constitution of the United States in 1787.

judicial interpretation: The process by which federal courts interpret the meaning of laws passed by Congress.

ratification: The process of formally approving something, such as a treaty, constitution, or constitutional amendment.

separation of powers: Division of the powers of government into different branches to prevent one branch from having too much power.

Supreme Court: The highest court in the federal judiciary. The judiciary is the branch of government responsible for resolving legal disputes and interpreting laws on a case-by-case basis.

A third weakness of the national government concerned the judiciary. Congress had the power to create a court for resolving cases in which private American vessels captured enemy merchant vessels. Congress, however, lacked the effective power to enforce the court's decisions. Moreover, Congress could not create a general judiciary for handling cases under the nation's laws.

Seven states sent delegates to a convention in Annapolis, Maryland, in September 1786 to discuss America's commercial problems under the Articles of Confederation. The delegates decided to ask Congress to call a national convention for revising the Articles. Congress issued the call in February 1787, and the Constitutional Convention met in Philadelphia, Pennsylvania, from May to September

Future president James Monroe believed that the Preamble would be an important part of the U.S. Constitution. Library of Congress.

that year. Instead of just revising the Articles, however, it recommended scrapping them entirely in favor of a whole new Constitution.

Separation of powers

There was much debate and disagreement between the delegates to the four-month Constitutional Convention in 1787. They agreed, however, that the Constitution should separate the powers of government into three branches: a legislature for making the laws, an executive for enforcing the laws, and a judiciary for deciding cases under the laws.

Nathaniel Chipman (1752–1843) was an assistant justice of the Supreme Court of Vermont when the Convention met in Philadelphia. In 1793, he published *Sketches of the Principles of Government,* in which (as reprinted in *The Founders' Constitution*) he explained the importance of separating the judiciary from the executive and legislative branches:

> There are very obvious reasons, why these powers should be committed to separate departments in the state, and not be entrusted unitedly to one man, or body of men. Different abilities are necessary for the making, judging, and executing of laws.... To commit their exercise to a single man, or body of men, essentially constitutes a monarchy, or aristocracy, for the time being. By giving them the power of avoiding all constitutional enquiry, it places them above a sense of accountability for their conduct. They have it in their power, either in the enacting, the interpretation, or the execution of the laws, to skreen [screen] themselves, and every member of their body, from account or punishment. The situation itself suggests to them, views and interests, different from those of the people, and leaves no common judge between them. It places them, in respect to the people, in that state of independence, which is often called a state of nature. In such case, the people, hopeless under oppression [domination], sink into a state of abject [hopeless] slavery, or roused to a sense of their injuries, assume their natural right, in such

situation, oppose violence to violence, and take exemplary [appropriate] vengeance of their oppressors. . . .

A separation and precise limitation of the legislative, judiciary, and executive powers, with frequent, free, and uncorrupted elections, is the only remedy for these evils. Those who exercise the legislative power, must be subjected to their own laws, and amenable [accountable] for a violation, equally with the plainest citizen. They must, by the express provision of the constitution, be confined to the consideration of general laws, and forever excluded the right of enacting particular penalties, privileges, or exemptions. Such

The Preamble

The preamble of the U.S. Constitution says:

> We, the People of the United States, in order to form a more perfect union, establish justice, insure domestic tranquility, provide for the common defence, promote the general welfare, and secure the blessings of liberty to ourselves and our posterity, do ordain and establish this Constitution for the United States of America.

In the middle of the Constitutional Convention of 1787, the delegates formed a Committee of Detail to draft language for the Constitution. The "Records of the Federal Convention" (as reprinted in *The Founders' Constitution*) reveal that during their meetings, committee members discussed the reason for including a preamble in the Constitution:

> The object of our preamble ought to be briefly to declare, that the present foederal government is insufficient to the general happiness; that the conviction of this fact gave birth to this convention; and that the only effectual mode which they can devise, for curing this insufficiency, is the establishment of a supreme legislative executive and judiciary. . . .

In 1788, Virginia delegate and future U.S. president James Monroe (1758–1831) wrote *Observations upon the Proposed Plan of Federal Government*. There (as reprinted in *The Founders' Constitution*), Monroe expressed his opinion that the preamble would be an important part of the Constitution: "The introduction, like the preamble to a law, is the Key of the Constitution. Whenever federal power is exercised, contrary to the spirit breathed by this introduction, it will be unconstitutionally exercised, and ought to be resisted by the people."

Forty-five years later, U.S. Supreme Court justice Joseph Story (1779–1845) wrote partial laws are the first beginnings of an attack on the equal rights of man, and a violation of the laws of nature. . . .

To prevent both legislative and executive abuses, the intervention of an independent judiciary is of no small importance. To the judges, the ministers of this power, it belongs to interpret all acts of the legislature, agreeably to the true principles of the constitution, as founded in the principles of natural law [the idea that human laws must conform to a higher law—one of nature, often believed to come from God], and to make an impartial application, in all cases of disputed right. By this provision, the

in *Commentaries on the Constitution* (as reprinted in *The Founders' Constitution*) that the preamble's "true office [function] is to expound [explain] the nature, and extent, and application of the powers actually conferred [presented] by the constitution."

The U.S. Supreme Court, however, has given no weight to the preamble when interpreting the Constitution. In the 1904 case of *Jacobson v. Massachusetts,* for example, the Reverend Henning Jacobson claimed that the preamble's "blessings of liberty" made it illegal for Massachusetts to force him to have a smallpox vaccination. The Supreme Court rejected the notion. It said, "Although that preamble indicates the general purposes for which the people ordained and established the Constitution, it has never been regarded as the source of any substantive power conferred on the government of the United States."

U.S. Supreme Court justice Joseph Story wrote about the Preamble of the U.S. Constitution in 1833. Getty Images.

rights and interest of the legislative and executive branches will be kept in union with the rights and interests of the individual citizens. . . .

Alexander Hamilton (1757–1804) was a delegate from New York at the Constitutional Convention. After the Convention submitted its proposed Constitution to Congress in September 1787, Hamilton joined fellow delegates James Madison (1751–1836) and John Jay (1745–1829) to write a series of essays urging the states to adopt it as the framework for American government. They signed the essays as the "Federalist," a reference to the Federalist Party, which wanted a strong national government for America. In "Federalist No. 78" (as reprinted in *The Founders' Constitution*), Hamilton wrote of the importance of an independent judiciary:

> This independence of the judges is equally requisite [required] to guard the constitution and the rights of individuals from the effects of those ill humours [whims] which the arts of designing [scheming] men, or the influence of particular conjunctures [combinations of interest], sometimes disseminate among the people themselves, and which, though they speedily give place to better information and more deliberate reflection, have a tendency in the mean time to occasion dangerous innovations in the government, and serious oppressions of the minor party in the community. . . .
>
> But it is not with a view to infractions of the constitution only that the independence of the judges may be an essential safeguard against the effects of occasional ill humours in the society. These sometimes extend no farther than to the injury of the private rights of particular classes of citizens, by unjust and partial laws. Here also the firmness of the judicial magistracy [office] is of vast importance in mitigating [minimizing] the severity, and confining the operation of such laws. It not only serves to moderate the immediate mischiefs of those which may have been passed, but it operates as a check upon the legislative body in passing them; who, perceiving that obstacles to

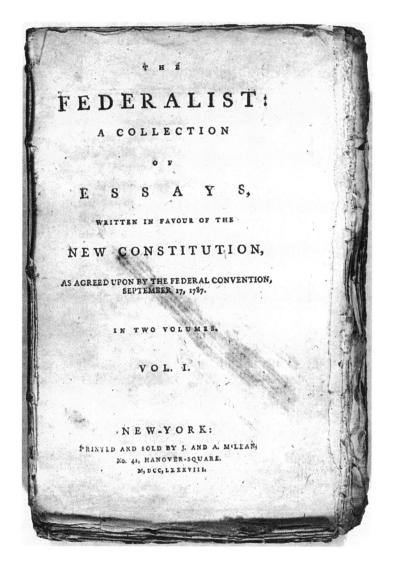

Title page from The Federalist. *Alexander Hamilton, James Madison, and John Jay were the authors.* William L. Clements Library, University of Michigan.

THE

FEDERALIST:

A COLLECTION

OF

ESSAYS,

WRITTEN IN FAVOUR OF THE

NEW CONSTITUTION,

AS AGREED UPON BY THE FEDERAL CONVENTION, SEPTEMBER 17, 1787.

IN TWO VOLUMES.

VOL. I.

NEW-YORK:

PRINTED AND SOLD BY J. AND A. M'LEAN, No. 41, HANOVER-SQUARE. M,DCC,LXXXVIII.

the success of an iniquitous [unjust] intention are to be expected from the scruples [ethics] of the courts, are in a manner compelled by the very motive of the injustice they mediate, to qualify their attempts.... Considerate men of every description ought to prize whatever will tend to beget or fortify that temper in the courts; as no man can be sure that he may not be tomorrow the victim of a spirit of injustice, by which he may be a gainer to-day. And every man must now feel that the inevitable [unavoidable] tendency of such a spirit is to sap the foundations of public and private confidence, and to introduce in its stead, universal distrust and distress.

In short, Hamilton believed judges were supposed to protect minorities from unfair treatment by legislative majorities. Hamilton was particularly concerned that legislative majorities would treat wealthy men unfairly. The spirit of Hamilton's idea, however, allows federal judges to use the Constitution to protect all kinds of minorities—property, racial, and otherwise—from legislative injustice.

Supreme Court and inferior courts

Article III of the Constitution covers the judicial branch of the federal government. It begins, "The judicial power of the United States, shall be vested in one supreme court, and in such inferior courts as the Congress may from time to time ordain and establish."

The Supreme Court is the only federal court the Constitution requires. Some delegates to the Constitutional Convention believed America would not need any more courts. Others disagreed. One of their many compromises was to leave it up to Congress to decide whether to create federal courts below the Supreme Court.

Judicial power: what kinds of cases does it cover?

Article III, Section 2, contains a list of the kinds of cases and controversies to which the judicial power "shall extend." If a case does not fall into a category in the list, the federal judiciary cannot hear it. Congress may not expand judicial power by adding cases to the list. The only way to change it is by constitutional amendment.

The U.S. Constitution, laws, and treaties The federal judiciary has the power to hear cases "in law and equity, arising under this constitution, the laws of the United States, and treaties made, or which shall be made, under their authority...." Treaties are agreements between nations. Cases "in law" refers to cases involving legal rights and responsibilities. Cases in "equity" means cases in which the courts create special remedies when the law is inadequate to resolve a private dispute.

Ambassadors, public ministers, and consuls The federal judicial power extends "to all cases affecting ambassadors, other public ministers and consuls...." Ambassadors are people who represent a nation in its relations with other nations and organizations around the world. Public ministers are government officials other than ambassadors who work in diplomacy. Consuls are government officials who represent a country's commercial interests in another nation.

Admiralty and maritime jurisdiction The judicial power covers "all cases of admiralty and maritime jurisdiction." Admiralty and maritime cases arise from the use of navigable waters, which includes oceans, seas, great lakes, and navigable rivers.

United States in lawsuit The federal judicial power covers controversies to which the United States is a party. That means lawsuits in which the United States as an entity is a participant.

Cases between states and citizens The federal judicial power initially covered "controversies between two or more states, between a state and citizens of another state, between citizens of different states, between citizens of the same state claiming lands under grants of different States, and between a state, or the citizens thereof, and foreign states, citizens or subjects."

America changed this provision with the Eleventh Amendment in 1798. The amendment prevents federal courts from hearing cases in which a state citizen sues another state, or in which a citizen or subject of a foreign nation sues one of the American states.

Original and appellate jurisdiction

After listing the kinds of cases the federal judiciary can hear, Article III, Section 2, says, "In all cases affecting ambassadors, other public ministers, and consuls, and those in which a state shall be a party, the supreme court shall have original jurisdiction. In all the other cases before mentioned, the supreme court shall have appellate jurisdiction, both as to law and fact, with such exceptions, and under such regulations as the Congress shall make."

Original jurisdiction Jurisdiction means the power of a court to hear and decide a case. Original jurisdiction gives a court the power to hold trials. Appellate jurisdiction gives a court the power to review trials and appeals from lower courts.

The Supreme Court's original jurisdiction gives it power to hold trials in cases involving ambassadors and other public ministers and consuls, and in cases in which a state is a party. Congress cannot take this power away from the Supreme Court. It is designed to ensure that ambassadors, public ministers, consuls, and states can file cases directly in the Supreme Court without having to go through lower federal courts or state courts.

Appellate jurisdiction The Constitution gives the Supreme Court appellate jurisdiction in all cases except those involving ambassadors, public ministers and consuls, and states. This means such cases must begin in either a state court or a lower federal court. The Supreme Court hears these cases only after trial, when the losing party appeals. In deciding appeals, the Supreme Court's job is to make sure judges in lower courts do not make serious mistakes concerning the meaning of the law or the procedure for holding a trial.

Congressional exceptions The Constitution says the Supreme Court has appellate jurisdiction "with such exceptions, and under such regulations as the Congress shall make." Some scholars think this means Congress can revoke all of the Supreme Court's appellate jurisdiction. Doing so would leave the Supreme Court to hear only cases under its original jurisdiction, meaning those involving ambassadors, other public ministers and consuls, and states.

In 1868, Congress revoked the Supreme Court's appellate jurisdiction to prevent it from deciding a specific case. The case involved a portion of the Reconstruction Acts, which were laws Congress passed after the American Civil War (1861–65) for bringing the Confederate States back into the United States. In March 1868, Congress feared the Supreme Court was going to use the case to strike down the Reconstruction Acts as unconstitutional. To prevent this, Congress passed a bill revoking the Supreme Court's power to review the kind of case the Court was considering.

The Supreme Court soon dismissed the case, saying it no longer had the power to decide it. In a unanimous written opinion, the Supreme Court said Congress had acted lawfully in revoking the Court's appellate power: "The power to make exceptions to the appellate jurisdiction of this Court is given by express words.... Without jurisdiction the Court cannot proceed at all in any cause. Jurisdiction is power to declare the law, and when it ceases to exist, the only function remaining to the Court is that of announcing the fact and dismissing the cause."

As of 2005, this is the only time Congress has revoked the Supreme Court's appellate jurisdiction to prevent it from deciding a pending case. Over the years, members of Congress have introduced bills for revoking the Supreme Court's power to review state supreme court decisions and to hear cases involving congressional investigations, the rights of accused criminals, and state laws concerning abortion and school prayer. None of these bills ever made it through Congress to become law.

Scholars debate whether Congress can lawfully revoke the Supreme Court's appellate jurisdiction. On the one hand, the language in the Constitution is clear, and the Supreme Court itself has ruled that such action by Congress is lawful.

On the other hand, the Constitution contains a list of the kinds of cases to which the judicial power "shall extend." This list includes those cases that fall under the Court's appellate jurisdiction. The phrase "shall extend" might be mandatory language that allows Congress to regulate the Court's appellate jurisdiction without revoking it. Some scholars think allowing Congress to control the Supreme Court's appellate power destroys the independence of the federal judiciary. Still others think the men who wrote the Constitution did not mean to give Congress such power.

Judicial power: what is it?

The Constitution gives "the judicial power" to the Supreme Court and to any lower courts Congress creates. The Constitution, however, does not define "the judicial power." Clues appear in other constitutional clauses, the records of the Constitutional Convention, and writings of the people who wrote and adopted the Constitution. Judicial power includes the power to hold trials, hear appeals, issue writs of habeas corpus, interpret laws, and review government conduct for compliance with the Constitution.

Trials It was widely accepted in 1787 that the judicial power included the power to hold trials in civil and criminal cases. Civil cases are disputes between private people or businesses, or noncriminal disputes between a person or business and a government. Criminal cases involve violations of criminal laws.

The Constitution of 1787 contains specific directions for criminal trials. Article III, Section 2, says, "The trial of all crimes, except in cases of impeachment, shall be by jury; and such trial shall be held in the state where the said crimes shall have been committed; but when not committed within any state, the trial shall be at such place or places as the Congress may by law have directed."

This clause requires all federal criminal trials to be by jury. A jury is a random group of citizens from the community in which a trial is held. During criminal trials, juries hear and see evidence, including documents, other physical evidence, and the testimony of witnesses. Next, the judge explains the law that applies to the case. Then the jury moves to a private room to decide whether the defendant is guilty under the applicable law.

Treason is one of the many crimes that may be tried in federal courts. The men who wrote the Constitution defined treason very specifically. Article III, Section 3, says, "Treason against the United States, shall consist only in levying war against them, or in adhering to their enemies, giving them aid and comfort. No person shall be convicted of treason unless on the testimony of two witnesses to the same overt [open] act, or on confession in open court." The men who wrote the Constitution defined treason specifically to prevent it from being used unfairly as a political weapon, including against presidents.

The Constitution of 1787 does not contain specific provisions concerning civil trials. The list of cases the judiciary has the power to hear, however, includes cases of a civil

American Revolution general Benedict Arnold is perhaps the American historical figure best known for committing the crime of treason. After an unsuccessful plot to surrender West Point to England, Arnold began fighting for the British. Library of Congress.

nature, such as "controversies ... between citizens of different states." So the federal judiciary clearly has the power to hold civil trials.

Appeals After a trial in a civil or criminal case, the court enters a judgment in favor of the winning party. The losing party usually can appeal the case to an appellate court. Appellate courts review trials to make sure judges and juries do not make serious mistakes. The U.S. Supreme Court also reviews decisions by lower appellate courts.

The kinds of mistakes appellate courts look for are misapplication of the law, errors in the admission of evidence for the jury to consider, and errors in the general procedure of the trial. By giving the Supreme Court "appellate jurisdiction," the Constitution clearly gives the federal judiciary the power to hear and decide appeals.

The 1969 case of *Tinker v. Des Moines Independent Community School District* illustrates the appeals process. As noted in *Supreme Court Drama,* the *Tinker* case happened during the Vietnam War (1954–75), a war between North and South Vietnam. The United States entered the war in the 1960s to fight for South Vietnam to protect it from communism. The war became unpopular as tens of thousands of American soldiers died with no indication that North Vietnam could be defeated. Protests against the war became common in America.

In Des Moines, Iowa, sixteen-year-old Christopher Eckhardt, fifteen-year-old John P. Tinker, and thirteen-year-old Mary Beth Tinker decided to protest the war by wearing black armbands with a peace symbol to their high school and junior high school. A former student from the high school had died in the war, and some students said they would wear different colored armbands to support the war. When the school principals learned of the plans, they announced that anyone wearing a black armband to school would be told to remove it and suspended for refusal to do so. Eckhardt and the Tinkers were suspended under this policy.

With help from their parents, the students filed a lawsuit in a federal district court. They asked the court to stop the schools from enforcing the "no armband" policy. They said the policy violated their rights under the First Amendment of the U.S. Constitution, which says the government may not abridge, or limit, the freedom of speech. The federal district court disagreed, ruling that the schools were allowed to enforce the "no armband" policy to prevent disturbances. The students appealed to the Court of Appeals for the Eighth Circuit, but it affirmed the district court's decision, so the students appealed to the U.S. Supreme Court.

In a 7-2 decision, the Supreme Court ruled in favor of the students. Writing for the Court, Justice Abe Fortas (1910–1982) said wearing armbands to protest a war is a form of speech called "symbolic" speech. Symbolic speech is speech that conveys ideas with symbols or actions instead of words. The First Amendment protects many kinds of speech, including symbolic speech. Justice

Fortas said, "Students in school as well as out of school are 'persons' under our Constitution." Because the students had not disrupted school activities, their protest was protected by the First Amendment. The federal district court had been wrong to approve the "no armband" policy.

Privilege of the writ of habeas corpus A writ of habeas corpus is an order that forces the executive branch to explain why a person has been imprisoned. People who believe they have been imprisoned illegally can ask a court to issue a writ. If the court agrees the imprisonment is illegal, it can set the prisoner free.

The U.S. Supreme Court has ruled that the federal judiciary has the power to issue writs of habeas corpus only when Congress gives it such power. Article I, Section 9, of the Constitution, however, says, "The privilege of the writ of habeas corpus shall not be suspended, unless when in cases of rebellion or invasion the public safety may require it." The phrase "shall not be suspended" arguably means federal courts must have the power to issue such writs. In any event, congressional law has continuously given federal courts this power since 1789.

Judicial interpretation In a criminal trial, a jury decides whether the defendant has violated the law. In a civil trial, a judge or jury decides whether one party has violated the legal rights of another party. In both cases, the judge must decide which law or laws apply to the situation. In jury trials, the judge explains the law to the jury before it makes a decision. In civil trials without a jury, called bench trials, the judge alone applies the law to the case.

Judicial interpretation is the act of deciding what a law means and how it applies to a particular case. Trial judges engage in judicial interpretation each time they instruct the jury on the applicable law in jury trials and each time they apply the law themselves in bench trials. Appellate judges interpret the law every time they review whether a trial judge or lower appellate judge applied the law properly in a specific case.

Judicial interpretation involves many kinds of laws. Judges interpret the Constitution, laws passed by Congress, regulations passed by federal agencies, and treaties with foreign nations. Judges also interpret the common law. Common law is law made by English and American judges on a case-by-case basis to govern private relationships between people. Examples of common law include the law of contracts and the law of torts. (A contract is an agreement between two or more people. A tort is a civil wrong or injury, such as assault and battery.)

Original Intent

Interpreting the Constitution is one of the most important duties of the federal judiciary. It is also one of the most difficult, because the Constitution is not always clear.

There are many methods for interpreting the Constitution. One is called the doctrine of original intent. Original intent means trying to figure out what the men who wrote the Constitution meant by the words they used.

There are a number of ways to interpret the Constitution through original intent. One is to study just the language of the Constitution. Another is to study the records of the Constitutional Convention. Yet another is to study the writings of the men who wrote the Constitution.

Interestingly, one of the primary authors of the Constitution felt the records of the Constitutional Convention should play no role in interpreting the document. Writing a letter in 1821, former president James Madison (1751–1836; served 1809–17), who also served as a Virginia convention delegate, said (as reprinted in *The Founders' Constitution*):

> As a guide in expounding [interpreting] and applying the provisions of the Constitution, the debates and incidental decisions of the Convention can have no authoritative character. However desirable it be that they should be preserved as a gratification to the laudable curiosity felt by every people to trace the origin and progress of their political Institutions, & as a source perhaps of some lights on the Science of Govt. the legitimate meaning of the Instrument must be derived from the text itself; or if a key is to be sought elsewhere, it must not be in the opinions or intentions of the Body which planned & proposed the Constitution, but in the sense attached to it by the people in their respective State Conventions where it recd. [received] all the Authority which it possesses.

Madison, in fact, took more notes during the Convention than any other delegate. According to Leonard W. Levy in *Original Intent and the Framers' Constitution*, Madison "was present every day and never absent for more than 'a casual fraction of an hour in any day,' so that he heard every speech. He sat center front so that he could hear everything, and every evening he wrote out his daily notes. He told a friend that the labor 'almost killed him' but he determined to finish the task, and he did."

Madison decided not to allow his notes to be published until after all the Convention delegates died. As it turned out, Madison was the last delegate to die, in 1836, so his notes were not published until 1840. Since then, courts and scholars have used them to interpret what the Constitution means.

Massachusetts delegate Elbridge Gerry, who would become the nation's fifth vice president in 1813, joined fellow delegate Rufus King in opposing the idea of members of the Supreme Court serving on a council with the president for vetoing laws passed by congress. © Bettmann/Corbis.

The Constitution does not specifically say federal courts have the power to interpret the law. Judicial interpretation, however, was generally accepted as a responsibility of trial and appellate judges in 1787.

Judicial review Judicial review is the power to determine whether a congressional law or executive action violates the Constitution. Federal judges exercise this power by striking down laws, regulations, and other government conduct they find unconstitutional.

The power of judicial review is controversial. The Constitution does not specifically give the federal judiciary this power. Many disagree strongly over whether it is proper for federal courts to exercise judicial review.

Some who favor judicial review find support for it in the Supremacy Clause of the Constitution. It says, "This constitution, and the laws of the United States which shall be made in pursuance thereof; and all treaties made, or which shall be made, under the authority of the United States, shall be the supreme law of the land. . . ." Supporters of judicial review say only courts can determine whether congressional laws are "made in pursuance" of the Constitution.

Many delegates at the Constitutional Convention believed the federal judiciary would have the power of judicial review. On June 4, 1787, the delegates discussed a proposal that members of the Supreme Court serve on a council with the president for vetoing, or rejecting, laws passed by Congress. According to the *Records of the Federal Convention* (as reprinted in *The Founders' Constitution*), delegates Elbridge Gerry (1744–1814) and Rufus King (1755–1827) opposed the idea:

> Mr. Gerry doubts whether the Judiciary ought to form a part of [the council for vetoing legislation], as they will have a sufficient check agst. [against] encroachments on their own department by their exposition [interpretation] of the laws, which involved a power of deciding on their Constitutionality. In some States the Judges had actually set aside laws as being agst. the Constitution. This was done too with general approbation [approval]. It was quite foreign from the nature of ye.

New York delegate Rufus King was against the idea of Supreme Court justices serving on a council with the president for rejecting laws passed by Congress. Library of Congress.

[the] office to make them judges of the policy of public measures....

Mr. King seconds the motion [to defeat the council], observing that the Judges ought to be able to expound [interpret] the law as it should come before them, free from the bias of having participated in its formation.

The delegates ultimately rejected the idea of the council, and gave the president the sole power to veto laws passed by Congress.

Hamilton was another delegate who believed federal courts would have the power of judicial review. Writing in one of his "Federalist" essays, Hamilton said that as the Constitution is the supreme law of the land, any law that violates the Constitution must fall. The judiciary, Hamilton believed, would be the only branch capable of deciding whether a law violated the Constitution. Otherwise, there would be no check on the constitutionality of congressional conduct.

Contrary to Gerry's suggestion, however, the exercise of judicial review by state courts was not beyond controversy. Today some scholars and citizens believe that Congress, as the branch of government representative of the people, is the one that should determine whether government conduct is constitutional or not. In 1803, however, the U.S. Supreme Court settled the question, declaring its power to strike down unconstitutional laws. Since then, Congress has considered bills and constitutional amendments to strip the judiciary of the power of judicial review, but such proposals have not become law as of 2005.

Impeachment trials of presidents

Article II, Section 4, says the president, vice president, and other civil officers may be removed from office only upon impeachment for and conviction of treason, bribery, or other high crimes and misdemeanors. Under Article I, the House of Representatives has the power of impeachment. Impeachment is an official accusation of wrongdoing that can lead to conviction and removal from office by the Senate. The Senate has the power to try, convict, and remove civil officers impeached in the House.

The vice president of the United States serves as president of the Senate, even during impeachment trials. The one exception is impeachment trials of presidents. Because the vice president replaces a president who is removed from office, it would not be appropriate for the vice president to oversee presidential impeachment trials. In such cases, the chief justice of the Supreme Court presides over the Senate trial.

The chief justice is the head of the Supreme Court. When the chief justice presides over a presidential impeachment trial, his primary role is to interpret and enforce the Senate's rules for conducting the trial. The Senate, however, can overrule a ruling by the chief justice. The chief justice, moreover, does not get to vote whether to convict the president who is being tried.

Appointment, compensation, and removal of justices and judges

The Constitution gives the president the power to nominate, or appoint, people to serve as justices of the Supreme Court and judges of the lower federal courts. The Senate, however, must approve the president's nominations by a simple majority. The Constitution contains no qualification requirements for people appointed to the judiciary.

Article III, Section 1, says, "The judges, both of the supreme and inferior courts, shall hold their offices during good behavior, and shall, at stated times, receive for their services, a compensation, which shall not be diminished during their continuance in office." This provision is designed to make the federal judiciary independent from the executive and legislative branches. The compensation provision prevents Congress from controlling judges by threatening to lower their salaries.

The provision on good behavior prevents the president from controlling judges by threatening to fire them. Instead, judges keep their jobs as long as they want during "good behavior." This means judges can only be removed from office by impeachment or conviction in Congress for treason, bribery, and other high crimes and misdemeanors. As of 2005, Congress has removed just seven judges from office through impeachment.

For More Information

BOOKS

Biskupic, Joan, and Elder Witt. *The Supreme Court at Work.* Washington, DC: Congressional Quarterly, Inc., 1997.

Brannen, Daniel E., and Richard Clay Hanes. *Supreme Court Drama: Cases That Changed America.* Detroit: UXL, 2001.

Goebel, Julius, Jr. *Antecedents and Beginnings to 1801.* Vol. I. New York: Macmillan, 1971.

Kelly, Alfred H., and Winfred A. Harbison. *The American Constitution: Its Origins and Development.* 5th ed. New York: W. W. Norton & Co., 1976.

Kurland, Philip B., and Ralph Lerner. *The Founders' Constitution.* 5 vols. Indianapolis: Liberty Fund, 1987.

Levy, Leonard W. *Original Intent and the Framers' Constitution.* New York: Macmillan, 1988.

McClenaghan, William A. *Magruder's American Government 2003.* Needham, MA: Prentice Hall School Group, 2002.

Schwartz, Bernard. *A History of the Supreme Court.* New York: Oxford University Press, 1993.

Shelley, Mack C., II. *American Government and Politics Today.* 2004–2005 ed. Belmont, CA: Wadsworth Publishing, 2003.

Surrency, Erwin C. *History of the Federal Courts.* 2nd ed. Dobbs Ferry, NY: Oceana Publications, 2002.

Volkomer, Walter E. *American Government.* 8th ed. Upper Saddle River, NJ: Prentice Hall, 1998.

Young, Roland. *American Law and Politics: The Creation of Public Order.* New York: Harper & Row, 1967.

CASES

Jacobson v. Massachusetts, 197 U.S. 11 (1904).

Tinker v. Des Moines Independent Community School District, 393 U.S. 503 (1969).

WEB SITES

Supreme Court of the United States. http://www.supremecourtus.gov (accessed on February 18, 2005).

U.S. Courts: The Federal Judiciary. http://www.uscourts.gov (accessed on March 23, 2005).

Changes in the Judicial Branch

In 1787, delegates from twelve American states wrote the Constitution of the United States. The Constitution divided the government into three branches. The legislative branch, Congress, makes the nation's laws. The executive branch, headed by the president, enforces the laws. The judicial branch, headed by the Supreme Court, holds trials and decides cases under the laws.

The Constitution gives the Supreme Court the power to hold trials in cases involving ambassadors, public ministers, consuls, and states. Public ministers are diplomatic officials other than ambassadors. Consuls are government officials who represent a country's commercial interests in another country.

In all other kinds of cases, the Supreme Court has the power to hear appeals from state courts and lower federal courts. An appeal is when a court reviews whether a judge or jury in a lower court made any serious mistakes. The Supreme Court has the power to decide appeals in cases arising under the Constitution and federal laws and treaties, cases involving vessels on navigable, or crossable, waters, cases in which the United States as an entity is a participant, and cases between citizens.

The Supreme Court is the only court the federal judiciary is required to have under the Constitution. The Constitution gives Congress the sole power to decide whether to create any courts below the Supreme Court. The history of the federal judiciary since 1787 involves growth of the federal judicial system and its powers.

Words to Know

checks and balances: The specific powers in one branch of government that allow it to limit the powers of the other branches.

civil case: A case that involves a dispute between private parties or a noncriminal dispute between a private party and a government.

Constitution of the United States of America: The document written in 1787 that established the federal government under which the United States of America has operated since 1789. Article III covers the judicial branch.

criminal case: A case in which a person is charged with violating a criminal law.

Founding Fathers: General term for the men who founded the United States of America and designed its government. The term includes the men who signed the Declaration of Independence in 1776 and the Constitution of the United States in 1787.

judicial interpretation: The process by which federal courts interpret the meaning of laws passed by Congress.

judicial review: The process by which federal courts review laws to determine whether they violate the U.S. Constitution. If a court finds that a law violates the Constitution, it declares the law unconstitutional, which means the executive branch is not supposed to enforce it anymore. Congress can correct such a defect by passing a new law that does not violate the Constitution.

ratification: The process of formally approving something, such as a treaty, constitution, or constitutional amendment.

separation of powers: Division of the powers of government into different branches to prevent one branch from having too much power.

Supreme Court: The highest court in the federal judiciary. The judiciary is the branch of government responsible for resolving legal disputes and interpreting laws on a case-by-case basis.

Judiciary Act of 1789

The First Congress under the Constitution met in April 1789. Members of the Federalist Party had majority control of both chambers, the House of Representatives and the Senate. Federalists wanted to construct a strong national government under the Constitution. Their main rivals, called Anti-Federalists, wanted state governments to be stronger than the national government.

One of the most important bills the first Congress passed was "An Act to Establish the Federal Courts of the United States." The act became known as the Judiciary Act of 1789. President George Washington (1732–1799; served 1789–97) signed it into law on September 24, 1789.

The Judiciary Act created a federal judiciary with trial courts and appellate courts to serve under the Supreme Court.

It was a victory for Federalists, who wanted an extensive federal judiciary. Anti-Federalists wanted state courts to handle trials, even in cases concerning federal laws.

District and circuit courts The Judiciary Act of 1789 created two types of trial courts—district courts and circuit courts. There were thirteen district courts. Eleven covered each of the eleven states that had ratified, or formally approved, the Constitution by then. (North Carolina did not ratify until November 1789, and Rhode Island did not ratify until May 1790.) Two district courts covered Maine and Kentucky, which were part of Massachusetts and Virginia, respectively, at the time.

Each district court had one judge. The district courts had the power to hold trials in cases involving admiralty law and minor federal crimes. Admiralty cases involve the use of navigable waters, such as oceans, seas, great lakes, and rivers. District courts could also hold trials in minor civil cases filed by the United States. A civil case is a noncriminal dispute between private parties or between a private party and the government.

The Judiciary Act grouped the eleven states into three circuits—eastern, middle, and southern—and created one circuit court for each circuit. Two Supreme Court justices and one district court judge served each circuit. Circuit courts held trials in civil cases between citizens of different states, major civil cases filed by the United States, and cases involving major crimes. Circuit courts also heard appeals from certain trials in the district courts.

Supreme Court The Constitution makes the Supreme Court the highest court in the federal judiciary. It also requires a chief justice to be head of the Court. The Constitution is silent, however, on how many justices must serve on the Court. The Judiciary Act of 1789 set the number at six, and assigned them in pairs to sit as trial judges in the three circuit courts.

The Constitution gives the Supreme Court the power to hold trials in cases involving ambassadors, public ministers, consuls, and states. The Judiciary Act of 1789 repeated this provision.

The Constitution says the Supreme Court may hear appeals in cases arising under the Constitution and federal laws and treaties, admiralty cases, cases in which the United States is a party, and cases between citizens. Congress, however, may make exceptions to this appellate power. In the Judiciary Act of 1789, Congress gave the Supreme Court the power to hear appeals mostly in civil cases involving more than $2,000. The Supreme Court did not get general power to hear appeals in criminal cases until the 1890s.

Section 25 of the Judiciary Act contained a controversial provision. It gave the Supreme Court the power to hear appeals from the highest court of each state in cases involving interpretation of the federal Constitution. Anti-Federalists disliked the notion that the Supreme Court could reverse a decision by a state court. This, however, has remained part of the Supreme Court's power of judicial review ever since.

Office of the attorney general The Judiciary Act of 1789 created the position of attorney general, who is the lead attorney for the United States. The president appoints the attorney general with approval by a simple majority of the Senate. The Judiciary Act also authorized the president to appoint U.S. attorneys to assist the attorney general with the government's caseload. In 1870, the attorney general became head of the U.S. Department of Justice, one of the major departments in the executive branch.

Bill of Rights

A bill of rights is a law protecting the basic rights of citizens. When the state delegates began debating in 1787 whether to ratify the Constitution, Anti-Federalists wanted the Constitution to have a bill of rights. Federalists agreed to seek a bill of rights if the Anti-Federalists would vote to ratify the Constitution. Such promises led to ratification by eleven of the thirteen American states by July 1788.

During the first Congress in 1789, U.S. representative (and future president) James Madison (1751–1836) of Virginia drafted twelve proposed amendments. On September 24, 1789, the House of Representatives voted to submit them to the states for consideration, and the Senate voted similarly the next day. Eleven states ratified ten of the amendments by the end of 1791, making them part of the Constitution. Those ten came to be

Amos Tappan Akerman, who served as attorney general during the Ulysses S. Grant administration from 1870 to 1871.

called the Bill of Rights. Many of the amendments affect the work of the federal judiciary.

The Fourth Amendment The executive branch is responsible for enforcing the nation's laws. Enforcement often involves searching a home or other place for evidence of a crime, seizing evidence, and arresting suspected criminals. The Fourth Amendment usually requires federal law enforcement agents to get a warrant from a court before conducting a search, seizure, or arrest.

The Fourth Amendment says, "No Warrants shall issue, but upon probable cause, supported by Oath or affirmation,

The Law of the Land or the Law of the Living?

The U.S. Constitution has been the framework for American government since its adoption in 1788. In 1789, future president Thomas Jefferson wrote a letter to future president James Madison, sharing his opinion on the duration of the Constitution:

> [No] society can make a perpetual [ongoing] constitution, or even a perpetual law. The earth belongs always to the living generation. They may manage it then, and what proceeds from it, as they please, during their usufruct [right to use something without destroying it]. They are masters too of their own persons, and consequently may govern them as they please. But persons and property make the sum of the objects of government.

The constitution and the laws of their predecessors extinguished then in their natural course with those who gave them being. This could preserve that being till it ceased to be itself, and no longer. Every constitution then, and every law, naturally expires at the end of 19 years. If it be enforced longer, it is an act of force, and not of right.

As of 2005, the Constitution has been in effect for 217 years. It has been amended twenty-seven times during that time. Some believe the Constitution is a living document, the words of which are flexible enough to allow their meaning to change over time to serve the needs of a changing country. Others think the Constitution can serve America well enough as it was written in 1787, without flexible, changing interpretations. Still others think the Constitution is outdated and ought to be rewritten entirely.

and particularly describing the place to be searched, and the persons or things to be seized." Probable cause means that federal courts cannot issue warrants unless there is good reason to believe a crime has been committed and that the search or seizure might produce evidence of it. Courts must base this determination on sworn testimony or affidavits (signed statements) of witnesses or law enforcement agents. A warrant must specifically describe the place to be searched or the person or thing to be seized. Law enforcement agents are supposed to obey these limitations.

The famous case of *Mapp v. Ohio* illustrates how the Fourth Amendment works. In May 1957, police in Cleveland, Ohio, had information that a bombing suspect was hiding in the home of Dollree Mapp. They also thought the house had illegal gambling equipment. When the police went to Mapp's house, she would not let them in, so they forced their way in without a search warrant. They did not find the bombing suspect or any gambling

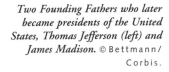

Two Founding Fathers who later became presidents of the United States, Thomas Jefferson (left) and James Madison. © B e t t m a n n /
C o r b i s .

equipment, but they found obscene material that was illegal to have under Ohio law. A state court convicted Mapp for having the obscene material and put her in prison.

Mapp appealed her conviction to the Ohio Supreme Court. That court affirmed her conviction, so she appealed again to the U.S. Supreme Court. With a 6-3 decision in 1961, the Supreme Court reversed Mapp's conviction. Writing for the majority, Justice Tom Campbell Clark (1899–1977) said the police violated Mapp's Fourth Amendment rights by searching her home without first getting a search warrant. Under a Supreme Court doctrine called the exclusionary rule, evidence found during an illegal search may not be used to convict a suspect. Because police found the obscene material during an illegal search, they were not allowed to use it to convict Mapp of violating Ohio's obscenity law.

The Fifth Amendment The Fifth Amendment prevents a person from being tried for a capital or infamous crime unless a grand jury finds good reason for the charge. A grand jury is a random group of citizens from the community, often more than the twelve who typically sit on a regular jury for a full criminal trial. Federal courts supervise federal grand jury proceedings.

The Fifth Amendment says a person may not be tried twice for the same crime or be forced to be a witness against him- or herself. The amendment prevents the federal government from taking away a person's life, liberty, or property without due process of law, which means fair legal proceedings. Finally, it prevents the government from taking a person's private property without giving him or her fair compensation. Federal judges are required to enforce these rights in the cases they hear.

The Sixth Amendment The Constitution says all federal criminal trials must be by jury in the state where the crime was committed. The Sixth Amendment expanded the rights of defendants in criminal trials. It requires criminal trials to be public and speedy. Criminal defendants have the right to know the charges against them, to question the witnesses against them, to force favorable witnesses to testify for them, and to be assisted by an attorney. Federal judges are supposed to enforce these rights for criminal defendants in federal criminal trials.

The Seventh Amendment The Constitution of 1787 did not contain specific provisions for civil trials. The Seventh Amendment changed this. It preserves the common law right to jury trials in cases involving more than $20. Common law is law made by English and American judges on a case-by-case basis to decide cases between private individuals, such cases involving breach of contract, defamation of character, and negligence. (Defamation is when one person wrongfully harms another's reputation. Negligence is when one person harms another person or property through careless action). The Seventh Amendment also prevents federal courts from changing a jury's factual findings in civil cases except as allowed under common law.

The Eighth Amendment The Eighth Amendment says, "Excessive bail shall not be required, nor excessive fines imposed, nor cruel and unusual punishments inflicted." Bail is a legal payment criminal defendants must make to be free prior to their trials. Defendants get the money back when they appear for trial. Fines are punishments for violating civil and criminal laws. Punishments are not cruel and unusual, according to the Supreme Court, when society generally approves them.

Eleventh Amendment

The Constitution gave the federal judiciary the power to hear cases "between a state and citizens of another state." Such cases could be filed directly in the Supreme Court.

When Americans debated whether to ratify the Constitution, Anti-Federalists were concerned about this provision. They thought requiring states to appear in federal courts would threaten the sovereignty, or independent power, of the states. According to Alfred H. Kelly and Winfred A. Harbison in *The American Constitution,* prominent Federalists assured the Anti-Federalists that this provision would not apply to cases filed against states unless the states agreed to be sued in federal court.

The Federalists, however, were wrong. Soon after construction of the federal judiciary in 1789, citizens began suing states in the Supreme Court. In one case, two citizens of South Carolina sued the state of Georgia to recover property that Georgia officials had confiscated, or taken. Georgia officials refused to appear in the Supreme Court. They sent a letter saying the Supreme Court had no power to hear a case filed against a state by a citizen of another state.

In 1793, the Supreme Court issued its decision in *Chisholm v. Georgia.* The Supreme Court rejected Georgia's argument that the Court lacked the power to hear the case, finding in favor of the citizens of South Carolina. The Court said the American states had consented to being sued in federal courts by state citizens when they ratified the U.S. Constitution.

Secretary of State James Madison was a key figure in the Marbury v. Madison *case.* © Corbis.

After the Court's decision, Anti-Federalists led a movement to change the Constitution with the Eleventh Amendment. Congress proposed the amendment in 1794. It says, "The Judicial power of the United States shall not be construed to extend to any suit in law or equity, commenced or prosecuted against one of the United States by Citizens of another State, or by Citizens or Subjects of any Foreign State." The Eleventh Amendment became part of the Constitution in January 1798.

Judicial review and *Marbury v. Madison*

Judicial review is the power to determine whether congressional laws and executive actions are valid under the Constitution. The Constitution does not specifically give the federal judiciary this power. It says that the Constitution, and laws and treaties made under it, are the supreme law of the land, and that state judges must obey them.

The Judiciary Act of 1789 enforced this requirement by giving the Supreme Court the power to hear appeals from state courts in particular cases. This power generally covered cases in which a state's highest court declared a federal law or treaty unconstitutional, ruled that a state law did not violate the Constitution, or ruled against a constitutional right.

The Judiciary Act did not specifically give the Supreme Court the power to determine whether laws passed by Congress were valid under the Constitution. The Supreme Court, however, announced this power in the 1803 case of *Marbury v. Madison.* Attorney William Marbury had sued Secretary of State James Madison in the Supreme Court. Marbury wanted the Court to force Madison to give him a commission for a justice-of-the-peace job to which President John Adams (1735–1826; served 1797–1801) had appointed Marbury just before leaving office in 1801. The Judiciary Act of 1789 said the Supreme Court could hold trials for orders, called writs of mandamus, to force government officials to do their jobs.

Chief Justice John Marshall (1755–1835) wrote the Court's decision in the case. Marshall said Marbury deserved the commission, but that the Court could not force Madison to deliver it. The reason was that the Constitution did not give the Supreme Court the power to hold trials for writs of mandamus.

When U.S. Supreme Court justice William Cushing (above) was ill in 1801, the Federalist-controlled Congress reduced the number of members on the Court from six to five to prevent incoming Democratic-Republican president Thomas Jefferson from getting to appoint a new justice if Cushing died. The number was raised back to six a year later, and Cushing wound up living until 1810. Supreme Court of the United States.

So the Judiciary Act of 1789 violated the Constitution by trying to give the Supreme Court this power. Marshall said federal courts must strike down congressional laws that violate the constitution.

Size of the Supreme Court

The Judiciary Act of 1789 set the number of Supreme Court justices at six. Between then and 1869, Congress raised the number five times and lowered it twice. The increases generally happened as the country grew and Congress created new circuit courts and district courts. Beginning in 1802, Congress assigned one Supreme Court justice to travel to each circuit to hear trials.

Increases also happened when Congress wanted to give a president power to appoint more justices to the Court. The Court reached its largest size to date in 1863, when Congress raised the number of justices to ten. This allowed President Abraham Lincoln (1809–1865; served 1861–65) to appoint a new justice, Stephen J. Field (1816–1899), at a time when Lincoln was stretching his constitutional powers to conduct the American Civil War (1861–65). Lincoln wanted the Court to have justices who would approve his war powers.

The first time Congress lowered the number of Supreme Court seats was in early 1801, when the Federalist-controlled Congress reduced the number from six to five. Congress did this to prevent the incoming Democratic-Republican president, Thomas Jefferson (1743–1826; served 1801–9), from getting to appoint someone if Justice William Cushing (1732–1810), who was ill, died. In 1802, after the Democratic-Republicans gained control in Congress, Congress raised the number of justices back to six. (Cushing lived until 1810, past Jefferson's two terms in office.)

In 1866, Congress reduced the number of Supreme Court seats from ten to seven. At the time, Congress had passed Reconstruction Acts for rebuilding the country after the American Civil War. President Andrew Johnson (1808–1875; served 1865–69) opposed many of Congress's policies, so Congress feared he might appoint justices who would strike down the acts as unconstitutional. Reducing the number of seats from ten to seven prevented Johnson from filling vacancies when

The appointment of Stephen J. Field (right) by President Abraham Lincoln in 1863 raised the total number of U.S. Supreme Court justices to ten, the largest size to date. Library of Congress.

two of the Court's justices, John Catron (1786–1865) and James M. Wayne (1790–1867), died.

Three years later, in 1869, Congress raised the number of Supreme Court seats from seven to nine, shortly after the inauguration of Ulysses S. Grant (1822–1885; served 1869–77). The number has been fixed there ever since.

The Thirteenth, Fourteenth, and Fifteenth Amendments

Near the end of the American Civil War in February 1865, Congress proposed a constitutional amendment to make slavery illegal in the United States. Twenty-seven states ratified it by the end of the year, making it the Thirteenth Amendment to the Constitution.

Ending slavery did not bring political equality to newly freed slaves. Many Southern states enacted so-called Black Codes, treating African Americans differently than white Americans under the law. The Black Codes had harsh vagrancy laws for African Americans. The codes set up apprenticeship, or training, programs that gave African Americans little more freedom at work than they had as slaves. Criminal punishment for African Americans was more severe than for white Americans. The laws established racial segregation, or separation, in schools and public facilities. Some laws prevented African Americans from testifying in courts of law.

To abolish the Black Codes and win political support from African Americans, Congress proposed the Fourteenth Amendment in June 1866. Section 1 declares that all people born or naturalized (legally declared a citizen) in the United States are citizens of the country and of the state in which they live. The Privileges and Immunities Clause says states may not pass laws that abridge, or lessen, the privileges and immunities, or rights, of American citizens. The Due Process Clause says states may not deprive people of life, liberty, or property without due process of law, which means fair legal proceedings. Finally, the Equal Protection Clause says states may not deny any person the equal protection of the laws.

The Fourteenth Amendment became part of the Constitution in June 1868. Southern states, however, continued to treat African Americans unfairly. One tactic was to prevent African Americans from voting in elections. In February 1869, Congress proposed the Fifteenth Amendment. It says, "The right of citizens of the United States to vote shall not be denied or abridged by the United States or by any State on account of race, color, or previous condition of servitude." The states ratified the Fifteenth Amendment by March 1870.

The Thirteenth, Fourteenth, and Fifteenth Amendments gave Congress the power to enforce them with appropriate legislation. If a state passes a law that violates one of the so-called Civil War Amendments, however, the federal judiciary is where citizens often turn for help. Under its power of judicial review, the

African American vagrants are rounded up in New Orleans, Louisiana, in 1864, a result of the enactment of the Black Codes in Southern states. Granger Collection, New York.

Supreme Court can strike down state laws that violate the Constitution and its amendments.

Judiciary Acts of 1869 and 1875

America had thirty-six states soon after the Civil War. Most of the states had one to three federal district courts, which continued to handle minor trials under federal law. As the country grew, backlogs in the district courts grew, too.

Congress divided the states into nine judicial circuits, each of which had a circuit court. Circuit courts continued to handle major trials plus some appeals from the district courts. Supreme Court justices still traveled to circuit courts for trials. There were not enough justices, however, to cover the circuits adequately, so in 1869 Congress added a circuit court judge to each circuit. As in the district courts, the circuit court dockets became backlogged with cases.

Congress began to reorganize the judiciary with the Judiciary Act of 1875. It shifted some kinds of trials from the circuit courts to the district courts and gave the circuit courts more responsibility for hearing appeals. It also expanded federal judicial power to almost the full extent allowed by the Constitution. Federal courts could now hear any cases concerning federal laws and involving more than $500.

Circuit Courts of Appeals Act of 1891

Congress passed the Circuit Courts of Appeals Act of 1891 to finish the reorganization it began in 1875. The act of 1891 had three main provisions. First, it transferred most federal trials to the district courts. The circuit courts continued holding some trials out of tradition, but lost all power to hear appeals. Congress eventually eliminated the circuit courts in 1911.

Second, the act created nine new circuit courts of appeals, one for each of the country's nine circuits. Each circuit court of appeals contained two circuit judges and one district judge. They had the power to hear almost all appeals from the district and circuit courts. In most cases, the decision by a circuit court of appeals was final.

The third main change affected the responsibilities of the Supreme Court. Under the act, the Supreme Court was required to hear only certain kinds of appeals from the district and circuit courts and from the circuit courts of appeals. Otherwise, the Supreme Court had discretion to choose whether or not to hear appeals. The effect was to reduce the Supreme Court's caseload and transfer most appellate responsibility to the circuit courts of appeals. The act also made circuit riding by Supreme Court justices optional, bringing an end to that tradition. (During the early years of the Supreme Court, justices had to travel across the country to hold trials in different federal circuits. This was known as circuit riding.)

The twentieth century

After Congress abolished circuit courts in 1911, the federal judiciary had district courts for trials, circuit courts of appeals for appeals, and the Supreme Court for final appeals. This structure

The Inalienable Rights of Mankind

In 1776, thirteen American colonies separated from Great Britain by signing the American Declaration of Independence. Written primarily by Thomas Jefferson, the Declaration contains these famous words about the rights of mankind:

> We hold these Truths to be self-evident, that all Men are created equal, that they are endowed by their Creator with certain unalienable Rights, that among these are Life, Liberty, and the Pursuit of Happiness. . . .

Although the Declaration spoke in terms of "men," the document has been celebrated as one of history's greatest statements of the inalienable rights of all people. Inalienable rights cannot be denied by government. They are rights that a fair government must preserve for its citizens.

The preamble to the Constitution of 1787 says one of its purposes is to "secure the blessings of liberty" to the people of America. The Constitution does not otherwise mention the inalienable rights of mankind. Some convention delegates were more concerned with defining the powers of American government than identifying the rights of its citizens. Others believed it was unnecessary to mention inalienable rights, since they cannot be denied. Jefferson, the author of the Declaration of Independence, was in Paris, France, at the time as American ambassador to France.

In 1788, America wrestled with whether to ratify the Constitution to make it the framework for American government. Delegates met in state conventions to hold debates on the proposed Constitution and to vote on ratification. Many delegates would not vote for ratification unless the Constitution's supporters agreed to seek amendments to add the basic rights of citizens to the document.

After ratification, congressman and future president James Madison drafted twelve proposed constitutional amendments. America adopted ten of them—the Bill of Rights—in 1791. Part of the Fifth Amendment says no person may "be deprived of life, liberty, or property, without due process of law. . . ." This language resembled Jefferson's celebration of life, liberty, and the pursuit of happiness, though it replaced happiness with property.

The Bill of Rights does not refer specifically to the inalienable rights of mankind. The Ninth Amendment, however, says, "The enumeration in the Constitution, of certain rights, shall not be construed to deny or disparage others retained by the people." This reflected the idea that people have inalienable rights that fair governments cannot take away. Nevertheless, the Ninth Amendment has been powerless as a restriction on the federal government.

Upon ratification in 1791, the Bill of Rights applied only to the federal government. State governments did not have to obey it. Moreover, despite its language of liberty, the Constitution made slavery legal in America. It did so in three ways. First, it specifically prevented Congress from outlawing the importation of slaves until 1808. Second, it required states to return escaped slaves to their masters. Third, it counted each slave as only three-fifths of a person for determining state populations for calculating the number of representatives each state got in the House of Representatives.

Over the next seventy-five years, people in the abolitionist (antislavery) movement worked to end slavery. They used the Declaration's inalienable rights to attack slavery as impossible in a free land. Slavery finally became illegal with the adoption of the Thirteenth Amendment in 1865.

After winning that battle, abolitionists turned to protecting the civil rights of newly freed slaves. In 1866, Congress proposed the Fourteenth Amendment, which, in Section 1, says:

> No State shall make or enforce any law which shall abridge the privileges or immunities of citizens of the United States; nor shall any State deprive any person of life, liberty, or

property, without due process of law; nor deny to any person within its jurisdiction the equal protection of the laws.

After Congress proposed the Fourteenth Amendment, Speaker of the House Schuyler Colfax (1823–1885) spoke in favor of Section 1, saying (as reprinted in the *Congressional Globe*), "I will tell you why I love it. It is because it is the Declaration of Independence placed immutably [absolutely] and forever in the Constitution."

Many Americans see a parallel between section 1 of the Fourteenth Amendment and the Declaration of Independence. The Fourteenth Amendment's "equal protection" clause resembles the Declaration's observation that "all Men are created equal." The Fourteenth Amendment's "privileges and immunities" resemble the Declaration's "unalienable rights." The Fourteenth Amendment's protection of "life, liberty, or property" resembles the Declaration's celebration of "Life, Liberty, and the Pursuit of Happiness." In "Completing the Constitution," scholar Robert J. Reinstein made the following observation about the adoption of the Fourteenth Amendment:

> [A] national political movement brought the Declaration of Independence "back into American life." The Declaration was the secular credo, or nonreligious doctrine, of the abolitionists. The Declaration not only supported their moral and political assaults on slavery but was the foundation of their constitutional theories.

America ratified the Fourteenth Amendment in 1868.

John Trumbull's painting shows the Founding Fathers gathered in 1776 to sign the Declaration of Independence.
National Archives and Records Administration.

has remained since then. Changes to the federal judiciary in the twentieth century concerned management of the judicial workload as the country grew in size and population.

Federal district courts and special courts As of 2005, the federal judiciary has ninety-four districts. Each district has at least one district court. Some districts are divided into divisions, each of which has a district court.

District courts handle criminal and civil trials under the nation's laws. District courts can also handle civil trials involving state law if the parties are citizens of different states and the amount of their dispute is more than $75,000. State civil cases below that amount must be filed in state courts.

The district courts have a system of courts for handling cases in which a person or business files for bankruptcy. (Bankruptcy allows a person who cannot pay his or her debts to pay what he or she can and then start over without any debts.) During the twentieth century, Congress also created federal courts for hearing special kinds of cases, such as the tax court and the court of international trade.

Courts of appeals In 1948, Congress changed the name of the circuit courts of appeals to courts of appeals for a given circuit. For example, the First Circuit Court of Appeals became the Court of Appeals for the First Circuit. As of 2005, the country has twelve courts of appeals covering twelve numbered, geographic circuits. There is also a court of appeals for the federal circuit, which hears appeals from around the country in cases involving special areas of the law.

The Supreme Court During the twentieth century, Congress decreased mandatory appeals and increased discretionary, or optional, appeals to the Supreme Court. Since 1988, almost all of the Supreme Court's caseload has been discretionary. If a party wants to appeal to the Supreme Court from a court of appeals, he or she must file a petition for a writ of certiorari, a petition that asks the Supreme Court to review the case. (A writ is a court order, and *certiorari* is a Latin word that means "to certify a court case for review.") At least four of the nine justices must vote to grant certiorari for the case to be appealed. Out of the thousands of petitions the Court receives each year, it selects only around one hundred of them.

The future

Under the Constitution, the president appoints justices to the Supreme Court and judges to the lower federal courts. The Senate reviews the appointments and either approves or rejects them. A simple majority is necessary for Senate approval.

Once appointed, federal justices and judges may serve as long as they want. The president has no power to remove a justice or judge from the bench. Congress can remove justices and judges only through impeachment in the House of Representatives and conviction in the Senate for treason, bribery, or other high crimes and misdemeanors.

Some citizens would like to change these procedures with elections and term limits. Elections would allow the people of America to select federal justices and judges. Term limits would limit the number of years a justice or judge could serve. Proponents say elections and term limits would encourage federal justices and judges to follow the will of the people. Opponents say justices and judges must be independent from popular will because part of their job is to protect the rights of minority groups in society.

For More Information

BOOKS

Biskupic, Joan, and Elder Witt. *The Supreme Court & the Powers of the American Government.* Washington, DC: Congressional Quarterly Inc., 1997.

Goebel, Julius, Jr. *Antecedents and Beginnings to 1801.* Vol. I. New York: Macmillan, 1971.

Kelly, Alfred H., and Winfred A. Harbison. *The American Constitution: Its Origins and Development.* 5th ed. New York: W. W. Norton & Co., 1976.

Kurland, Philip B., and Ralph Lerner. *The Founders' Constitution.* 5 vols. Indianapolis: Liberty Fund, 1987.

Levy, Leonard W. *Original Intent and the Framers' Constitution.* New York: Macmillan, 1988.

McClenaghan, William A. *Magruder's American Government 2003.* Needham, MA: Prentice Hall School Group, 2002.

Schwartz, Bernard. *A History of the Supreme Court.* New York: Oxford University Press, 1993.

Shelley, Mack C., II. *American Government and Politics Today.* 2004–2005 ed. Belmont, CA: Wadsworth Publishing, 2003.

Surrency, Erwin C. *History of the Federal Courts.* 2nd ed. Dobbs Ferry, NY: Oceana Publications, 2002.

Volkomer, Walter E. *American Government.* 8th ed. Upper Saddle River, NJ: Prentice Hall, 1998.

Wheeler, Russell R., and Cynthia Harrison. *Creating the Federal Judicial System.* Washington, DC: Federal Judicial Center, 1994.

Young, Roland. *American Law and Politics: The Creation of Public Order.* New York: Harper & Row, 1967.

PERIODICALS

Congressional Globe, 39th Cong., 1st Sess. 2459 (1866).

Reinstein, Robert. J. "Completing the Constitution: The Declaration of Independence, Bill of Rights and Fourteenth Amendment." *Temple Law Review* (1993).

CASES

Mapp v. Ohio, 367 U.S. 643 (1961).

WEB SITES

Supreme Court of the United States. http://www.supremecourtus.gov (accessed on February 18, 2005).

U.S. Courts: The Federal Judiciary. http://www.uscourts.gov (accessed on March 23, 2005).

Key Positions in the Judicial Branch

The judiciary is the branch of the federal government that decides cases under the nation's laws. It is made up of various courts. The main courts are the federal district courts, the circuit courts of appeals, and the U.S. Supreme Court.

Federal district courts hold trials in criminal and civil cases. A criminal case is one in which the federal government charges a person or business with violating a federal criminal law. A civil case is a noncriminal dispute between people or businesses, or between the government and a person or business.

Federal district courts cover ninety-four geographic districts in the United States. The party, or participant, who loses a case in a district court may appeal to the appropriate circuit court of appeals.

Courts of appeals review trials to make sure district court judges and juries do not make serious mistakes. There are thirteen courts of appeals in the federal system. Twelve of them cover geographic regions, and one handles special kinds of appeals from across the nation.

A party who loses in a court of appeals may ask the U.S. Supreme Court to review the case. Most of the time, the Supreme Court has discretion, or power, to choose whether or not to review a case. If it reviews a case, the Supreme Court usually limits review to a major question of law of national importance.

The key positions in the federal judiciary are the justices who serve on the Supreme Court, the judges who serve on the courts of appeals and district courts, and the magistrates who

Words to Know

checks and balances: The specific powers in one branch of government that allow it to limit the powers of the other branches.

circuit court of appeals: A court in the federal judicial system that handles appeals from the trial courts, called federal district courts. The United States is divided into twelve geographic areas called circuits, and each circuit has one court of appeals that handles appeals from the federal district courts in its circuit. A party who loses in a circuit court of appeals may ask the Supreme Court to review the case.

civil case: A case that involves a dispute between private parties or a noncriminal dispute between a private party and a government.

Constitution of the United States of America: The document written in 1787 that established the federal government under which the United States of America has operated since 1789. Article III covers the judicial branch.

criminal case: A case in which a person is charged with violating a criminal law.

district courts: The courts in the federal judicial system that handle trials in civil and criminal cases. Each state is divided into one or more federal judicial districts, and each district has one or more federal district courts. A party who loses in a federal district court may appeal to have the case reviewed by a circuit court of appeals.

judge: A public official who presides over a court and who often decides questions brought before him or her.

judicial interpretation: The process by which federal courts interpret the meaning of laws passed by Congress.

judicial review: The process by which federal courts review laws to determine whether they violate the U.S. Constitution. If a court finds that a law violates the Constitution, it declares the law unconstitutional, which means the executive branch is not supposed to enforce it anymore. Congress can correct such a defect by passing a new law that does not violate the Constitution.

justice: One of nine jurists who serve on the U.S. Supreme Court. The chief justice serves as the head of the Supreme Court; the other eight are called associate justices.

separation of powers: Division of the powers of government into different branches to prevent one branch from having too much power.

Supreme Court: The highest court in the federal judiciary. The judiciary is the branch of government responsible for resolving legal disputes and interpreting laws on a case-by-case basis.

serve in the district courts. Other key positions include law clerks, court clerks, court stenographers, and the reporter of decisions.

Supreme Court justices

The jurists who serve on the Supreme Court are called justices. The Constitution does not specify how many justices the Court should have. Instead, Congress sets the number by law. In the Judiciary Act of 1789, Congress set the number at six. The number fluctuated up and down over the next eighty years. Since 1869, the number has been fixed at nine.

Appointment, compensation, and removal of justices There are no requirements in the Constitution that a person must satisfy to serve as a Supreme Court justice. Article II, Section 2, simply gives the president the power to appoint justices with advice and consent from the Senate. This means the Senate must approve a president's appointment, or nomination, by a simple majority vote. Before the Senate votes, the Senate Judiciary Committee holds hearings to make a recommendation.

The Constitution says justices must be paid for their services. Congress determines this amount by law. The Constitution makes it illegal for a justice's salary to be lowered during his or her service. This prevents Congress and the president from trying to control justices by threatening to change their salaries.

The Constitution says justices "shall hold their offices during good behavior." This means justices can serve as long as they want. Nobody, including the president, Congress, and other justices, can fire them from their jobs.

Justices, however, can be impeached, or officially accused of wrongdoing, and removed from office by Congress if they commit treason, bribery, or other high crimes and misdemeanors. Treason means levying war against the United States or giving aid and comfort to its enemies. Bribery means accepting a gift for official conduct. The Constitution does not define "high crimes and misdemeanors," and scholars disagree over its meaning. Because Congress has the sole authority to remove a justice by impeachment, Congress gets to decide whether a justice has committed a high crime or misdemeanor.

Removal by impeachment has two phases. During the first phase, the House of Representatives holds hearings and votes on whether to impeach a justice. A simple majority in the House of Representatives must vote in favor of a justice's impeachment.

Once impeached, a justice faces trial in the Senate. At the end of the trial, a two-thirds majority of senators must vote for conviction to remove the justice from office.

Samuel Chase was the only Supreme Court justice to be impeached, though he remained on the bench because the Senate failed to reach a two-thirds majority necessary to remove him. He served from 1796 to 1811. Maryland Historical Society.

As of 2005, Justice Samuel Chase (1741–1811) is the only Supreme Court justice to have been impeached by the House. The House impeached Chase by a vote of 73–32 in March 1804 for political speeches he made during courtroom proceedings. Justices are not supposed to allow politics to affect their fair conduct of cases. In March 1805, after the impeachment trial in the Senate, the Senate vote exceeded a simple majority, but it failed to reach the two-thirds majority necessary to convict and remove Chase.

The U.S. Supreme Court on October 23, 1967: (front row, left to right) John Marshall Harlan, Hugo Black, Earl Warren, William O. Douglas, and William J. Brennan Jr.; (back row, left to right) Abe Fortas, Potter Stewart, Byron R. White, and Thurgood Marshall. © B e t t m a n n / C o r b i s .

The chief justice and associate justices One of the nine justices on the Supreme Court is the chief justice. The other eight are called associate justices. When a chief justice resigns or dies, the president nominates someone to fill his or her place. The replacement can be one of the associate justices or someone who is not yet on the Court. The Senate must approve the president's nomination by a simple majority.

The chief justice is the symbolic leader of the Supreme Court. He or she sits at the center of the bench when the Court hears oral arguments from attorneys. (As of 2005, all of the chief justices were men.) When the justices meet to discuss the cases they have to decide, the chief justice leads the discussion. If the chief justice is part of the majority of justices in deciding a particular case, he chooses the justice who writes the opinion for the Court.

The chief justice has special administrative duties. He chairs the Judicial Conference of the United States and the board of the Federal Judicial Center, and he supervises the Administrative Office of the United States Courts. The Judicial Conference and the Administrative Office are responsible for running the federal judiciary. The Federal Judicial Center conducts research, training, and planning for the federal judiciary.

Under Article I, Section 3, of the Constitution, the chief justice presides over the Senate during impeachment trials of U.S. presidents. In this role, the chief justice helps the Senate apply its rules for impeachment trials. The chief justice does not get to vote on whether to convict an impeached president.

There have been two presidential impeachment trials in U.S. history. Chief Justice Salmon P. Chase (1808–1873) presided over the 1868 trial of President Andrew Johnson (1808–1875; served 1865–69); Chief Justice William Rehnquist (1924–) presided over the 1999 trial of President Bill Clinton (1946–; served 1993–2001).

When it comes to deciding cases, the chief justice does not have any more power than the associate justices. He has one vote in deciding whether the Supreme Court should accept a case for review, and one vote in the decision of a case. Chief justices get paid more than associate justices because of their extra administrative duties. They are appointed and removed, however, the same way as associate justices.

Accepting, hearing, and deciding cases The main work of the Supreme Court involves selecting cases to review, hearing the cases it accepts, and deciding them. Parties who want the Supreme Court to review a case from a lower federal court or from the highest court of a state file a petition for a writ of certiorari, a petition that asks the Supreme Court to review the case. (A writ is a court order, and *certiorari* is a Latin word that means "to certify a court case for review.") The petition explains why the case is important enough for the Court's consideration. If at least four justices vote to grant the petition, the Court hears the case.

Chief Justice William H. Rehnquist presided over the impeachment trial of President Bill Clinton in 1999.
Supreme Court of the United States.

Hearing a case has two main phases. In the first phase, the parties file written briefs explaining their sides of the case. In the second phase, the parties appear before the Court in public to present oral argument. This gives the justices a chance to ask the parties specific questions about the case. Most of the time, attorneys do the work of writing briefs and presenting oral argument for the parties.

After reading the briefs and hearing oral argument, the justices meet in a private conference to discuss the case. These discussions are not recorded, and the public never gets to see them. After discussing the case, the justices vote on how to decide it.

At least five justices must vote for reversal to change the result from the lower courts. Otherwise, the original result remains unchanged.

Serving in Different Branches

The U.S. Constitution prevents members of Congress from holding office in another branch of the government while they serve in Congress. Technically, the Constitution does not prevent members of the executive branch from serving in the judicial branch at the same time. Such dual service, however, would seem to violate the separation of powers for which the Constitution stands.

Nothing prevents one person from serving in all three branches at different times, and a number of Americans have accomplished this feat. Chief Justice John Marshall (1755–1835) served as a congressman from Virginia and then secretary of state under President John Adams (1735–1826; served 1797–1801). Justice James F. Byrne (1879–1972) was a congressman and senator from South Carolina who also served as secretary of state under President Harry Truman (1884–1972; served 1945–53). Other justices who also served in both Congress and the executive branch include Salmon P. Chase, Nathan Clifford (1803–1881), Lucius Q. Lamar (1825–1893), and Sherman Minton (1890–1965)

As of 2005, William Howard Taft (1857–1930) is the only person who served both as president of the United States and as a justice of the Supreme Court. Taft was president from 1909 to 1913. Then he served as chief justice of the Supreme Court, his lifelong ambition, from 1921 to 1930. Taft died in 1930, a month after resigning from the Court.

Many future presidents served in the legislative branch before taking on the highest office in the land. A more unusual circumstance, however, is a *former* president serving in another branch of government. Only three have done it. Besides Taft's

service in the judiciary, former president John Quincy Adams (1767–1848; served 1825–29) served in the U.S. House of Representatives from 1831 to 1848. Former president Andrew Johnson was a U.S. senator for nearly five months before his death in 1875. One other ex-president, John Tyler (1790–1862; served 1841–45), was elected to the Confederate House of Representatives in 1861, but he died before Congress assembled.

William Howard Taft, the only person to serve as both a U.S. president and a justice of the U.S. Supreme Court. © Bettmann/Corbis.

If the chief justice is in the majority, he assigns himself or another justice in the majority the task of drafting an opinion explaining the Court's decision. If the chief justice is in the minority, the associate justice in the majority with the most years of service on the Court assigns a justice from the majority to draft the opinion.

Justices may write their own opinions either agreeing or disagreeing with the Court's result. A justice who agrees writes a concurring opinion. A justice who disagrees writes a dissenting opinion.

The justices share drafts of their opinions with each other to give everyone a chance to suggest changes. When the opinions are finished, the Court releases its official decision and any concurring or dissenting opinions to the parties and the public.

Court of appeals judges

The courts immediately below the Supreme Court in the federal judiciary are called circuit courts of appeals. There are thirteen such courts. Twelve of them cover geographic regions, including eleven numbered regions and one in the District of Columbia. These courts hear appeals from the federal district courts in their circuits.

The thirteenth court of appeals is called the Court of Appeals for the Federal Circuit. It is located in Washington, D.C. It hears appeals from federal district courts nationwide in cases involving special matters. It also hears appeals from special federal trial courts, including the U.S. Court of International Trade and the U.S. Court of Federal Claims.

Appointment, compensation, and removal of circuit court judges Each court of appeals has a number of judges fixed by congressional law. One of the judges is the chief judge. He or she is the symbolic head of the circuit with administrative duties much like those of the chief justice of the Supreme Court.

Courts of appeals judges are appointed by the president with advice and consent from the Senate, just like Supreme Court justices. They get compensation, or salaries, that cannot be lowered while they are in office, and they stay in office during good behavior until they die or decide to resign. Congress has the sole

The Circuit Courts of Appeals

There are thirteen circuit courts of appeals in the federal judiciary. One is called the Court of Appeals for the Federal Circuit. It sits in Washington, D.C., to hear appeals from district courts nationwide in special kinds of federal cases and from special federal trial courts.

The other twelve courts of appeals cover twelve geographic regions, or circuits. One covers the District of Columbia, and the others cover numbered circuits that contain U.S. states and territories. Each circuit court of appeals hears appeals from the federal district courts in its circuit:

★ The Court of Appeals for the First Circuit covers federal district courts in Maine, Massachusetts, New Hampshire, Puerto Rico (a U.S. territory), and Rhode Island.

★ The Second Circuit covers Connecticut, New York, and Vermont.

★ The Third Circuit covers Delaware, New Jersey, Pennsylvania, and the Virgin Islands (a territory).

★ The Fourth Circuit covers Maryland, North Carolina, South Carolina, Virginia, and West Virginia.

★ The Fifth Circuit covers Louisiana, Mississippi, and Texas.

★ The Sixth Circuit covers Kentucky, Michigan, Ohio, and Tennessee.

★ The Seventh Circuit covers Illinois, Indiana, and Wisconsin.

★ The Eighth Circuit covers Arkansas, Iowa, Minnesota, Missouri, Nebraska, North Dakota, and South Dakota.

★ The Ninth Circuit covers Alaska, Arizona, California, Guam (a territory), Hawaii, Idaho, the Northern Mariana Islands (a territory), Montana, Nevada, Oregon, and Washington.

★ The Tenth Circuit covers Colorado, Kansas, New Mexico, Oklahoma, Utah, and Wyoming.

★ The Eleventh Circuit covers Alabama, Florida, and Georgia.

★ The Court of Appeals for the District of Columbia hears appeals from the Federal District Court for the District of Columbia.

authority to remove circuit judges through the impeachment process. Otherwise, circuit judges cannot be fired.

The work of circuit court judges The work of the courts of appeals resembles the work of the Supreme Court, with some exceptions. In most cases, parties can automatically appeal a case from a federal district court to the appropriate court of appeals without getting permission. A court of appeals usually reviews more issues than the Supreme Court does.

Court of appeals judges hear and decide cases in panels of three. The panels receive written briefs, hear oral arguments, and discuss and decide cases much like the justices on the Supreme Court. At least two of the three judges must vote for reversal to change the result from the federal district court.

Sometimes a party who loses before a panel of three judges can ask all the judges in the circuit to rehear the case before appealing to the Supreme Court. Such a rehearing is called en banc review.

District court judges

Congressional law divides the United States into ninety-four districts for the organization of federal trial courts. Each district contains at least one court with a set number of district court judges. Some districts are divided into divisions, each of which has a court with a number of district court judges.

Appointment, compensation, and removal of district court judges

The constitutional provisions for the appointment, compensation, and removal of district court judges are the same ones that apply to circuit judges and Supreme Court justices. Presidents appoint district court judges with advice and consent from the Senate. Judges serve for life during good behavior until they die or resign, and get a salary that cannot be lowered. Only Congress can remove a district court judge through the impeachment process.

The work of district court judges

District court judges handle trials in criminal and civil cases. Trials have five main phases. In the first phase of a civil case, a person or business, called a plaintiff, files a complaint against a defendant. In the first phase of a criminal case, the government files criminal charges against a defendant. The parties in both kinds of cases might disagree over whether the court has the power to decide the case. This gives the district court judge his or her first opportunity to make a decision in the case.

If a court has the power to hear a case, the parties go through the second main phase, called discovery. In discovery, each party must share information he or she has about the case with the other parties. The purpose of discovery is to help the parties agree on issues that are not in dispute, and narrow the issues on which they disagree. Parties sometimes refuse to share information during discovery. At that point, district court judges hear motions to decide whether or not the information has to be shared under federal law and the rules of the court.

The third main phase of a civil trial is called summary judgment. In this phase, one or both sides ask the judge to decide the case without holding a trial. If the evidence is so one-sided that one party deserves to win as a matter of law, the judge enters summary judgment in favor of that party.

Summary judgment avoids the need to hold a time-consuming and costly trial. The party who loses summary judgment, however, can appeal the decision to the appropriate circuit court of appeals. The court of appeals can reverse the summary judgment decision if the district court judge made a mistake. Criminal trials do not have summary judgment proceedings because defendants have a constitutional right to be tried by a jury.

The fourth main phase is the actual trial. Trials happen when parties fail to settle their disagreement along the way. In jury trials, parties chose a jury from citizens in the community. To choose the jury, attorneys for both sides question potential jurors. The purpose is to determine whether a potential juror might have beliefs that would prevent him or her from being a fair juror. The parties can exclude jurors with such beliefs from serving on a jury. There is no limit to the number of such exclusions. Parties may also exclude a fixed number of potential jurors who do not have specific beliefs that would prevent them from being fair. This allows parties to exclude people whom they feel might be unfair, even though they lack a good reason for the feeling. Parties, however, cannot exclude jurors because of their race, gender, or other such features. In the most serious kinds of cases, such as murder, jury selection can be a long, complicated process.

After jury selection, the parties present their cases to the jury. The jury is responsible for deciding who wins the case. The district court judge oversees the trial. He or she controls what evidence the jury is allowed to hear under the law. He or she also instructs the jury on the law it must apply when deciding who wins the case.

In bench trials, parties present their case to the judge without a jury. The judge decides the case like a jury would have done. Whether a judge or jury decides a case, the result is called a verdict.

The fifth phase of a civil trial happens after a jury or judge decides a case. The losing party can ask the judge to reverse the verdict or to hold a new trial. Judges can reverse a jury verdict when the jury's decision is unreasonable, though this happens only occasionally. Judges can grant a new trial when there was an error during trial, even one made by the judge, that unfairly affected the losing party's case. Because criminal defendants have a constitutional right to be tried only once by a jury, judicial control over criminal verdicts is much more limited.

In civil cases, judges enter judgments in favor of the winning party after resolving any post-trial motions. In criminal cases, judges enter judgments in favor of defendants who are found not guilty. When a defendant is found guilty, the judge imposes a sentence in accord with federal law. At this stage in both civil and criminal cases, the parties decide whether to accept the results or appeal to the circuit court of appeals. The federal government, however, cannot appeal a verdict of not guilty in a criminal case.

District court magistrate judges

In 1968, Congress passed the Federal Magistrates Act. The law gave district courts the power to appoint magistrate judges to help district court judges do their jobs.

Magistrate judges are usually lawyers, but they do not always have to be. They receive a salary for their services. Unlike regular judges, magistrate judges are appointed for fixed terms and can be fired by a court for good cause, or reason.

District courts control the power of the magistrate judges who work for them. Many magistrate judges handle pretrial hearings in both criminal and civil cases. The purpose of pretrial hearings is to resolve certain issues before the parties present their cases at trial. Magistrate judges can hold trials in criminal cases involving both felonies and misdemeanors if the defendant agrees. Misdemeanors are less serious than felonies, which are the most serious kind of crimes. For example, under federal law, assaulting another person on federal property by simply striking, beating, or wounding him or her is a misdemeanor punishable by six months in prison. Assaulting someone on federal property with a deadly weapon or in a way that causes serious bodily injury is a felony punishable by up to ten years in prison.

Magistrate judges also help district court judges with civil cases. Magistrate judges often hear and resolve discovery disputes if parties disagree over what information they must share. They hold informal trials and recommend results to the district court judges. If the parties to a civil case agree, magistrate judges can hold full trials without district court judges.

Law clerks

Law clerks are lawyers who help justices and judges with legal research and writing. They are usually young lawyers who have just graduated from law school, but they can also be lawyers with more experience.

Each Supreme Court justice usually hires four law clerks. These law clerks tend to be lawyers who graduated near the top of their classes at the most prestigious law schools in the nation. Many of them serve as law clerks in lower courts before getting to the Supreme Court. They usually serve as Supreme Court law clerks for one year. The positions carry with them invaluable experience.

Supreme Court law clerks have three main responsibilities. They analyze the thousands of petitions the Supreme Court receives each year asking it to review cases. Law clerks write memoranda about the petitions to help the justices decide which cases to accept for review.

Supreme Court law clerks also write memoranda to prepare the justices to hear oral arguments in the cases they accept for review. Finally, law clerks read briefs, conduct legal research, and write memoranda to help the justices decide the cases they have accepted for review. Sometimes law clerks draft opinions for the justices. The justices, however, always review the drafts and make changes before issuing them as official, concurring, or dissenting opinions.

Court of appeals judges usually hire two or three law clerks. These law clerks have duties similar to those of the Supreme Court law clerks. They preview appeals to help the judges decide which cases can be handled quickly and which require more work. They write memoranda to prepare the judges to hear oral arguments. They read briefs, conduct legal research, write memoranda, and draft opinions to help circuit judges decide cases.

Lucille Lomen, the first woman to serve as a law clerk for a U.S. Supreme Court justice. She worked for Associate Justice William O. Douglas in 1944 and 1945. © Bettmann/Corbis.

District court judges and magistrate judges usually have one or two law clerks. These clerks read briefs, conduct legal research, write memoranda, and draft opinions to help the judges and magistrates decide motions in criminal and civil trials. A motion is a request for the court to decide a particular issue relating to a case.

Clerk of the court

Every court in the federal judiciary has a clerk. The clerk of the court runs an office that administers the day-to-day business of the court. This includes administering case schedules, receiving and filing papers in cases, distributing papers to the justices and judges, collecting filing fees and court fees, and preparing and distributing court orders. Court clerks also help attorneys with informal procedures that do not appear in the court's official rules.

Court stenographers

Court stenographers are people who record every word spoken during a hearing or trial in district court and during oral argument in appellate courts. Stenographers do this entirely by hand using a device called a stenotype machine, which looks like a typewriter. Today, many courts record courtroom proceedings rather than use stenographers. Either way, the process gives judges and parties a record of what happened in court.

Attorneys

Attorneys, or lawyers, are people who represent parties in court cases, both in the federal and state judicial systems. Most attorneys are not employed by the courts. All attorneys, however, are considered officers of the courts. This means they must comply with court rules for proper behavior in the judicial systems.

There are three main kinds of attorneys in the federal judicial system: U.S. attorneys, federal public defenders, and private attorneys. U.S. attorneys represent the federal government in federal courts. They serve as prosecutors in criminal cases. They also represent the government's side of the case in civil cases, whether the government is a plaintiff suing someone else or a defendant being sued.

U.S. attorneys are employed by the U.S. Department of Justice, which is a department under the president in the executive branch of the government. As of 2005, there were ninety-three U.S. attorneys representing the federal government in ninety-four geographic regions called districts.

Each U.S. attorney gets help from a number of assistant U.S. attorneys.

When a case involving the federal government reaches the U.S. Supreme Court, a special attorney called the solicitor general handles the case for the government. Like the U.S. attorneys, the solicitor general is employed by the Department of Justice and has many assistant attorneys helping him or her.

The second main kind of attorney in the federal judicial system is the federal public defender. Federal public defenders represent criminal defendants who cannot afford an attorney. They are employed by the federal court in which they serve. Like U.S. attorneys, federal public defenders receive help from assistant federal public defenders.

Private attorneys are the third main kind of attorney in the federal judicial system. Some work for law firms, others work for businesses, and others work for nonprofit organizations. Private attorneys have to obey court rules for proper behavior just like attorneys employed by the federal government.

Reporter of decisions

The official versions of Supreme Court decisions are published in *United States Reports*. The person who prepares the Court's opinions for publication is called the reporter of decisions. As of early 2005, fifteen reporters of decisions have served the Court since 1790.

The official versions of decisions by the circuit courts of appeals are published in *Federal Reporter*. The official versions of decisions by the federal district courts are published in *Federal*

Four attorneys involved in the Microsoft monopoly case in 1999: (left to right) U.S. attorney general Janet Reno, U.S. assistant attorney general Joel Klein, Connecticut attorney general Richard Blumenthal, and U.S. Justice Department trial attorney David Boies. Photograph by Brendan McDermid. ©Reuters/Corbis.

Court stenographer Dorothy Siegal records testimony on a stenotype machine during the 1935 trial of Bruno Hauptmann, who was charged with the kidnapping and murder of the son of famed pilot Charles A. Lindbergh.
©Bettmann/Corbis.

Supplement. A private company called West Publishing Company publishes both.

For More Information

BOOKS

Abraham, Henry J. *Justices, Presidents, and Senators.* Lanham, MD: Rowman & Littlefield Publishers, 1999.

Baum, Lawrence. *The Supreme Court.* Washington, DC: Congressional Quarterly Inc., 1998.

Biskupic, Joan, and Elder Witt. *The Supreme Court at Work.* Washington, DC: Congressional Quarterly, Inc., 1997.

Carp, Robert A., and Ronald Stidham. *The Federal Courts.* 2nd ed. Washington, DC: Congressional Quarterly Inc., 1991.

Choper, Jesse H., ed. *The Supreme Court and Its Justices.* 2nd ed. Chicago: American Bar Association, 2001.

McClenaghan, William A. *Magruder's American Government 2003.* Needham, MA: Prentice Hall School Group, 2002.

Schwartz, Bernard. *A History of the Supreme Court.* New York: Oxford University Press, 1993.

Shelley, Mack C., II. *American Government and Politics Today.* 2004–2005 ed. Belmont, CA: Wadsworth Publishing, 2003.

Surrency, Erwin C. *History of the Federal Courts.* 2nd ed. Dobbs Ferry, NY: Oceana Publications, 2002.

Volkomer, Walter E. *American Government.* 8th ed. Upper Saddle River, NJ: Prentice Hall, 1998.

Wasby, Stephen L. *The Supreme Court in the Federal Judicial System.* 2nd ed. New York: Holt, Rinehart and Winston, 1984.

WEB SITES

O'Hara, James B. "Court History Quizzes." *Supreme Court Historical Society.* http://www.supremecourthistory.org/ 02_history/subs_history/02_f.html (accessed on March 30, 2005).

Supreme Court of the United States. http://www.supremecourtus.gov (accessed on February 18, 2005).

United States Department of Justice. http://www.usdoj.gov/ (accessed on February 12, 2005).

U.S. Courts: The Federal Judiciary. http://www.uscourts.gov (accessed on March 23, 2005).

Daily Operations of the Judicial Branch

The federal judiciary has trial courts for handling cases under the nation's laws. The trial courts are called federal district courts. Federal district judges are in charge of cases in the district courts. Appellate courts called circuit courts of appeals review the work of the trial courts. Circuit judges are in charge of cases in the courts of appeals. The highest appellate court, the U.S. Supreme Court, reviews the work of both the courts of appeals and the district courts. The jurists on the Supreme Court are called justices.

The federal judiciary has special courts for hearing particular kinds of cases. These include the U.S. Court of International Trade and the U.S. Court of Federal Claims. The judiciary also has offices that handle administration and planning for the federal court system, including the Judicial Conference of the United States, the Administrative Office of the United States Courts, and the Federal Judicial Center.

Federal district courts

The United States and its territories are divided into ninety-four geographic districts. Each district has at least one federal district court. Some districts are divided into divisions, each of which has a federal district court. U.S. attorneys handle cases for the federal government in each district.

Federal district courts handle trials in criminal, civil, and bankruptcy cases. Criminal cases involve the violation of federal criminal laws. Civil cases are noncriminal disputes between private parties or between a private party and the government.

Words to Know

checks and balances: The specific powers in one branch of government that allow it to limit the powers of the other branches.

circuit court of appeals: A court in the federal judicial system that handles appeals from the trial courts, called federal district courts. The United States is divided into twelve geographic areas called circuits, and each circuit has one court of appeals that handles appeals from the federal district courts in its circuit. A party who loses in a circuit court of appeals may ask the Supreme Court to review the case.

civil case: A case that involves a dispute between private parties or a noncriminal dispute between a private party and a government.

Constitution of the United States of America: The document written in 1787 that established the federal government under which the United States of America has operated since 1789. Article III covers the judicial branch.

criminal case: A case in which a person is charged with violating a criminal law.

district courts: The courts in the federal judicial system that handle trials in civil and criminal cases. Each state is divided into one or more federal judicial districts, and each district has one or more federal district courts. A party who loses in a federal district court may appeal to have the case reviewed by a circuit court of appeals.

judge: A public official who presides over a court and who often decides questions brought before him or her.

judicial interpretation: The process by which federal courts interpret the meaning of laws passed by Congress.

judicial review: The process by which federal courts review laws to determine whether they violate the U.S. Constitution. If a court finds that a law violates the Constitution, it declares the law unconstitutional, which means the executive branch is not supposed to enforce it anymore. Congress can correct such a defect by passing a new law that does not violate the Constitution.

justice: One of nine jurists who serve on the U.S. Supreme Court. The chief justice serves as the head of the Supreme Court; the other eight are called associate justices.

legislative courts: Courts created by Congress to handle some of its lawmaking powers under Article I of the U.S. Constitution.

separation of powers: Division of the powers of government into different branches to prevent one branch from having too much power.

Supreme Court: The highest court in the federal judiciary. The judiciary is the branch of government responsible for resolving legal disputes and interpreting laws on a case-by-case basis.

Bankruptcy cases involve people or businesses who cannot pay their bills or debts.

Criminal cases Criminal cases begin when a U.S. attorney files federal criminal charges against a defendant. (State courts handle cases involving state criminal laws.) For some kinds of federal crimes, the U.S. attorney must first get an indictment, or formal charge, from a grand jury. A grand jury is a group of citizens who review whether the government has enough evidence to charge someone with a criminal violation. If so, the grand jury issues an indictment. Federal district judges oversee grand jury proceedings.

When a person is charged with a crime, a federal judge orders him or her to appear in district court for arraignment. During arraignment, the judge reads the charges to the defendant and asks whether the defendant pleads guilty or not guilty. If the defendant pleads guilty, he or she normally pays a fine, gets probation (court supervision), or goes to jail for a period of time. If the defendant pleads not guilty, he or she forces the government to prove the charges at a trial. Defendants have a constitutional right to be represented by an attorney at all criminal proceedings, hearings, and trials, including arraignment.

Federal district judges oversee trials of defendants who plead not guilty. The parties, meaning the government and the defendant, begin by selecting a jury of twelve people who have been called randomly from the community for jury service. The parties give opening statements to the jury, explaining what they plan to prove during their cases. Next, each side gets to question witnesses and present physical evidence to the jury. During this phase, the judge applies rules of evidence to decide what testimony and physical evidence the jury is allowed to see and hear. The rules are supposed to prevent unreliable, irrelevant, and illegally obtained evidence from getting to a jury so the jury can make its decision based on lawful, reliable evidence. For example, courts are not supposed to allow juries to hear evidence the government gets by violating a person's Fourth Amendment right to be free from unreasonable searches and seizures. Near the end of the trial, the parties make closing arguments, explaining to the jury what they want the jury to decide.

After the parties present their evidence and make their arguments, it is time for the jury to decide the case. The federal district judge instructs the jury on the law that applies to the case. Then the jury retires to a private room to discuss the case. All twelve jurors must agree on a verdict to find the defendant guilty or not guilty.

If a jury finds a defendant not guilty, the government must accept the verdict. It cannot appeal, and it cannot try the

Legislative Courts

Article III of the U.S. Constitution covers the federal judiciary. The U.S. Supreme Court, circuit courts of appeals, and federal district courts get their powers from Article III. These courts are sometimes called Article III courts, or constitutional courts.

Article I of the Constitution covers Congress, which is the legislative branch of the government. Congress makes the nation's laws. Section 8 of Article I defines Congress's lawmaking power.

Congress has created special courts to handle cases that pertain to its lawmaking power. Such courts are called Article I courts, or legislative courts. They include the U.S. Court of Appeals for the Armed Forces, the U.S. Court of Appeals for Veterans Claims, and the U.S. Tax Court.

The U.S. Court of Appeals for the Armed Forces hears appeals in cases involving members of America's armed forces, including the Army, Navy, Air Force, and Marines. Congress created the court under its Article I power "to make rules for the government and regulation of the land and naval forces."

Cases involving members of the armed forces normally begin with court-martial proceedings in one of the military branches. A court-martial happens when a member of the military is accused of violating the Uniform Code of Military Justice, which contains the rules for military service. A court-martial may be appealed to the U.S. Court of Appeals for the Armed Forces, and from there to the U.S. Supreme Court.

The U.S. Court of Appeals for Veterans Claims hears cases involving veterans' rights. Such cases begin in the U.S. Department of Veterans Affairs, a department under the president in the executive branch of government. In the department, the Board of Veterans Appeals issues decisions concerning veterans' rights. Veterans may appeal board decisions to the U.S. Court of Appeals for Veterans Claims, and from there to the U.S. Court of Appeals for the Federal Circuit (an Article III court) and ultimately to the U.S. Supreme Court.

Congress created the U.S. Tax Court under its Article I power "to lay and collect taxes." The court hears cases under the Internal Revenue Code, which contains the nation's tax laws. A case begins when the commissioner of internal revenue in the executive branch determines that a person owes federal taxes. If the person disagrees with the decision, he or she may file a petition to have the U.S. Tax Court hear the case. Parties may appeal the court's decision to a U.S. court of appeals and ultimately to the U.S. Supreme Court.

Legislative courts have judges, but the judges do not have the rights of judges on constitutional courts. Legislative judges are appointed by the president for a fixed term of service. Instead of holding office for life, like Article III judges do, Article I judges may be fired for good cause, or a good reason. Finally, their salaries are subject to more congressional control than the salaries of Article III judges.

defendant again for the same crime. If the jury finds the defendant guilty, the judge sentences the defendant with a fine, probation, jail time, or a combination thereof. A defendant can accept the sentence or else appeal the jury's verdict based on errors made in the government's investigation, handling, and trial of the case. When the jurors' votes are not unanimous, the result is called a hung jury. If a jury is hung, the government can try the defendant again for the same crime.

Criminal defendants have a constitutional right to a jury trial in most federal cases. Defendants may, however, waive that right and be tried by a judge instead. Such trials are called bench trials. A defendant might choose a bench trial when the case is complicated or when he or she thinks a judge might be more lenient. Bench trials involve opening statements, presentation of evidence, and closing arguments, just like jury trials. The judge, however, decides the case instead of a jury. Sentencing and appeals happen the same way as in jury trials.

Civil cases Civil cases begin when one party, called the plaintiff, files a complaint against another party, called the defendant. Complaints explain the legal dispute between the parties. Federal district courts handle civil cases arising under federal laws. They also handle civil cases arising under state laws when the parties are from different states and (as of 2005) the amount of their dispute is more than $75,000. Civil cases usually involve business disputes or cases in which one person injures another person or some property.

Defendants file an answer, disputing the charges in the plaintiff's complaint. Sometimes a defendant files a motion to dismiss a complaint. Such a motion challenges whether the plaintiff has a genuine legal dispute or whether the federal district court has the power to hear the case. District court judges hear such motions to decide whether a case may proceed or must be dismissed.

If the defendant answers the complaint and the court does not dismiss it, the parties proceed to discovery. Discovery requires both sides of the case to share any information they have about the case. Discovery involves answering written questions, sharing documents and evidence, and answering oral questions during depositions, or testimonies. In discovery, parties often disagree over what information they must share. Federal district judges apply rules of procedure to decide what evidence the parties must share and what they may keep to themselves. In general, parties must share all evidence that relates to the issues for trial. Parties, however, may keep evidence that is irrelevant to the case. They also do not have to share information protected by a privilege, such as statements they have made to their lawyers.

Most parties settle civil cases by agreement before getting to trial. If the parties fail to settle, the district judge holds a trial. Civil trials are much like criminal trials. The parties select a jury, give opening statements, present their cases through witnesses and physical evidence, and make closing arguments. The jury, which can have fewer than twelve people, decides the case based on the law explained by the judge. If the parties waive a jury trial, the judge decides the case without a jury. The party who loses may appeal to the U.S. court of appeals for the circuit in which the federal district court sits.

Bankruptcy cases U.S. federal district courts have special courts and judges who handle bankruptcy cases. Bankruptcy is for individuals and business owners who do not have enough money to pay their bills and other debts. In a bankruptcy proceeding, a federal district judge helps the person or business divide the money he or she has among creditors. Creditors are people and businesses to whom the bankrupt person owes money. After going through bankruptcy, a person is able to eliminate most of his or her debts and bills without paying them fully. It is a chance to "start over" financially. A person who goes through bankruptcy, however, ends up with a poor credit rating, which makes it hard to get loans for automobiles, homes, and other expensive items. Under congressional law, federal courts have sole power to handle bankruptcy cases. State courts cannot handle them.

Circuit courts of appeals

The United States and its territories are divided into twelve geographic circuits. Eleven of them are numbered, each covering more than one state or territory. The twelfth covers the District of Columbia. Each circuit has a court of appeals with many circuit judges who handle the court's workload.

There is a thirteenth court of appeals called the U.S. Court of Appeals for the Federal Circuit. It sits in Washington, D.C., to hear appeals in cases involving patents, international trade, and money claims against the federal government. A patent gives a person or business a protected right in a product or process. International trade is business that takes place across national borders.

Purpose of appeals A person who loses his or her case in a federal district court may appeal the case to the court of appeals for the circuit in which the district court sits. A person begins an appeal by filing a notice of appeal. When it gets a notice of appeal, the federal district court transfers its record of the case to the court of appeals for review.

In an appeal, the court of appeals determines whether the federal district court judge or jury made any major errors in a case. A number of things can go wrong at the trial level. A judge might apply the wrong law when deciding a motion or instructing the jury. A judge might let the jury hear evidence that should have been kept out, or keep out evidence that the jury should have seen. A jury or judge might decide a case in a way that is unsupported by the evidence. In an appeal, the losing party asks the appellate court to reverse the district court's decision based on such errors.

Briefing, oral argument, and decisions Appeals have three main stages. The first begins when the parties, usually represented by attorneys, file written briefs explaining their sides of the case. The person who filed the appeal, called the appellant, writes a brief explaining how the district court judge or jury made an error that needs to be corrected. The other side, called the appellee, files a brief explaining why he or she thinks the trial judge or jury did not make a serious mistake.

The second stage of an appeal is called an oral argument. An oral argument is a chance for the parties to appear before the judges who will decide the appeal. Normally, a panel of three circuit judges hears each case in the courts of appeals. Sometimes the court hears a case "en banc," which means every judge hears and decides it. (The U.S. Court of Appeals for the Second Circuit, for example, has a total of thirteen active judges as of March 2005.) During the oral argument, the judges get to ask the parties questions about the case. Attorneys for the parties usually write the briefs and handle the oral argument, but a person can do it alone.

After the oral argument, the panel meets in private to discuss the case. If they all agree on a result, the result is unanimous. If only two judges agree, they are called the majority. Normally, one of the judges in the three- or two-judge majority writes an opinion explaining the court's decision. A judge on the

Charles Evans Hughes, U.S. Supreme Court chief justice from 1930 to 1941. Getty Images.

panel who agrees with the decision can write a concurring opinion to explain his or her position. A judge on the panel who disagrees with the decision can write a dissenting opinion, explaining why he or she thinks the court's decision is wrong.

Judicial interpretation According to Dexter Perkins in *Charles Evans Hughes and American Democratic Statesmanship,* Chief Justice Charles Evans Hughes (1862–1948) once said, "We are under a Constitution but the Constitution is what the judges say it is." Chief Justice Hughes was referring to judicial interpretation, which is the task of deciding what the Constitution and federal laws mean. Judicial interpretation is one of the most important tasks of the federal judiciary. Circuit court judges who write opinions affect future cases by interpreting the meaning of the federal Constitution and federal laws and regulations. Since most cases do not make it to the Supreme Court, circuit judges carry a lot of power when they engage in judicial interpretation.

Judicial review Judicial review is the task of reviewing congressional laws, federal regulations, and executive action to determine whether they violate the Constitution. The Constitution does not specifically give this power to the federal judiciary. Instead, the U.S. Supreme Court declared the power for the judiciary in the 1803 case of *Marbury v. Madison.*

Judicial review is very controversial. Some believe that the people should have the final say on the constitutionality of government action. Federal judges are not elected by the people and cannot be removed from office once appointed by the president and the Senate. This means it is hard for the people to change a constitutional decision made by a court of appeals or the Supreme Court.

Supreme Court

The Supreme Court is the only court specifically mentioned in the Constitution. It is the highest court in the federal judiciary. Nine justices serve on the Court. The head of the Court is called the chief justice, and the other eight are called associate justices.

The Supreme Court hears appeals, much like the circuit courts of appeals. People who lose in a circuit court of appeals or in the highest court of a state can ask the Supreme Court to

An illustration of the 1983 U.S. Supreme Court in session. Justices of that Court were (in alphabetical order) Harry Blackmun, William J. Brennan Jr., Warren Burger, Thurgood Marshall, Sandra Day O'Connor, Lewis Powell, William Rehnquist, John Paul Stevens, and Byron White. © Franklin McMahon/Corbis.

review the case. Sometimes a party can appeal directly from a federal district court to the Supreme Court without going through a court of appeals.

Writs of certiorari Unlike the circuit courts of appeals, the Supreme Court does not have to hear every appeal it receives. Instead, the Court normally has the power to pick which appeals to hear. It does so using a device called a writ of certiorari. (A writ is a court order, and *certiorari* is a Latin word that means "to certify a court case for review.")

A writ of certiorari is an order for a lower court to transmit the record in a case to the Supreme Court for review. Parties who want the Supreme Court to review a case file a petition, asking the Supreme Court to issue a writ for their case. The petition is a brief that explains why the case is important enough for the Court to consider.

The Court typically chooses to hear a case only if it involves issues of law that have national importance. If the Court grants a petition, it normally limits review to those specific issues instead of reviewing every issue the parties want to present. The Supreme Court grants a petition for a writ of certiorari only if at least four of the nine justices want to review the case.

The Supreme Court and the Presidential Election of 2000

Under the U.S. Constitution, presidents get elected through the electoral system. The Constitution does not give the Supreme Court a direct role in the process. In the election of 2000, however, the electoral system allowed the Supreme Court to play a role in the outcome.

Under the electoral system, each state gets a number of electors equal to the total number of senators and representatives they have in Congress. (Additionally, the District of Columbia gets a number of electors equal to the senators and representatives it would have if it was a state.) Each state gets to determine how to choose its electors.

As of 2005, the states allow voters to choose electors on election day in November of each election year. In December, after the November election results for choosing electors are final, the electors gather in their state capitals to vote for the next president and vice president. The presidential and vice presidential candidates

who get the most electoral votes win the election.

The electoral system makes it possible for the result in one state to affect the outcome of the entire election. This is what happened in 2000. After election night on November 7, 2000, Texas governor George W. Bush (1946–) was just hundreds of votes ahead of Vice President Al Gore (1948–) in Florida. The candidate who won Florida was going to win the electoral vote in December, making him the next president.

Some of the counties in Florida had problems with their ballots, making it hard to determine which hole a voter had punched in making his or her selection. This made it possible that the official count in Florida was wrong. When an election is as close as the one in Florida was, the loser can ask for a recount. Gore requested recounts in four counties. Bush filed lawsuits to stop the recounts, and Gore filed lawsuits to force the recounts.

One of the lawsuits made it all the way to the U.S. Supreme Court. In *Bush v. Gore*, Bush

Briefing and oral argument After the Supreme Court accepts a case for review, briefing and oral argument are much like in the circuit courts of appeals. Both sides file briefs explaining why they think the lower courts were right or wrong in how they decided the issues being reviewed. Then both sides appear for oral argument before the Court. Normally all nine justices hear and decide every case, so attorneys and people who argue before the Court can face questioning from nine justices at a time.

Conferences and decisions After the justices read the briefs and hear oral argument, they meet in private conference to discuss the

asked the Court to stop the Florida recounts. Bush's lawyers said the recounts would violate the U.S. Constitution, which says a state may not violate a person's right to equal protection of the laws. The Bush team said recounting ballots without a clear standard for which ballots should count and which should not count would violate the equal protection rights of the people who had punched their ballots clearly.

On December 12, 2000, the U.S. Supreme Court issued its 5-4 decision in the case. The Court sided with Bush and ordered the recounts in Florida to stop. This allowed Bush to win Florida, officially by 537 votes out of the almost six million cast in Florida. Bush became president of the United States in January 2001.

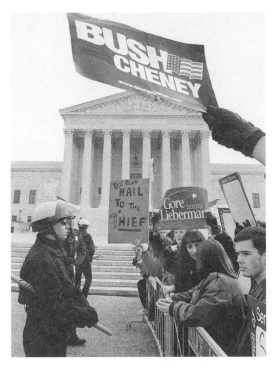

Supporters for Vice President Al Gore and Texas governor George W. Bush square off in front of the U.S. Supreme Court building on December 11, 2000, amidst the fight over who would be victorious in the 2000 presidential election. © Reuters/Corbis.

case. The conferences are not recorded, and the public never gets to see them. The chief justice normally begins by sharing his or her thoughts about a case. Then the associate justices speak in order of seniority, meaning how long they have served on the Court.

After discussion, the justices vote on how to decide the case. It takes at least five justices to change the result from the lower courts. If the chief justice is part of the majority, he or she assigns

The Labor Amendment

After the American Civil War (1861–65), the United States adopted the Thirteenth Amendment to the Constitution to outlaw slavery. It says, "Neither slavery nor involuntary servitude ... shall exist within the United States, or any place subject to their jurisdiction. Congress shall have the power to enforce this [amendment] by appropriate legislation."

The Thirteenth Amendment clearly makes slavery illegal in the United States. It also makes involuntary servitude illegal. Involuntary servitude means being forced to work for someone against your will.

Some believe the Thirteenth Amendment is a labor amendment that gives workers constitutional rights. In *Building Unions,* Peter Kellman wrote:

> [Workers] believed that freedom meant the abolition [elimination] of the condition of involuntary servitude both on and off the job. They reasoned that it was Congress's responsibility to make the amendment a reality in working-class life. They argued that denial of freedom of speech, assembly and organization on the job, or of the right to strike [stop working] and boycott [stop buying], was tantamount [equal] to involuntary servitude.

In Thirteenth Amendment cases, the Supreme Court has usually not supported workers' rights. The 1897 case of *Robertson v. Baldwin* is an example. In that case, two men signed contracts to serve as seamen on the private vessel *Arago* from San Francisco, California, for as long as the voyage might last. In Astoria, Oregon, the two men left the vessel because they were dissatisfied with their jobs.

Under a federal law, seamen who left a private vessel before their contracts ended could be arrested, forced to return to the vessel to work, and punished by imprisonment. The master of the *Arago* had the two men arrested and returned to the ship against their will. The two men still refused to work, so the *Arago* dropped them off in San Francisco, where they were arrested to be tried for federal crimes.

The men filed for a writ of habeas corpus, which is a document asking a court to release a person who is being imprisoned in violation of his or her rights. The seamen said imprisoning them for refusing to work violated the Thirteenth Amendment. The trial court rejected their argument and dismissed the writ, so the seamen appealed to the U.S. Supreme Court.

In a 7-1 decision (one justice did not participate), the U.S. Supreme Court affirmed the trial court's decision. Writing for the Court, Justice Henry B. Brown one of the justices in the majority to write the Court's opinion to explain its decision. If the chief justice is not in the majority, the most senior justice in the majority assigns one of the majority justices to write the Court's opinion. As in the courts of appeals, other justices may write concurring and dissenting opinions, agreeing or disagreeing with the result.

Justices circulate their opinions before finishing them to give the other justices a chance to suggest changes. When the opinions are

(1836–1913) said forcing seamen to fulfill their private contracts did not violate the Thirteenth Amendment, for two reasons. First, the seamen made the contracts voluntarily, so the work could not be called involuntary servitude. Second, countries worldwide forced seamen to fulfill their contracts, and punished them with imprisonment for not doing so, as far back as 900 BCE. According to Justice Brown, this meant America did not mean to outlaw such arrangements with the Thirteenth Amendment.

Justice John M. Harlan wrote a dissenting opinion, disagreeing with the Court's decision. Justice Harlan observed that the two seamen from the *Arago* "were seized, somewhat as runaway slaves were in the days of slavery, and committed to jail without bail, 'until the *Arago* was ready for sea.'" Justice Harlan said a seaman who breaks a contract should have to pay damages like any other person who unlawfully breaks a contract. Forcing a seaman to serve against his will, however, was plainly involuntary servitude, according to Harlan.

In response to the idea that seamen had been forced to fulfill their contracts throughout history, Harlan wrote, "Those laws, whatever they may have been, were enacted at a time when no account was taken of a man as man, when human life and human liberty were regarded as of little value, and when the powers of government were

employed to gratify the ambition and the pleasures of despotic [unfair] rulers rather than promote the welfare of the people."

U.S. Supreme Court justices Henry B. Brown (left) and John Marshall Harlan. Getty Images.

finished, the justice who wrote the Court's opinion usually announces the decision by reading a summary of it from the bench. At the same time, the Court distributes written copies of the full opinions.

U.S. Court of International Trade

The U.S. Court of International Trade is a special court that holds trials in civil cases involving international trade issues. International trade means business between a person or company in the United States and a person or company in another country. International trade cases can involve private disputes between such parties, or trade disputes between a private party and a government.

The U.S. Court of International Trade has headquarters in New York City. As of 2005, nine judges serve on the court. The head of the court, called the chief judge, assigns one judge to handle most trials. Sometimes a panel of three judges handles a case. Although the court sits in New York City, it can hold trials in federal courthouses across the nation.

A person who loses in the U.S. Court of International Trade may appeal to the U.S. Court of Appeals for the Federal Circuit. A party who loses there may ask the U.S. Supreme Court to review the case.

U.S. Court of Federal Claims

The U.S. Court of Federal Claims is a special court that sits in Washington, D.C. It holds trials in all cases, except tort cases, in which a party seeks money damages from the federal government. (Torts are injuries caused when someone violates a duty or obligation to another person. Examples include battery, defamation, and negligence. Battery is an unlawful physical encounter. Defamation is harming someone's reputation. Negligence is injury caused by carelessness.) One of the court's sixteen judges normally handles each trial. The party who loses may appeal to the U.S. Court of Appeals for the Federal Circuit. The party who loses there may ask the Supreme Court to review the case.

Administration and planning for the federal judiciary

The federal judiciary is an enormous operation with hundreds of judges and tens of thousands of employees nationwide. Each court has a clerk's office that handles administration for that specific court. To handle nationwide administration and planning for the federal judiciary, Congress created a number of government offices. These include the Judicial Conference of the United States, the Administrative Office of the United States Courts, and the Federal Judicial Center.

Judicial Conference of the United States The Judicial Conference of the United States makes policies for administration of the federal judiciary. It is composed of the chief justice of the Supreme Court, the chief judges of the thirteen circuit courts of appeals, one district judge from each of the twelve geographic circuits, and the chief judge of the U.S. Court of International Trade. Staff from the Administrative Office of the United States Courts helps the Judicial Conference do its job.

The Judicial Conference has a number of statutory duties. It surveys the condition of business in the federal courts and makes recommendations for better management. It makes plans for the assignment of judges to the courts of appeals and federal district courts. It studies the operation and effect of court rules for handling cases. Finally, it directs and supervises the Administrative Office of the United States Courts.

Administrative Office of the United States Courts The Administrative Office of the United States Courts handles overall administration for and management of the federal judiciary. The chief justice of the Supreme Court appoints a director and deputy director to run the Administrative Office. In addition to administration, the Office runs federal judicial programs, makes policy recommendations to the Judicial Conference, and communicates with Congress on budget issues and other matters.

Federal Judicial Center The Federal Judicial Center is the research and training arm of the federal judiciary. It is led by a board that consists of the chief justice of the Supreme Court, two circuit court judges, three district court judges, and the director of the Administrative Office of the U.S. Courts. The Federal Judicial Center studies the operation of the federal judiciary and makes policy recommendations to the Judicial Conference. It also runs training programs for judges and personnel of the federal judiciary.

For More Information

BOOKS

Baum, Lawrence. *The Supreme Court.* Washington, DC: Congressional Quarterly Inc., 1998.

Biskupic, Joan, and Elder Witt. *The Supreme Court & the Powers of the American Government.* Washington, DC: Congressional Quarterly Inc., 1997.

Biskupic, Joan, and Elder Witt. *The Supreme Court at Work.* Washington, DC: Congressional Quarterly, Inc., 1997.

Carp, Robert A., and Ronald Stidham. *The Federal Courts.* 2nd ed. Washington, DC: Congressional Quarterly, Inc., 1991.

Choper, Jesse H., ed. *The Supreme Court and Its Justices.* 2nd ed. Chicago: American Bar Association, 2001.

Irons, Peter. *A People's History of the Supreme Court.* New York: Penguin Books, 1999.

Kellman, Peter. *Building Unions: Past, Present, and Future.* New York: Apex Press, 2001.

Lazarus, Edward P. *Closed Chambers.* New York: Times Books, 1998.

McClenaghan, William A. *Magruder's American Government 2003.* Needham, MA: Prentice Hall School Group, 2002.

O'Connor, Sandra Day. *The Majesty of the Law.* New York: Random House, 2003.

Perkins, Dexter. *Charles Evans Hughes and American Democratic Statesmanship.* Boston: Little Brown, 1956.

Schwartz, Bernard. *A History of the Supreme Court.* New York: Oxford University Press, 1993.

Shelley, Mack C., II. *American Government and Politics Today.* 2004–2005 ed. Belmont, CA: Wadsworth Publishing, 2003.

Surrency, Erwin C. *History of the Federal Courts.* 2nd ed. Dobbs Ferry, NY: Oceana Publications, 2002.

Volkomer, Walter E. *American Government.* 8th ed. Upper Saddle River, NJ: Prentice Hall, 1998.

Wasby, Stephen L. *The Supreme Court in the Federal Judicial System.* 2nd ed. New York: Holt, Rinehart and Winston, 1984.

CASES

Bush v. Gore, 531 U.S. 98 (2000).

Robertson v. Baldwin, 165 U.S. 275 (1897).

WEB SITES

Federal Judicial Center. http://www.fjc.gov/ (accessed on March 31, 2005).

Supreme Court of the United States. http://www.supremecourtus.gov (accessed on February 18, 2005).

United States Court of International Trade. http://www.cit.uscourts.gov/ (accessed on March 31, 2005).

United States Tax Court. http://www.ustaxcourt.gov/ (accessed on March 31, 2005).

U.S. Court of Appeals for the Armed Forces. http://www.armfor.uscourts.gov/ (accessed on March 31, 2005).

U.S. Court of Appeals for Veterans Claims. http://www.vetapp.gov/ (accessed on March 31, 2005).

U.S. Court of Federal Claims. http://www.cit.uscourts.gov/ (accessed on February 12, 2005).

U.S. Courts: Administrative Office of the United States Courts. http://www.uscourts.gov/adminoff.html (accessed on March 31, 2005).

U.S. Courts: Judicial Conference of the United States. http://www.uscourts.gov/judconf.html (accessed on March 31, 2005).

U.S. Courts: The Federal Judiciary. http://www.uscourts.gov (accessed on March 23, 2005).

U.S. Courts: U.S. Bankruptcy Courts. http://www.uscourts.gov/bankruptcycourts.html (accessed on March 31, 2005).

Judicial-Executive Checks and Balances

The U.S. Constitution divides the government into three branches: legislative, executive, and judicial. Generally speaking, the legislative branch, Congress, makes the nation's laws. The executive branch enforces the laws through the president and various executive offices. The judicial branch, made up of the Supreme Court and lower federal courts, decides cases that arise under the laws.

This division of government is called the separation of powers. The separation of powers is supposed to prevent tyranny. Tyranny is arbitrary (random) or unfair government action that can result when one person has all the power to make, enforce, and interpret the laws.

In addition to the broad separation of powers into three branches, the Constitution keeps the judicial and executive branches separate with two specific provisions. Under Article III, Section 1, judges of the Supreme Court and lower federal courts "hold their offices during good behavior." This means the president cannot remove judges from office. Instead, only Congress can remove judges through impeachment and conviction for treason, bribery, and other high crimes and misdemeanors under Article II, Section 4. The Constitution defines treason as levying war against America or giving aid and comfort to its enemies. Bribery is an illegal payment to influence official action.

Likewise, the president can be removed from office only through impeachment and conviction by Congress. The Supreme Court and lower federal courts do not hear impeachment cases. This ensures that only Congress, which is accountable for its

Words to Know

checks and balances: The specific powers in one branch of government that allow it to limit the powers of the other branches.

circuit court of appeals: A court in the federal judicial system that handles appeals from the trial courts, called federal district courts. The United States is divided into twelve geographic areas called circuits, and each circuit has one court of appeals that handles appeals from the federal district courts in its circuit. A party who loses in a circuit court of appeals may ask the Supreme Court to review the case.

Constitution of the United States of America: The document written in 1787 that established the federal government under which the United States of America has operated since 1789. Article III covers the judicial branch.

federal district courts: The courts in the federal judicial system that handle trials in civil and criminal cases. Each state is divided into one or more federal judicial districts, and each district has one or more federal district courts. A party who loses in a federal district court may appeal to have the case reviewed by a circuit court of appeals.

judicial review: The process by which federal courts review laws to determine whether they violate the U.S. Constitution. If a court finds that a law violates the Constitution, it declares the law unconstitutional, which means the executive branch is not supposed to enforce it anymore. Congress can correct such a defect by passing a new law that does not violate the Constitution.

judiciary: The branch of the federal government that decides cases that arise under the nation's law. The federal judiciary includes the Supreme Court of the United States, circuit courts of appeals, and federal district courts.

president: The highest officer in the executive branch of the federal government, with primary responsibility for enforcing the nation's laws.

separation of powers: Division of the powers of government into different branches to prevent one branch from having too much power.

Supreme Court: The highest court in the federal judiciary. The judiciary is the branch of government responsible for resolving legal disputes and interpreting laws on a case-by-case basis.

actions at election time, can remove a president from office. Supreme Court justices and lower court judges, who are appointed by the president and so are free from popular control, cannot remove a president.

Checks and balances

The men who wrote the Constitution in 1787 wanted each branch's power to be separate, but not absolute. They considered absolute power, even over just a portion of the government, to be dangerous.

To prevent the power of any one branch from being absolute, the Founding Fathers wrote the Constitution to contain a system of checks and balances. These are powers that each branch has for limiting the power of the other branches. Some scholars say the system of checks and balances actually creates a government of shared powers instead of one with separated powers.

The judiciary's main powers over the president are judicial review and judicial interpretation. Judicial review is the power to review executive action to determine if it violates the Constitution. Judicial interpretation is the power to determine the validity and meaning of executive agency regulations. Other judicial checks include the writ (judicial order) of habeas corpus, the writs of mandamus and prohibition, and the chief justice's role in impeachment of the president. A writ of habeas corpus is a procedure that prisoners can use to get released if they are being held in violation of the law. The writ requires a jailer to bring the prisoner before a court, where a judge can set the prisoner free if he or she is being held in violation of constitutional rights. A writ of mandamus is a court order that forces government officials to do their jobs. A writ of prohibition is a court order preventing a government official from doing something prohibited by law.

The executive branch's main powers over the judiciary are the appointment power, executive privilege, and the power to issue pardons and reprieves.

Judicial review

Judicial review is the power to review government action for compliance with the Constitution. The Constitution does not specifically give the federal judiciary this power. Instead, the Supreme Court assumed the power in its decision in *Marbury v. Madison* in 1803.

The case began in 1801, in the waning days of the administration of President John Adams (1735–1826; served 1797–1801). One of the last things Adams did as president was sign commissions, or orders, appointing people to serve as justices of the peace in the District of Columbia. Adams's secretary of state, John Marshall (1755–1835), was supposed to deliver the commissions to the appointees. Marshall failed to deliver all of them before Adams left office.

When President Thomas Jefferson (1743–1826; served 1801–9) took office in March 1801, he did not want the people appointed by Adams to take office because they were members of the Federalist Party, the main rival to Jefferson's Democratic-Republican Party. When William Marbury and other appointees

Ducking the Separation of Powers?

In 2001, Vice President Dick Cheney (1941–) headed a task force called the National Energy Policy Development Group. The task force developed energy policy for the administration of President George W. Bush (1946–; served 2001–). Energy policy is a country's plan for developing energy resources, such as oil, coal, wind, and other sources of power.

In July 2001, an organization called Judicial Watch filed a lawsuit against Cheney and the task force. Judicial Watch wanted Cheney to produce documents from the task force's work. A federal law required government task forces to reveal their records unless the task force was made entirely of federal officials. Judicial Watch said the task force had members who were executives from energy corporations, such as Enron.

Cheney and the task force refused to disclose the records. Cheney said executive privilege allowed him to maintain the secrecy of records relating to the development of government policy. Joined by another organization called the Sierra Club, Judicial Watch fought with Cheney in various court proceedings to force him to disclose the records.

The case reached the Supreme Court at the end of 2003. The Court had to decide a technical issue relating to a federal district court's decision in the case. Three weeks after the Supreme Court agreed to hear the case, Cheney went on a duck hunting and fishing trip with Justice Antonin Scalia (1936–).

Scalia flew with Cheney to the vacation on a government airplane.

Many Americans thought it was inappropriate for Cheney and Scalia to socialize when the Supreme Court was set to hear a case in which Cheney was a party. Eight of the ten largest newspapers in the country, and twenty of the largest thirty, published editorials asking Scalia to recuse himself from the case. (Recuse means to refrain from participating in the decision of a case.) Some editorials said even if Justice Scalia could decide the case fairly, the hunting trip made his participation in the case seem inappropriate.

The Sierra Club filed a motion in the Supreme Court, officially asking Scalia to recuse himself. A federal law said judges must recuse themselves when their fairness could "reasonably be questioned." The Sierra Club said Scalia's hunting trip made it reasonable for Americans to wonder whether he could decide the case fairly. The Sierra Club used the newspaper editorials to support its position. Judicial Watch did not join the motion, and publicly said it did not think Scalia had to recuse himself.

The Supreme Court's practice for recusal motions is to have the justice being questioned decide the motion himself. On March 18, 2004, Justice Scalia decided not to recuse himself. Scalia said there was no reasonable way to question his fairness in the Cheney case. Scalia said he and Cheney were never alone during the hunting trip and never discussed the case. Even though Scalia and Cheney are friends, Scalia said recusal is only required when a case involves a friend's personal finances or liberty asked the new secretary of state, James Madison (1751–1836), to give them their commissions, Madison refused under orders from Jefferson.

Marbury sued Madison in the Supreme Court. The Judiciary Act of 1789 gave the Supreme Court the power to hear

interests. The task force case involved Cheney's official actions as vice president of the United States, not his personal matters.

Scalia rejected the notion that the newspaper editorials made it reasonable to question his fairness. Scalia said the editorials were misinformed about the facts of the case. Some of them said Scalia was Cheney's guest on the trip, when in fact both Scalia and Cheney were guests of a private person. Some of the editorials said Scalia and Cheney hunted together in the same blind (a place where hunters hide from their prey), when that was untrue, too, according to Scalia. Near the end of his opinion, Scalia wrote:

> The question, simply put, is whether some-one who thought I could decide this case impartially [fairly] despite my friendship with the Vice President would reasonably believe that I *cannot* decide it impartially because I went hunting with that friend and accepted an invitation to fly there with him on a Government plane. If it is reasonable to think that a Supreme Court Justice can be bought so cheap, the Nation is in deeper trouble that I had imagined.

In June 2004, the Supreme Court decided the technical questions then at issue in the litigation. The Court directed the federal district court to review and decide whether documents Cheney sought to conceal were protected by executive privilege. That autumn, the district court ordered Cheney and the task force to release any documents not protected by any privilege,

and to produce a list of documents they thought were protected by privilege. The Court could then decide whether those documents really deserved to be protected from disclosure.

As of early 2005, almost four years after Judicial Watch filed the lawsuit, the parties continued to fight over the issue in federal court.

U.S. Supreme Court justice Antonin Scalia, who found himself involved in a 2003 controversy that included his friend, Vice President Dick Cheney. Supreme Court of the United States.

cases for writs of mandamus. Marbury wanted the Supreme Court to force Madison to give him his commission.

The Supreme Court did not get to decide the case until 1803. The same John Marshall who had neglected to deliver Marbury's commission in the first place was now chief justice, or leader, of the Supreme Court. (Historians generally agree that if a situation similar to this case came up today, Marshall would disqualify himself due to a clear conflict of interest.) Marshall wrote the court's opinion, saying that Marbury deserved the commission and that Madison should deliver it. The Supreme Court, however, could not issue a writ of mandamus to force Madison to do his job. Marshall said the Judiciary Act of 1789 violated the Constitution because the Constitution does not allow people to sue in the Supreme Court for writs of mandamus. Such cases must begin in a lower federal court and be appealed to the Supreme Court if necessary.

Since *Marbury v. Madison,* the Supreme Court has used judicial review to scrutinize acts of Congress and actions of the executive branch in cases before it. The main limitations on executive power in such cases are the limitations on searches and seizures under the Fourth Amendment and the rights of criminal defendants under the Fifth and Sixth Amendments.

Searches and seizures: the Fourth Amendment America adopted the Fourth Amendment of the Constitution in 1791, three years after adopting the Constitution itself. The Fourth Amendment says:

> The right of the people to be secure in their persons, houses, papers, and effects, against unreasonable searches and seizures, shall not be violated, and no Warrants shall issue, but upon probable cause, supported by Oath or affirmation, and particularly describing the place to be searched, and the persons or things to be seized.

The Fourth Amendment is supposed to restrict the law enforcement activities of the executive branch. Law enforcement agents who investigate crimes often have to search houses, seize possible evidence, and arrest people. The Fourth Amendment says law enforcement must do these things reasonably.

Law enforcement agents often need to get a warrant to conduct a search, seize evidence, or arrest a person. A warrant is a court order authorizing such action. The Fourth Amendment says courts should not issue warrants without testimony or the sworn statement of a witness demonstrating probable cause. Probable cause is a reasonable belief that the search or seizure could produce evidence of a crime. Courts check the power of law enforcement by denying warrant applications when the government does not have enough evidence to support a search, seizure, or arrest.

After law enforcement conducts an investigation, federal prosecutors decide whether to file criminal charges against a suspect. The trial process is another chance for the federal judiciary to check the law enforcement power of the executive branch. Sometimes law enforcement agents collect evidence of a crime by violating the Fourth Amendment. For example, they might search a house or seize evidence without a warrant, or in a manner that violates the terms of the warrant they have

When law enforcement agents gather evidence by violating the Fourth Amendment, criminal defendants ask the court to enforce the exclusionary rule. The exclusionary rule is a rule created by the U.S. Supreme Court. In general, it prevents the federal government from using evidence at a criminal trial that it got by violating the Fourth Amendment. Enforcement of the exclusionary rule can result in dismissal of criminal charges, even against guilty defendants. In this way, the exclusionary rule encourages law enforcement authorities to obey the Fourth Amendment.

Rights of criminal defendants: the Fifth Amendment Criminal defendants have other rights under the Fifth and Sixth Amendments, also adopted in 1791. The Fifth Amendment says:

> No person shall be held to answer for a capital, or otherwise infamous crime, unless on presentment or indictment of a Grand Jury, except in cases arising in the land or naval forces, or in the Militia, when in actual service in time of War or public danger; nor shall any person be subject for the same offence to be twice put in jeopardy of life or limb; nor shall be compelled in any criminal case to be a witness against himself, nor be deprived of life, liberty, or property, without due process of law. . . .

The federal judiciary checks the law enforcement power of the executive branch by enforcing this amendment in cases against criminal defendants. Under the Grand Jury Clause, the executive branch must use grand juries to charge criminal defendants with capital or infamous crimes. Capital crimes are crimes that may be punishable by death, meaning the death penalty. For example, first degree murder, which means premeditated or preplanned murder, is a capital crime. Infamous crimes are crimes that, under the common law, made a person incapable of testifying in court because of untrustworthiness. Under the common law (judge-made law in English and early-American courts), infamous crimes included treason, felonies, and crimes involving dishonesty, such as perjury. Treason means an act of war against the United States. Felonies refer to the most serious kinds of crime, usually punishable by either death or imprisonment for more than one year. Perjury is lying under oath. A grand jury is a group of citizens who review the evidence against a suspect to make sure there is enough to hold a criminal trial. Federal judges oversee grand jury proceedings to make sure they comply with the law.

The Fifth Amendment's Double Jeopardy Clause says a person may not be tried twice for the same crime. Federal courts enforce this clause against prosecutors. Sometimes a case against a defendant is stopped before the case is finished. In such instances, federal courts must decide whether the first case went far enough to make a second case illegal under the Double Jeopardy Clause.

The Fifth Amendment prevents prosecutors from forcing a criminal defendant to testify at his or her own trial. This is called the privilege against self-incrimination. This privilege also allows criminal suspects to refuse to answer questions during investigations, a practice commonly referred to as "taking the fifth." In criminal cases, federal courts sometimes have to decide whether investigators or prosecutors got evidence from a defendant by violating the privilege against self-incrimination. Under the exclusionary rule, courts are not supposed to allow prosecutors to use such evidence against the person whose privilege was violated.

The Due Process Clause of the Fifth Amendment says the government may not take a person's life, liberty, or property without due process of law. Generally, due process requires a criminal defendant to have notice of the charges against him or her and a chance to present a defense in a fair proceeding. Federal courts check the power of law enforcement by enforcing this clause in criminal prosecutions.

Rights of criminal defendants: the Sixth Amendment The Sixth Amendment says:

> In all criminal prosecutions, the accused shall enjoy a right to a speedy and public trial, by an impartial jury of the State and district wherein the crime shall have been committed, which district shall have been previously ascertained by law, and to be informed of the nature and cause of the accusation; to be confronted with the witnesses against him; to have compulsory [required] process for obtaining witnesses in his favor, and to have the Assistance of Counsel for his defence.

Congress has passed federal laws concerning a defendant's constitutional right to have a speedy public trial by a fair jury in the district where the crime was committed. Federal courts check the power of the executive branch by enforcing these laws in criminal cases. The courts also make sure defendants have fair notice of the charges against them.

Under the Confrontation Clause, a defendant has the right to face the witnesses against him or her. This means that, generally, witnesses have to testify against defendants in open court, and defendants cannot be banned from court during the testimony. Defendants also have the right to force witnesses with favorable evidence to appear in court to testify during criminal trials. Federal courts enforce this right with subpoenas, which are court orders for witnesses to appear in court to give testimony.

Judicial interpretation

Judicial interpretation is the act of deciding what a congressional law or executive regulation means. In theory, judicial interpretation is not supposed to be a check on congressional or executive power. Instead, it is supposed to determine and enforce the will of Congress or the executive branch. In practice, however, interpreting laws and regulations gives courts considerable power to determine what they mean, which can affect the exercise of congressional and executive power.

Judicial interpretation affects the regulatory work of executive agencies. Agencies are executive offices responsible for enforcing specific areas of federal law. The Environmental Protection Agency (EPA), for example, enforces congressional laws that regulate the pollution of air, land, and water.

Executive agencies get their power from such congressional laws. Congress, for instance, has given the EPA the power to enforce the Clean Air Act and the Clean Water Act (among other laws). These laws contain very general standards concerning the pollution of air and water. To enforce them, the EPA writes regulations. Regulations are like congressional laws, but they contain much more detail.

People and businesses in America must obey both congressional laws and executive regulations. If the EPA thinks someone has violated a law or regulation, it can file a civil or criminal case against the offender. The EPA usually resolves such cases by agreements with the offenders or by holding administrative hearings in EPA offices.

Occasionally, however, these cases end up in the federal courts. When they do, federal judges have to interpret the agency's regulations. Interpretation requires the judge to decide whether the agency had the power to adopt the regulation under the relevant congressional law. In this way, interpretation acts as a check on executive power by making sure the agency has not done something Congress did not authorize it to do.

If a regulation was lawfully adopted under congressional law, the judge must decide what the regulation means, and whether the defendant violated it. This process gives the federal judiciary considerable power over the regulatory actions of the executive branch.

Writs of habeas corpus

Federal authorities sometimes arrest, imprison, or convict a person in a way that violates his or her rights under the Constitution or federal law. When this happens, the person can apply to a federal court for a writ of habeas corpus. The writ requires federal authorities to bring the accused to court so he or she can ask the court to decide whether the imprisonment is illegal. If the court agrees with the prisoner, it can order him or her to be released, even if he or she is guilty of a crime.

According to the U.S. Supreme Court, federal courts only have the power to issue writs of habeas corpus if congressional law gives them the power. The court, however, might be wrong about this. Article I, Section 9, of the Constitution says, "The privilege of the writ of habeas corpus shall not be suspended, unless when in cases of rebellion or invasion the public safety may require it." This arguably means Americans have a constitutional right to seek writs of habeas corpus, whether or not Congress authorizes the power. Congressional law, however, has authorized writs of habeas corpus since the federal government began to operate under the Constitution in 1789.

Writs of mandamus and prohibition

A writ of mandamus is a court order forcing a government official to do something required by his or her job. A writ of prohibition is a court order preventing a government official from doing something prohibited by his or her job.

The U.S. Constitution does not mention writs of mandamus and prohibition. Instead, Congress has passed laws giving the federal courts such power. Use of this power acts as a check on the powers of the executive branch.

Courts generally issue writs of mandamus only to compel government officials to do ministerial acts. A ministerial act is one that does not involve discretion, or judgment. Instead, it is action clearly required by the law. An example is issuance of a permit or license to an applicant who qualifies for it.

A discretionary act is an act that requires a government official to exercise judgment. An example is a U.S. attorney's decision whether to prosecute a suspected criminal. Courts generally will not issue writs to compel discretionary conduct because judges are not supposed to substitute their judgment for that of government officials.

In practice, federal judges rarely issue writs of mandamus or prohibition. Instead, if they think a writ is necessary, they write an opinion explaining why and give the government official a chance to correct his or her conduct without being compelled by a writ.

The chief justice's role in presidential impeachments

Under Article II, Section 4, executive officials may only be removed from office by impeachment for and conviction of

U.S. Supreme Court chief justice Salmon P. Chase presided over the impeachment trial of Andrew Johnson in 1868. Library of Congress.

treason, bribery, and other high crimes and misdemeanors. Under Article I, Congress has the sole authority to conduct the process. The House of Representatives can impeach officials by vote of a simple majority. Impeachment serves as an accusation of misconduct. Once impeached, an official faces trial in the Senate, which can remove the official by vote of at least a two-thirds majority. The federal judiciary plays no role in the process.

There is one small exception to this rule. Normally, the vice president presides over Senate impeachment trials because he is officially the president of the Senate under Article I, Section 3, of the Constitution. When the president faces an impeachment trial in the Senate, however, the chief justice of the Supreme Court presides instead of the vice president. Because the vice president stands to get the job of a president who is removed from office, it would not be fair to let him or her preside over the trial. In this way, the chief justice serves as a check on the vice president's senatorial power and, therefore, a check on the legislative branch as well.

The chief justice, who is the leader of the Supreme Court, has a limited role in presidential impeachment trials. He or she does not get to vote whether to convict and remove the president. The chief justice mainly interprets and enforces the Senate's rules for conducting the trial. Under the rules, the Senate can overrule an interpretation or decision by the chief justice. The chief justice's presence, however, lends an air of credibility and authority to the controversial business of trying to remove a president from office. In American history, there have been only two times that a president has been impeached: Andrew Johnson (1808–1875; served 1865–69) in 1868 and Bill Clinton (1946–; served 1993–2001) in 1998. Neither was removed from office, though Johnson retained his position by only a single vote.

Appointment power

Under Article II, Section 2, of the Constitution, presidents have the power to nominate people to serve on the Supreme Court and lower federal courts. The Senate gets to vote whether to approve or reject these nominations. A simple majority is all that is required to approve the president's choices.

Supreme Court justices and lower federal judges serve as long as they want unless impeached and convicted by Congress for treason, bribery, or other high crimes and misdemeanors. This means presidents cannot remove them from office. Presidents get to appoint new justices and judges only when one retires or when Congress creates a new seat on a court.

The power to appoint justices and judges to the Supreme and lower courts, however, acts as a check on the power of the Court. This is especially true when the president's political philosophy differs greatly from those of the Supreme Court justices.

Sandra Day O'Connor is sworn in as the first woman on the U.S. Supreme Court in September 1981. Husband John J. O'Connor holds two family Bibles as Chief Justice Warren Burger swears in his new colleague. AP/Wide World Photos.

When justices retire, the president can affect the Supreme Court's decisions for years or decades into the future by nominating justices who agree with his philosophies, as long as the Senate approves the nominations.

Executive privilege

The executive branch often faces demands that it produce information about its conduct. Congress might ask for information on how an executive agency is functioning under federal law. A special prosecutor might demand information on whether a president or other executive official has violated the law. Citizens can request information under a law called the Freedom of Information Act (FOIA). When a government office gets a FOIA request from a citizen, it must respond to the request in a certain amount of time. Much of the time, the office has to release the information requested. The FOIA law, however, allows the government to keep certain kinds of information secret. Examples include information relating to national security, and private business information of individual companies. Citizens and the government frequently end up in lawsuits over whether the government must release information requested under the FOIA.

If an executive official resists a demand for information, the person seeking the information can sue for it. Federal courts can force an official to produce information if production is required or allowed under the applicable law. Serving in this role, federal courts act as a check on the secret exercise of executive power.

When executive officials defend such cases, they have two main strategies. First, they often argue that the applicable law does not require them to produce the desired information. Second, they sometimes argue that they have a privilege, called executive privilege, that allows them to keep the information secret.

The executive privilege is a right to keep information secret for national safety or the public good. The Constitution does not give the executive branch an executive privilege. Instead, presidents have created it themselves, and the Supreme Court has approved it. When an executive official successfully keeps information secret, he or she checks the power of Congress, the courts, and the citizens to require access to governmental information. Some scholars and citizens consider such secrecy to be an abuse of executive power. Others think it is necessary for the executive branch to handle important government matters. Richard Nixon (1913–1994; served 1969–74), for instance, unsuccessfully tried to use executive privilege amidst the Watergate scandal. His participation in the cover-up of a burglary of the Democratic National Committee headquarters in 1972 led to his resignation in 1974.

Pardons and reprieves

Article II, Section 2, gives the president the power to grant pardons and reprieves for offenses against the United States. A pardon is complete forgiveness for a crime. It prevents the criminal from being punished by the law. A reprieve suspends a sentence, or punishment, to give a criminal time to ask the court to change the sentence. The pardon power checks the power of the courts by allowing a president to forgive a criminal if he

United States v. Nixon

The 1974 case of *United States v. Nixon* illustrates the separation of powers between the executive and judicial branches. The case grew out of the 1972 presidential race between the Republican contender, President Richard Nixon (1913–1994; served 1969–74), and his Democratic opponent, U.S. senator George McGovern (1922–) of South Dakota. Nixon won the election in November by a wide margin.

On June 17, 1972, months before the election, five burglars broke into offices of the Democratic National Committee in the Watergate building in Washington, D.C. The five men, plus two more who planned the break-in, stood trial for burglary in January 1973. In March 1973, one of the seven, James W. McCord Jr., accused the Nixon administration of trying to prevent investigation of the incident.

Under pressure from these allegations, Nixon appointed a special prosecutor, Archibald Cox (1912–2004), to investigate whether there was a cover-up. During the investigation, White House aide Alexander Butterfield (1926–) revealed that Nixon had installed an audiotape system in the Oval Office, to secretly tape conversations with advisors for historical purposes. Cox issued a subpoena, or court order, directing Nixon to give Cox some of the tapes. Nixon responded by firing Cox. Public outrage forced Nixon to appoint another prosecutor, Leon Jaworski (1905–1982), to continue the investigation.

On March 1, 1974, a grand jury charged U.S. attorney general John N. Mitchell (1913–1988) and six other officials from the Nixon administration with conspiracy to obstruct investigation of the Watergate burglary. Nixon was named as one of the conspirators, but he was not charged as an accused criminal.

In April 1974, Jaworski issued a subpoena, again asking Nixon to produce tape recordings of Oval Office conversations. Jaworski said he needed the tapes for the criminal trial of Mitchell and Nixon's other officials. This time, Nixon asked the Federal District Court for the District of Columbia to quash, or strike down, the subpoena.

Through his attorneys, Nixon argued that as president, he had an executive privilege that allowed him to maintain the secrecy of conversations with his advisors. He also argued that the federal courts, as a separate branch of the government, had no power to dispute his interpretation of his executive privilege.

On May 31, 1974, District Judge John Sirica (1904–1992) denied Nixon's request. Nixon appealed the case straight to the U.S. Supreme Court. The Court heard arguments on July 8, 1974, and issued its decision weeks later, on July 24.

In an 8–0 opinion written by Chief Justice Warren E. Burger (1907–1995), the Court ordered Nixon to give the tapes to Judge Sirica. Judge Sirica was to review them to decide if they contained evidence for the pending criminal trial. Such information would be turned over to prosecutor Jaworski.

The Court rejected Nixon's argument that it lacked power to interpret the meaning of Nixon's executive privilege. The Constitution does not explicitly give the president an executive privilege. This means that if it exists at all, the privilege must be an implied part of the president's powers under the Constitution. The Supreme Court said that because its job is to interpret the meaning of the laws, including the Constitution, the Court had the power to interpret the extent of Nixon's executive privilege.

The Court also rejected Nixon's argument that his executive privilege was absolute. An absolute privilege is one that cannot be broken. The Court suggested presidents have an absolute privilege "to protect military, diplomatic, or sensitive national security secrets." Nixon was not arguing that his recorded White House conversations contained such secrets.

The Court ruled that when a president's secret information does not involve military, diplomatic, or sensitive national security secrets, courts can order presidents to produce information needed for a criminal trial. In such cases, the need for the information outweighs the president's need for secrecy. Chief Justice Burger said courts will rarely need to force presidents to produce information for criminal trials. This meant that breaking the executive privilege in such cases would not prevent executive officials from being honest in their advice to the president.

Nixon's tenuous hold on the presidency unravelled quickly. Less than three weeks later, Nixon resigned, the first U.S. president in history to do so.

President Richard Nixon sits in front of secret Oval Office recordings that the U.S. Supreme Court ruled unanimously on July 24, 1974, should be released to Watergate prosecutors. Nixon had attempted to keep them from being turned over, citing executive privilege. The tapes contained damning evidence against the president, and he resigned from office less than a month later. AP/Wide World Photos.

thinks the court's sentence was unfair. On December 24, 1992, outgoing president George Bush (1924–; served 1989–93) pardoned six members of the administration of Ronald Reagan (1911–2004; served 1981–89) who were involved in the Iran-Contra arms-for-hostages investigation, including former defense secretary Caspar Weinberger (1917–). According to U.S. Information Agency writer Dian McDonald, Bush pardoned the men, who had not gone to trial, because the "common denominator of their motivation—whether their actions were right or wrong—was patriotism."

For More Information

BOOKS

Beard, Charles A. *American Government and Politics.* 10th ed. New York: Macmillan Co., 1949.

Biskupic, Joan, and Elder Witt. *The Supreme Court & the Powers of the American Government.* Washington, DC: Congressional Quarterly Inc., 1997.

Congressional Quarterly Inc. *Powers of the Presidency.* 2nd ed. Washington, DC: Congressional Quarterly Inc., 1997.

Dougherty, J. Hampden. *Power of Federal Judiciary over Legislation.* New York: Putnam's Sons, 1912. Reprint, Clark, NJ: Lawbook Exchange, 2004.

Janda, Kenneth, Jeffrey M. Berry, and Jerry Goldman. *The Challenge of Democracy.* 5th ed. Boston: Houghton Mifflin Company, 1997.

McClenaghan, William A. *Magruder's American Government 2003.* Needham, MA: Prentice Hall School Group, 2002.

Nelson, Michael, ed. *The Presidency and the Political System.* 7th ed. Washington, DC: CQ Press, 2003.

Parenti, Michael. *Democracy for the Few.* 6th ed. New York: St. Martin's Press, 1995.

Roelofs, H. Mark. *The Poverty of American Politics.* 2nd ed. Philadelphia: Temple University Press, 1998.

Shelley, Mack C., II. *American Government and Politics Today.* 2004–2005 ed. Belmont, CA: Wadsworth Publishing, 2003.

Volkomer, Walter E. *American Government.* 8th ed. Upper Saddle River, NJ: Prentice Hall, 1998.

CD-ROM

21st Century Complete Guide to U.S. Courts. Progressive Management, 2003.

CASES

Marbury v. Madison, 1 Cranch 137 (1803).

Youngstown Sheet and Tube Co. v. Sawyer, 343 U.S. 579 (1952).

WEB SITES

McDonald, Dian. "Bush Pardons Weinberger, Five Others Tied to Iran-Contra." *Federation of American Scientists.* http://www.fas.org/news/iran/1992/921224-260039.htm (accessed on February 23, 2005).

Sabato, Larry J. "Feeding Frenzy: Judge Douglas Ginsburg's Marijuana Use—1987." *Washington Post.* http://www.washingtonpost.com/wp-srv/politics/special/clinton/frenzy/ginsburg.htm (accessed on February 18, 2005).

Supreme Court of the United States. http://www.supremecourtus.gov (accessed on February 18, 2005).

U.S. Courts: Federal Judiciary. http://www.uscourts.gov (accessed on February 18, 2005).

The White House. http://www.whitehouse.gov (accessed on February 16, 2005).

Judicial-Legislative Checks and Balances

*T*he U.S. Constitution divides the powers of government into three branches: legislative, executive, and judicial. Generally speaking, the legislative branch, Congress, makes the nation's laws. The executive branch enforces the laws through the president and various executive offices. The judicial branch, made up of the Supreme Court and lower federal courts, decides cases that arise under the laws.

This division of government is called the separation of powers. The separation of powers is supposed to prevent tyranny. Tyranny is random or unfair government action that can result when one person has all the power to make, enforce, and interpret the laws.

In addition to the broad separation of powers into three branches, the Constitution keeps the judicial and legislative branches separate with various specific provisions. Article I, Section 5, says the chambers of Congress, namely the House of Representatives and the Senate, are the sole judge of who wins congressional elections and who is qualified to serve there. The same part of the Constitution gives the House and Senate sole authority to make their rules of operation.

Article I, Section 6, the so-called Speech and Debate Clause, says representatives and senators cannot be punished for speeches made in Congress, and cannot be arrested while in office, except for treason, felony, and breach of the peace. (Treason is defined as levying war against America or giving aid and comfort to its enemies. A felony is the most serious kind of crime, usually punishable by imprisonment for more than a year.)

Words to Know

bicameralism: The practice of dividing the legislative, or lawmaking, power of government into two chambers.

checks and balances: The specific powers in one branch of government that allow it to limit the powers of the other branches.

circuit court of appeals: A court in the federal judicial system that handles appeals from the trial courts, called federal district courts. The United States is divided into twelve geographic areas called circuits, and each circuit has one court of appeals that handles appeals from the federal district courts in its circuit. A party who loses in a circuit court of appeals may ask the Supreme Court to review the case.

Congress: The legislative, or lawmaking, branch of the federal government. Congress has two chambers, the Senate and the House of Representatives.

Constitution of the United States of America: The document written in 1787 that established the federal government under which the United States of America has operated since 1789. Article III covers the judicial branch.

federal district courts: The courts in the federal judicial system that handle trials in civil and criminal cases. Each state is divided into one or more federal judicial districts, and each district has one or more federal district courts. A party who loses in a federal district court may appeal to have the case reviewed by a circuit court of appeals.

judicial review: The process by which federal courts review laws to determine whether they violate the U.S. Constitution. If a court finds that a law violates the Constitution, it declares the law unconstitutional, which means the executive branch is not supposed to enforce it anymore. Congress can correct such a defect by passing a new law that does not violate the Constitution.

judiciary: The branch of the federal government that decides cases that arise under the nation's law. The federal judiciary includes the Supreme Court of the United States, circuit courts of appeals, and federal district courts.

separation of powers: Division of the powers of government into different branches to prevent one branch from having too much power.

Supreme Court: The highest court in the federal judiciary. The judiciary is the branch of government responsible for resolving legal disputes and interpreting laws on a case-by-case basis.

Article III, Section 1, of the Constitution says judges of the Supreme Court and lower courts "shall hold their offices during good behavior." This means they cannot be removed from office except by impeachment and conviction for treason, bribery, or other high crimes and misdemeanors under Article II, Section 4. Article III, Section 1, says judges must receive a salary for their services, which Congress sets. Congress cannot lower a judge's salary during the judge's service on the court.

Checks and balances

The men who wrote the Constitution in 1787 wanted each branch's power to be separate, but not absolute. They considered absolute power, even over just a portion of the government, to be dangerous.

To prevent the power of any one branch from being absolute, the Founding Fathers wrote the Constitution to contain a system of checks and balances. These are powers that each branch has for limiting the power of the other branches. Some scholars say the system of checks and balances actually creates a government of shared powers instead of one with separated powers.

The judiciary's main powers over Congress are judicial review and judicial interpretation. Judicial review is the power to review congressional laws to determine if they violate the Constitution. Judicial interpretation is the power to decide what congressional laws mean and how they apply in specific cases.

Congress's main checks on the judiciary include the power to amend the Constitution, pass new laws, approve the president's appointment of judges, control the number of justices on the Supreme Court, and impeach judges guilty of treason, bribery, or high crimes and misdemeanors.

Judicial review

The Constitution says "the judicial power of the United States, shall be vested in one supreme court, and in such inferior courts as the Congress may from time to time ordain and establish." The Constitution defines the kinds of cases to which the "judicial power" applies, including cases arising under the Constitution, laws, and treaties of the United States. Beyond hearing and deciding such cases, however, the Constitution does not define what the "judicial power" is.

Constitutionality of judicial review Scholars have debated whether the federal judicial power includes the power of judicial review. Judicial review means reviewing congressional laws (and executive action) to determine if they are valid under the Constitution.

The Constitution does not specifically give the federal judiciary the power of judicial review. Instead, the Supremacy

Clause of Article VI says, "This constitution, and the laws of the United States which shall be made in pursuance thereof; and all treaties made, or which shall be made, under the authority of the United States, shall be the supreme law of the land."

Some scholars believe that only the judicial branch can determine, on a case-by-case basis, whether congressional laws have been "made in pursuance" of, or in carrying out, the Constitution. Others believe that Congress and the president are responsible for deciding if their own actions are constitutional. Still others believe that the people of America, who elect Congress and, indirectly, the president, are ultimately responsible for deciding what is lawful under the Constitution and what is not.

Although the Constitution is unclear on judicial review, many of the men who wrote it in 1787 generally believed the judiciary would have this power. Foremost among them was Alexander Hamilton (1757–1804), who in 1789 became the first secretary of the treasury under President George Washington (1732–1799; served 1789–97). According to Joan Biskupic and Elder Witt in *The Supreme Court & the Powers of the American Government*, Hamilton wrote in No. 78 of *The Federalist Papers* in 1788:

> Limitations [on Congress] ... can be preserved in no other way than through the medium of courts of justice, whose duty it must be to declare all acts contrary to the manifest tenor of the Constitution void. Without this, all the reservations of particular rights or privileges would amount to nothing.... No legislative act, therefore, contrary to the Constitution, can be valid.... The interpretation of the laws is the proper and peculiar province of the courts. A constitution is, in fact, and must be regarded by the judges as, a fundamental law. It therefore belongs to them to ascertain [determine] its meaning as well as the meaning of any particular act proceeding from the legislative body. If there should happen to be an irreconcilable [conflicting] variance between the two, that which has the superior obligation and validity ought, of course, to be preferred; or, in other words, the Constitution ought to be preferred to the statute, the intention of the people to the intention of their agents [in Congress].

Marbury v. Madison In 1803, fifteen years after adoption of the Constitution, the Supreme Court officially answered the question of whether the federal judiciary has the power of judicial review. It did so in the famous case of *Marbury v. Madison*. The case was part of a political battle between Federalists, led by Chief Justice John Marshall (1755–1835), and Democratic-Republicans, led by President Thomas Jefferson (1743–1826; served 1801–9) and Secretary of State James Madison (1751–1836).

In the election of 1800, the Federalists lost control of both Congress and the presidency to the Democratic-Republicans. Before leaving office, Congress created sixteen new federal judgeships and authorized Federalist president John Adams (1735–1826; served 1797–1801) to name as many justices of the peace in the District of Columbia as he wished. Adams, in turn, named Federalists to fill the sixteen new federal judgeships plus forty-two justice of the peace positions. He also appointed Marshall, then serving as his secretary of state, to be the chief justice of the Supreme Court. (The chief justice is the head of the Supreme Court.)

One of Marshall's last duties before leaving office as secretary of state was to deliver the commissions, or official orders, to the people appointed to be justices of the peace in the District of Columbia. Somehow he failed to deliver four of them, including one to an attorney named William Marbury. When President Jefferson took office in March 1801, Marbury asked Jefferson's secretary of state, Madison, to give him the commission. Under orders from Jefferson, Madison refused to give the commission to Marbury.

Marbury decided to sue Madison in the Supreme Court. The Judiciary Act of 1789 gave the Supreme Court power to issue writs of mandamus. A writ of mandamus is an official court order for a government official to do his or her job. Marbury asked the Supreme Court to issue a writ of mandamus to Madison, ordering him to deliver the commission to Marbury.

Marshall, the very man who had failed to deliver the commission in the first place, helped to decide the case in 1803 as chief justice of the Supreme Court. Writing the Court's official opinion in the case, Marshall agreed that Marbury should get the commission. He also agreed that a writ of mandamus was the proper tool for forcing Madison to deliver the commission. Marshall surprised everyone, however, by concluding that the Supreme Court did not have the power to issue a writ of mandamus. His reason was that the Judiciary Act of 1789, which gave the Supreme Court power to issue the writ, violated the Constitution. The Constitution did not give the Supreme Court power to issue writs in such cases, so a congressional law trying to give the Supreme Court that power was in violation of the Constitution.

In the course of his written opinion, Marshall announced that the judiciary has the power of judicial review:

> It is a proposition too plain to be contested, that the constitution controls any legislative act repugnant [offensive] to it. . . . It is, emphatically, the province and duty of the judicial department to say what the law is. Those who apply the rule to particular cases, must of necessity expound [explain] and interpret that rule. If two laws conflict with each other, the courts must decide on the operations of each. . . . If then the courts are to regard the constitution, and the constitution is superior to any ordinary act of the legislature, the constitution, and not such ordinary act, must govern the case to which they both apply.

The case was a political victory for Marshall and the Federalists. Although he declared the Court incapable of giving Marbury the commission, Marshall assumed the greater power to review, in cases before the Court, laws passed by the Democratic-Republican controlled Congress.

Marshall's opinion on judicial review still stands, and federal courts routinely review congressional laws in the cases before them. Americans would probably have to enact a constitutional amendment to strip the federal judiciary of the power of judicial review.

As of 2005, the Supreme Court has struck down only around 125 federal laws and executive orders as unconstitutional. The mere existence of judicial review, however, can affect the laws that Congress passes.

Judicial interpretation

Deciding whether a law violates the Constitution is a part of the judiciary's job. Federal courts, however, do not engage in judicial view as often as they engage in judicial interpretation. This is the process of deciding what a law means and how it applies in a specific case.

Judicial interpretation becomes necessary for many reasons. Sometimes a situation arises that Congress did not envision when it wrote a law. Other times a law is written in a poor or confusing fashion. And in some instances, Congress purposefully writes a law in general terms, leaving it to the courts to apply the law to specific cases.

The judiciary has been called the least dangerous branch of the federal government in terms of how much power it has compared to the president and Congress. Judicial interpretation, however, can be very powerful. For example, in 1890 Congress passed the Sherman Antitrust Act. The act was meant to prevent business monopolies from dominating areas of commerce, or the economy. It declared that every contract, combination, or conspiracy that restrains trade is illegal. (A restraint of trade is something that interferes with the free operation of the economy.)

In 1920, the U.S. Supreme Court heard a case that required interpretation of the Sherman Antitrust Act. The Court decided that the act does not prohibit every restraint of trade, but only "unreasonable" restraints of trade. Deciding what is reasonable and what is unreasonable gives the federal courts great discretion in Sherman Act cases. Engaging in judicial interpretation, the Supreme Court has also used the Sherman Act to defeat activity by labor unions trying to protect the rights of workers, even though Congress passed the act to prevent unfair business activity.

Some scholars and citizens believe judicial interpretation gives the courts too much power, allowing them to make policies that Congress should make instead. For instance, in 1866, Congress proposed, and in 1868 America adopted, the Fourteenth Amendment of the Constitution. The amendment says all Americans are entitled to equal protection of the laws. One purpose of the amendment was to prevent unequal treatment of African Americans, who had been freed from slavery in 1865 under the Thirteenth Amendment.

In the 1896 case *Plessy v. Ferguson,* however, the Supreme Court decided that the Fourteenth Amendment did not prevent states from requiring whites and blacks to use separate railway cars. The Court ruled that "separate but equal" facilities satisfied the "equal protection" requirements of the Fourteenth Amendment. This rule stood until 1954, when the Supreme Court unanimously decided in *Brown v. Board of Education of*

Topeka that separate public services are not equal under the Fourteenth Amendment. The Fourteenth Amendment, however, did not change between 1896 and 1954; the Supreme Court's *interpretation* of it changed. Hence, it is sometimes hard to distinguish between the power of judicial interpretation and the power to make the laws.

Limitations on judicial review and interpretation

While judicial review and interpretation are powerful, they have limits. The strongest limit is the constitutional requirement that the Supreme Court decide only cases and controversies.

Citizenship for African Americans

The American Declaration of Independence makes the familiar statement that "all Men are created equal." The story of Dred Scott and equality for African Americans illustrates judicial interpretation and constitutional amendment, which are part of the checks and balances between Congress and the Supreme Court.

Dred Scott was a slave owned by Dr. John Emerson, an army surgeon who lived in St. Louis, Missouri. From 1834 to 1838, Scott went with Emerson during army assignments in Illinois, Wisconsin Territory, and back to Missouri. Illinois and Wisconsin were free areas where slavery was illegal.

In 1854, years after Emerson's death, Emerson's widow sold Scott to her brother, John F. A. Sanford. The sale was designed to allow Scott to sue Sanford to gain his freedom. Scott's attorney filed the suit in federal court in Missouri that year. He argued that Scott became a free citizen of the United States when he lived on free soil in Illinois and Wisconsin Territory from 1834 to 1838.

The case, *Scott v. Sandford,* made it to the U.S. Supreme Court. (Sanford's last name was misspelled during the case.) In a 7–2 decision in 1857, the Court decided that African Americans could not be citizens under the U.S. Constitution. In his opinion, Chief Justice Roger B. Taney (1777–1864) wrote that slaves "had for more than a century [before the Constitution was adopted] been regarded as being of an inferior order, and altogether unfit to associate with the white race, either in social or political relations; and so far inferior, that they had no rights which the white man was bound to respect; and that the negro [black people] might justly and lawfully be reduced to slavery for his benefit."

Four years later, America entered the Civil War (1861–65). At the end of that conflict, America adopted the Thirteenth Amendment to the U.S. Constitution, which made slavery illegal nationwide.

Southern states, however, passed laws to discriminate against newly freed slaves. These so-called Black Codes created harsher criminal penalties for African Americans and set up

Other limits have been created by the judiciary itself, which does not always abide by them.

Cases and controversies Article III, Section 2, of the Constitution contains a list of the "cases" and "controversies" to which the judicial power extends, or applies. It includes:

★ cases arising under the Constitution, laws, and treaties of the United States

★ cases affecting ambassadors and other public ministers

★ cases concerning the use of navigable, or crossable, waters

separate public facilities and schools for blacks and whites. The codes set up apprenticeship, or training, programs that gave African Americans little more freedom at work than they had as slaves. Some laws prevented African Americans from testifying in courts of law.

In 1866, to defeat the Black Codes, Congress proposed the Fourteenth Amendment to the Constitution. Section 1 says, "All persons born or naturalized in the United States, and subject to the jurisdiction [power] thereof, are citizens of the United States and of the State wherein they reside." When America adopted this amendment in 1868, it overturned the Supreme Court's 1857 decision that African Americans were not citizens.

African Americans continued to fight against legal public discrimination into the 1950s and 1960s. During those decades, the Supreme Court and Congress ended the American practice of providing separate facilities for black and white people. Still, the large numbers of African Americans in jails at the beginning of the twenty-first century led some people to conclude that official discrimination had not ended.

In Scott v. Sandford *in 1857, the U.S. Supreme Court ruled that former slave Dred Scott (above) was not a citizen of the United States because African Americans could not be citizens under the U.S. Constitution.*

Civil rights lawyers George Hayes, Thurgood Marshall, and James M. Nabrit congratulate each other following victory in the Brown v. Board of Education *case in 1954.*
Library of Congress.

★ controversies in which the United States is a party

★ controversies between two or more states, between citizens of different states, and between citizens of the same state claiming lands under grants from different states

★ controversies between a state (or its citizens) and a foreign state or nation (or its citizens or subjects)

The Supreme Court and lower federal courts have the power to resolve only those "cases" and "controversies" listed in the Constitution. This means that if someone files a federal lawsuit that does not come from this list of cases and controversies, the court cannot hear the case. It also means that if

Congress passes a law of which the Supreme Court disapproves, the Court cannot strike down the law on its own. Instead, it must wait until someone files an appropriate "case" or "controversy" to challenge the law. Likewise, the Court cannot express an official opinion on a question from another branch of the government. It can only speak through the opinions it issues in real cases or controversies.

Friendly suits and test cases Sometimes people who want to challenge a law or governmental action will create a lawsuit even though they do not have a real problem between them. The judiciary calls such lawsuits friendly suits or test cases.

Federal courts generally will not hear friendly suits or test cases. The reason is that such cases are not real "cases" or "controversies" under the Constitution. The Supreme Court and lower courts, however, occasionally break this rule, hearing friendly suits and test cases when the issues are important. This happened In the 1895 case of *Pollock v. Farmers' Loan and Trust Co.* In this lawsuit, a shareholder of a corporation sued the corporation to prevent it from paying an income tax passed by Congress. (A shareholder is a person who owns a portion of a corporation. An income tax is a tax on earnings.) The corporation and the shareholders both did not want to pay the tax, so there was no true dispute between them. The purpose of the lawsuit was to give the Supreme Court a chance to rule whether the income tax was lawful under the Constitution. The Supreme Court considered the case important enough to decide even though the lawsuit was really a friendly suit or test case. The Supreme Court declared the tax law unconstitutional, eliminating federal income taxes until the nation amended the Constitution to allow income taxes under the Sixteenth Amendment in 1913.

Ripeness and mootness Ripeness and mootness are doctrines the judiciary uses to limit the kinds of cases it will consider. Under the ripeness doctrine, a court will not hear a case until the law that applies to the case has been enforced. The reason is that the way in which an enforcement agency enforces or interprets a law might affect the way a court decides a case. Until then, the case is not ripe, or ready, for consideration.

Under the mootness doctrine, a court will not hear a case when the problem that resulted in the case has disappeared or has otherwise been resolved by the parties. Courts prefer to decide cases only when there is a problem to resolve. If the problem has been resolved, the case is considered moot, or dead.

Despite these doctrines, courts sometimes hear and decide cases that are moot or not ripe if the case is important enough to the judges or justices in charge.

Avoiding constitutional issues If a federal court can decide a case without interpreting the Constitution, it generally will do so. This is because courts usually prefer to save constitutional interpretation for cases that cannot be resolved any other way. The practice is supposed to protect the Constitution from being interpreted in an unnecessary fashion. This can be frustrating for parties and other citizens who want the courts to answer constitutional questions.

Political question doctrine Under the political question doctrine, a court will not review government action that is committed to the discretion, or sound judgment, of another branch. The political question doctrine comes from the separation of powers. The judicial branch usually believes that the separation of powers prevents it from reviewing discretionary action by the legislative and executive branches. An example of discretionary action in the executive branch is the decision to file or drop criminal charges against a suspected criminal. An example of discretionary action in the legislative branch is the decision to expel a senator or representative for misconduct.

Congressional power over the courts

Congress checks the power of the judiciary mainly through its power to propose constitutional amendments and pass new laws. Congress also has the power to confirm the president's appointments to the federal bench, change the number of justices on the Supreme Court, and impeach and convict judges who commit treason, bribery, or other high crimes and misdemeanors.

Proposed constitutional amendments Congress is the only branch that can officially propose a constitutional amendment. An amendment is a change to the Constitution. As of 2005, the

Constitution has been amended twenty-seven times since it was adopted in 1788.

To propose an amendment under Article V of the Constitution, either two-thirds of both chambers of Congress or two-thirds of the state legislatures must vote in favor of the proposal. A proposed amendment becomes part of the Constitution only if ratified, or approved, by either three-fourths of the state legislatures or three-fourths of the state constitutional conventions called to consider the amendment. Congress gets to determine whether ratification is by state legislatures or conventions.

The power to propose constitutional amendments can check the power of the judiciary when America ratifies an amendment that overturns a Supreme Court decision. As of 2005, America has ratified five constitutional amendments to overturn decisions of the U.S. Supreme Court. The Eleventh Amendment, adopted in 1798, overturned a Supreme Court decision that citizens of domestic and foreign states could sue state governments in federal court. The Fourteenth Amendment, adopted in 1868, overturned decisions that African Americans were not citizens and that Congress could not protect their civil rights. The Sixteenth Amendment, adopted in 1913, overturned a decision that Congress could not enact income tax laws. The Nineteenth Amendment, adopted in 1920, overturned a decision that women had no right to vote in elections. Finally, the Twenty-sixth Amendment, adopted in 1971, overturned a decision that Congress could not lower the voting age for state elections to eighteen. Previously, Congress had the power to require states to allow eighteen-year-olds to vote in national elections. A congressional law in the 1960s required states to register 18-year-olds for both federal and state elections. Oregon challenged the law, and the U.S. Supreme Court decided that Congress could not control the voting age for state elections. The Twenty-sixth Amendment reversed that.

Members of Congress frequently propose constitutional amendments, but such proposals rarely come to a vote in one chamber and even more rarely get passed by both chambers. This means the power to propose amendments is not a very useful tool for checking the power of the judiciary.

Legislative power If the Supreme Court makes an error when it interprets a law, or simply interprets a law in a manner with which Congress disagrees, Congress can pass a new law with language that corrects the Court's interpretation. The ability to do this comes from Congress's basic lawmaking power under Article I, Section 8, of the Constitution. The power to pass a new law to change a judicial interpretation is very useful. Congress uses this power much more than it uses the power to propose a constitutional amendment.

Confirmation power The president of the United States has the power to nominate, or appoint, people to serve as judges on the Supreme Court and lower federal courts. This power comes from Article II, Section 2, of the Constitution. The same provision gives the Senate the power to either confirm or reject the president's nominations. A simple majority of senators must vote for a president's nomination to confirm it.

Confirmation or rejection of a Supreme Court nominee can affect the result the Court reaches in future cases, because the Court decides cases by a simple majority vote of the nine justices who serve on it. As of March 2005, the Senate has rejected 28 of the 148 people presidents have nominated to serve on the Supreme Court since 1789.

The Senate also gets to confirm appointments to the lower federal courts. The process is guided by an informal practice called senatorial courtesy. Under this practice, the president checks with senators from the president's own political party before nominating a federal judge to serve on a federal court in the senators' state. Failure to employ senatorial courtesy reduces the chances of a president's nominee being accepted. In practice, the Supreme Court rejects nominations to the lower federal courts less frequently than it rejects nominations to the Supreme Court.

Number of Supreme Court justices The Constitution created a Supreme Court but did not specify the number of justices to serve on it. Instead, Congress sets the number by law under its power to make all laws necessary for the government to function.

In the Judiciary Act of 1789, Congress set the number of Supreme Court justices at six. Between then and 1869, Congress raised or lowered the number seven times, finally settling on nine

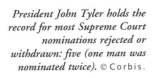
President John Tyler holds the record for most Supreme Court nominations rejected or withdrawn: five (one man was nominated twice). © Corbis.

justices in 1869. Lowering the number of justices is a way to prevent a president in office from getting to appoint new justices when old ones die or retire. Raising the number is a way to allow a president to fill the Court with justices who agree with the administration's philosophy of government.

Supreme Court justices decide cases by a simple majority vote. Congress has occasionally considered changing this practice to require either greater majorities or even unanimous votes for Court action. None of these proposals has come close to passing in Congress.

Judge G. Harrold Carswell was nominated in 1970 by President Richard Nixon as a U.S. Supreme Court justice, but was rejected by the U.S. Senate. © Bettmann/ Corbis.

Impeachment Judges on the Supreme Court and lower federal courts are appointed for life. Under Article II, Section 4, of the Constitution, the only way to remove a judge from office is by impeachment and conviction for treason, bribery, or other high crimes and misdemeanors.

The Constitution defines treason as levying war against America or giving aid and comfort to its enemies. Bribery is the act of giving money or something else of value to influence government conduct. The Constitution does not define the phrase "high crimes and misdemeanors." This essentially gives

Federal judge Alcee Hastings testifies during his impeachment hearing in 1989. He was convicted and removed from office. He later was elected to the U.S. House of Representatives in Florida.
AP/Wide World Photos.

Congress the power to impeach judges and other federal officers for political reasons, even if an officer has not committed a true crime.

The Constitution gives the House of Representatives the sole power to impeach a federal judge (or any other federal officer). Impeachment is a formal accusation that a judge has committed an impeachable offense. Once impeached, a judge faces trial in the Senate, which has the sole power to convict a judge (or any other federal officer) who has been charged by the House with an impeachable offense. Conviction by the Senate results in removal from office, and can result in being banned from serving in federal office in the future.

The House has impeached only one Supreme Court justice, Samuel Chase (1741–1811), in 1804. The Senate, however, voted not to convict Chase. As of 2005, the House has impeached only twelve lower court judges, and the Senate convicted just seven of them. The three most recent convictions were of Nevada federal district court judge Harry Claiborne (1917–2004) in 1986, Florida federal district court judge Alcee L. Hastings (1936–) in 1989, and Mississippi federal district court judge Walter L. Nixon Jr. in 1989.

Constitutional limitations on congressional power

The Constitution contains provisions that specifically limit Congress's power to check the judiciary. They include the preservation of writs of habeas corpus, prohibition of bills of attainder, and protection of the right to jury trials.

Writ of habeas corpus "Habeas corpus" is a Latin term meaning "to have the body." Habeas corpus procedures allow a prisoner to ask a court to investigate whether the prisoner is being held illegally. If so, the court can issue an order, a writ of habeas corpus, that the prisoner be released.

Article I, Section 9, of the Constitution says, "The privilege of the writ of habeas corpus shall not be suspended, unless when in cases of rebellion or invasion the public safety may require it." This means Congress cannot deprive the federal judiciary of its power to issue writs of habeas corpus, except during rebellions or invasions. As of 2005, the habeas corpus procedure has been suspended officially only four times: during the American Civil War (1861–65); in South Carolina during Reconstruction (1865–77) after the Civil War; in the Philippines in 1905 during American occupation of the nation subsequent to the Spanish-American War (1898); and in Hawaii during World War II (1939–45).

Bills of attainder Article I, Section 9, of the Constitution also prohibits Congress from passing bills of attainder. A bill of attainder is a law that inflicts punishment on someone without a trial. This provision checks Congress by protecting the right to jury trials in federal courts.

Jury trials and location Besides the prohibition of bills of attainder, other provisions in the Constitution protect the right

Impeachment of Supreme Court Justices

Judges on the U.S. Supreme Court and lower federal courts serve until they die or resign from office. The only way judges can be removed from office is by being impeached and convicted for "treason, bribery, or other high crimes and misdemeanors." Under the Constitution, the House of Representatives has the sole power to impeach, or formally accuse, a federal judge of such misconduct. The Senate, after holding a trial, has the sole power to convict and remove a judge who has been impeached.

As of 2005, Samuel Chase (1741–1811) is the only Supreme Court justice to have been impeached. He served on the Court from 1796 to 1811. Chase was a Federalist who was outspoken against both the Democratic-Republican Congress and the administration of Thomas Jefferson (1743–1826; served 1801–9). In March 1804, the House of Representatives voted 73–32 to impeach Chase for political misconduct during his duties as a judge. The vote went strictly along party lines.

The Senate held its impeachment trial in February 1805. On March 1, it voted not to convict Chase of any of the eight charges against him. The vote was closest on the charge that in May 1803, Chase had improperly lectured against the Jefferson administration to a grand jury in Baltimore, Maryland. A grand jury is a body of citizens who decide whether to charge a person with a crime. Judges are not supposed to let politics influence their conduct of grand jury or trial proceedings.

Since then, only two other Supreme Court justices have faced serious impeachment threats. In 1969, *Life* magazine reported that three years earlier, Justice Abe Fortas (1910–1982) received a $20,000 check from a nonprofit foundation formed by millionaire Louis E. Wolfson (1912–). Wolfson had since been convicted of violating securities laws. A code of conduct said judges should not use the power or prestige of their office to support businesses or charitable organizations. Under threat of impeachment for his involvement with Wolfson, Fortas resigned in May 1969. Fortas denied, however, that he had done anything wrong.

The other Supreme Court justice to face impeachment was William O. Douglas (1898–1980). Douglas, in fact, faced impeachment charges twice, once in 1953 and again in 1970. In both instances, Douglas refused to resign, and the House committees responsible for investigating Douglas failed to recommend impeachment, so the full House never voted. Douglas served on the Supreme Court until he retired for health reasons in November 1975.

Samuel Chase, the only U.S. Supreme Court justice to be impeached. In March 1805 (one year after the impeachment), the U.S. Senate voted not to convict Chase of his charges, and Chase remained on the bench. © Bettmann/Corbis.

to jury trials in federal courts. Article III, Section 2, says, "The trial of all crimes, except in cases of impeachment, shall be by jury; and such trial shall be held in the state where the said crimes shall have been committed." This provision is reinforced by the Sixth Amendment, which says, "In all criminal prosecutions, the accused shall enjoy the right to a speedy and public trial, by an impartial jury of the State and district wherein the crime shall have been committed." These provisions prevent Congress from eliminating jury trials in criminal cases.

The Seventh Amendment protects the right to jury trials in civil cases, which are cases between private citizens, businesses, or organizations. It says, "Where the value in controversy shall exceed twenty dollars, the right of trial by jury shall be preserved." As of 2005, however, Congress has passed a law that prevents parties with state law claims from suing in federal court unless the amount in controversy exceeds $75,000. Parties with federal law claims generally do not have to satisfy this requirement to sue in federal court.

For More Information

BOOKS

Beard, Charles A. *American Government and Politics.* 10th ed. New York: Macmillan Co., 1949.

Biskupic, Joan, and Elder Witt. *The Supreme Court & the Powers of the American Government.* Washington, DC: Congressional Quarterly Inc., 1997.

Dougherty, J. Hampden. *Power of Federal Judiciary over Legislation.* New York: Putnam's Sons, 1912. Reprint, Clark, NJ: Lawbook Exchange, 2004.

Janda, Kenneth, Jeffrey M. Berry, and Jerry Goldman. *The Challenge of Democracy.* 5th ed. Boston: Houghton Mifflin Company, 1997.

Loomis, Burdett A. *The Contemporary Congress.* 3rd ed. Boston: Bedford/St. Martin's, 2000.

McClenaghan, William A. *Magruder's American Government 2003.* Needham, MA: Prentice Hall School Group, 2002.

Parenti, Michael. *Democracy for the Few.* 6th ed. New York: St. Martin's Press, 1995.

Roelofs, H. Mark. *The Poverty of American Politics.* 2nd ed. Philadelphia: Temple University Press, 1998.

Shelley, Mack C., II. *American Government and Politics Today.* 2004–2005 ed. Belmont, CA: Wadsworth Publishing, 2003.

Volkomer, Walter E. *American Government.* 8th ed. Upper Saddle River, NJ: Prentice Hall, 1998.

Wolfensberger, Donald R. *Congress and the People.* Washington, DC, and Baltimore: Woodrow Wilson Center Press and Johns Hopkins University Press, 2000.

CD-ROM

21st Century Complete Guide to U.S. Courts. Progressive Management, 2003.

CASES

Brown v. Board of Education of Topeka, 347 U.S. 483 (1954).

Marbury v. Madison, 1 Cranch 137 (1803).

Plessy v. Ferguson, 163 U.S. 537 (1896).

Pollock v. Farmers' Loan and Trust Co. 158 U.S. 601 (1895).

Scott v. Sandford, 19 How. 393 (1857).

WEB SITES

Federal Judiciary. http://www.uscourts.gov (accessed on February 18, 2005).

Sabato, Larry J. "Judge Douglas Ginsburg's Marijuana Use—1987." *Washington Post.* http://www.washingtonpost.com/wp-srv/politics/special/clinton/frenzy/ginsburg.htm (accessed on March 18, 2005).

Supreme Court of the United States. http://www.supremecourtus.gov (accessed on February 18, 2005).

United States House of Representatives. http://www.house.gov (accessed on March 14, 2005).

United States Senate. http://www.senate.gov (accessed on March 14, 2005).

Appendix

THE CONSTITUTION OF THE UNITED STATES OF AMERICA

We the People of the United States, in Order to form a more perfect Union, establish Justice, insure domestic Tranquility, provide for the common defence, promote the general Welfare, and secure the Blessings of Liberty to ourselves and our Posterity, do ordain and establish this Constitution for the United States of America.

Article I.

SECTION 1. All legislative Powers herein granted shall be vested in a Congress of the United States, which shall consist of a Senate and House of Representatives.

SECTION 2. The House of Representatives shall be composed of Members chosen every second Year by the People of the several States, and the Electors in each State shall have the Qualifications requisite for Electors of the most numerous Branch of the State Legislature. No Person shall be a Representative who shall not have attained to the Age of twenty five Years, and been seven Years a Citizen of the United States, and who shall not, when elected, be an Inhabitant of that State in which he shall be chosen.

Representatives and direct Taxes shall be apportioned among the several States which may be included within this Union, according to their respective Numbers, which shall be determined by adding to the whole Number of free Persons, including those bound to Service for a Term of Years, and excluding Indians not taxed, three fifths of all other Persons. The actual Enumeration shall be made within three Years after the first Meeting of the Congress of the United States, and within every subsequent Term of ten Years, in such Manner as they shall by Law direct. The Number of Representatives shall not exceed one for every thirty Thousand, but each State shall have at Least one Representative; and until such enumeration shall be made, the State of New Hampshire shall be entitled to chuse three, Massachusetts eight, Rhode-Island and Providence Plantations one, Connecticut five, New-York six, New Jersey four, Pennsylvania eight, Delaware one, Maryland six, Virginia ten, North Carolina five, South Carolina five, and Georgia three.

When vacancies happen in the Representation from any State, the Executive Authority thereof shall issue Writs of Election to fill such Vacancies.

The House of Representatives shall chuse their Speaker and other Officers; and shall have the sole Power of Impeachment.

SECTION 3. The Senate of the United States shall be composed of two Senators from each State, chosen by the Legislature thereof, for six Years; and each Senator shall have one Vote.

Immediately after they shall be assembled in Consequence of the first Election, they shall be divided as equally as may be into three Classes. The Seats of the Senators of the first Class shall be vacated at the Expiration of the second Year, of the second Class at the Expiration of the fourth Year, and of the third Class at the Expiration of the sixth Year, so that one third may be chosen every second Year; and if Vacancies happen by Resignation, or otherwise, during the Recess of the Legislature of any State, the Executive thereof may make temporary Appointments until the next Meeting of the Legislature, which shall then fill such Vacancies.

No Person shall be a Senator who shall not have attained to the Age of thirty Years, and been nine Years a Citizen of the United States, and who shall not, when elected, be an Inhabitant of that State for which he shall be chosen.

The Vice President of the United States shall be President of the Senate, but shall have no Vote, unless they be equally divided.

The Senate shall chuse their other Officers, and also a President pro tempore, in the Absence of the Vice President, or when he shall exercise the Office of President of the United States. The Senate shall have the sole Power to try all Impeachments. When sitting for that Purpose, they shall be on Oath or Affirmation. When the President of the United States is tried, the Chief Justice shall preside: And no Person shall be convicted without the Concurrence of two thirds of the Members present.

Judgment in Cases of Impeachment shall not extend further than to removal from Office, and disqualification to hold and enjoy any Office of honor, Trust or Profit under the United States: but the Party convicted shall nevertheless be liable and subject to Indictment, Trial, Judgment and Punishment, according to Law.

SECTION 4. The Times, Places and Manner of holding Elections for Senators and Representatives, shall be prescribed in each State by the Legislature thereof; but the Congress may at any time by Law make or alter such Regulations, except as to the Places of chusing Senators. The Congress shall assemble at least once in every Year, and such Meeting shall be on the first Monday in December, unless they shall by Law appoint a different Day.

SECTION 5. Each House shall be the Judge of the Elections, Returns and Qualifications of its own Members, and a Majority of each shall constitute a Quorum to do Business; but a smaller Number may adjourn from day to day, and may be authorized to compel the Attendance of absent Members, in such Manner, and under such Penalties as each House may provide. Each House may determine the Rules of its Proceedings, punish its Members for disorderly Behaviour, and, with the Concurrence of two thirds, expel a Member. Each House shall keep a Journal of its Proceedings, and from time to time publish the same, excepting such Parts as may in their Judgment require Secrecy; and the Yeas and Nays of the Members of either House on any question shall, at the Desire of one fifth of those Present, be entered on the Journal.

Neither House, during the Session of Congress, shall, without the Consent of the other, adjourn for more than three days, nor to any other Place than that in which the two Houses shall be sitting.

SECTION 6. The Senators and Representatives shall receive a Compensation for their Services, to be ascertained by Law, and paid out of the Treasury of the United States. They shall in all Cases, except Treason, Felony and Breach of the Peace, be privileged from Arrest during their Attendance at the Session of their respective Houses, and in going to and returning from the same; and for any Speech or Debate in either House, they shall not be questioned in any other Place.

No Senator or Representative shall, during the Time for which he was elected, be appointed to any civil Office under the Authority of the United States, which shall have been created, or the Emoluments whereof shall have been encreased during such time; and no Person holding any Office under the United States, shall be a Member of either House during his Continuance in Office.

SECTION 7. All Bills for raising Revenue shall originate in the House of Representatives; but the Senate may propose or concur with Amendments as on other Bills.

Every Bill which shall have passed the House of Representatives and the Senate, shall, before it become a Law, be presented to the President of the United States: If he approve he shall sign it, but if not he shall return it, with his Objections to that House in which it shall have originated, who shall enter the Objections at large on their Journal, and proceed to reconsider it. If after such Reconsideration two thirds of that House shall agree to pass the Bill, it shall be sent, together with the Objections, to the other House, by which it shall likewise be reconsidered, and if approved by two thirds of that House, it shall become a Law. But in all such Cases the Votes of both Houses shall be determined by yeas and Nays, and the Names of the Persons voting for and against the Bill shall be entered on the Journal of each House respectively. If any Bill shall not be returned by the President within ten Days (Sundays excepted) after it shall have been presented to him, the Same shall be a Law, in like Manner as if he had signed it, unless the Congress by their Adjournment prevent its Return, in which Case it shall not be a Law.

Every Order, Resolution, or Vote to which the Concurrence of the Senate and House of Representatives may be necessary (except on a question of Adjournment) shall be presented to the President of the United States; and before the Same shall take Effect, shall be approved by him, or being disapproved by him, shall be repassed by two thirds of the Senate and House of Representatives, according to the Rules and Limitations prescribed in the Case of a Bill.

SECTION 8. The Congress shall have Power To lay and collect Taxes, Duties, Imposts and Excises, to pay the Debts and provide for the common Defence and general Welfare of the United

States; but all Duties, Imposts and Excises shall be uniform throughout the United States;

To borrow Money on the credit of the United States;

To regulate Commerce with foreign Nations, and among the several States, and with the Indian Tribes;

To establish an uniform Rule of Naturalization, and uniform Laws on the subject of Bankruptcies throughout the United States;

To coin Money, regulate the Value thereof, and of foreign Coin, and fix the Standard of Weights and Measures;

To provide for the Punishment of counterfeiting the Securities and current Coin of the United States;

To establish Post Offices and post Roads;

To promote the Progress of Science and useful Arts, by securing for limited Times to Authors and Inventors the exclusive Right to their respective Writings and Discoveries;

To constitute Tribunals inferior to the Supreme Court;

To define and punish Piracies and Felonies committed on the high Seas, and Offences against the Law of Nations;

To declare War, grant Letters of Marque and Reprisal, and make Rules concerning Captures on Land and Water;

To raise and support Armies, but no Appropriation of Money to that Use shall be for a longer Term than two Years;

To provide and maintain a Navy;

To make Rules for the Government and Regulation of the land and naval Forces;

To provide for calling forth the Militia to execute the Laws of the Union, suppress Insurrections and repel Invasions;

To provide for organizing, arming, and disciplining, the Militia, and for governing such Part of them as may be employed in the Service of the United States, reserving to the States respectively, the Appointment of the Officers, and the Authority of training the Militia according to the discipline prescribed by Congress;

To exercise exclusive Legislation in all Cases whatsoever, over such District (not exceeding ten Miles square) as may, by Cession of particular States, and the Acceptance of Congress, become the Seat of the Government of the United States, and to exercise like Authority over all Places purchased by the

Consent of the Legislature of the State in which the Same shall be, for the Erection of Forts, Magazines, Arsenals, dock-Yards, and other needful Buildings; –And

To make all Laws which shall be necessary and proper for carrying into Execution the foregoing Powers, and all other Powers vested by this Constitution in the Government of the United States, or in any Department or Officer thereof.

SECTION 9. The Migration or Importation of such Persons as any of the States now existing shall think proper to admit, shall not be prohibited by the Congress prior to the Year one thousand eight hundred and eight, but a Tax or duty may be imposed on such Importation, not exceeding ten dollars for each Person.

The Privilege of the Writ of Habeas Corpus shall not be suspended, unless when in Cases of Rebellion or Invasion the public Safety may require it.

No Bill of Attainder or ex post facto Law shall be passed.

No Capitation, or other direct, Tax shall be laid, unless in Proportion to the Census or Enumeration herein before directed to be taken.

No Tax or Duty shall be laid on Articles exported from any State.

No Preference shall be given by any Regulation of Commerce or Revenue to the Ports of one State over those of another; nor shall Vessels bound to, or from, one State, be obliged to enter, clear, or pay Duties in another.

No Money shall be drawn from the Treasury, but in Consequence of Appropriations made by Law; and a regular Statement and Account of the Receipts and Expenditures of all public Money shall be published from time to time.

No Title of Nobility shall be granted by the United States: And no Person holding any Office of Profit or Trust under them, shall, without the Consent of the Congress, accept of any present, Emolument, Office, or Title, of any kind whatever, from any King, Prince, or foreign State.

SECTION 10. No State shall enter into any Treaty, Alliance, or Confederation; grant Letters of Marque and Reprisal; coin Money; emit Bills of Credit; make any Thing but gold and silver Coin a Tender in Payment of Debts; pass any Bill of

Attainder, ex post facto Law, or Law impairing the Obligation of Contracts, or grant any Title of Nobility.

No State shall, without the Consent of the Congress, lay any Imposts or Duties on Imports or Exports, except what may be absolutely necessary for executing it's [sic] inspection Laws; and the net Produce of all Duties and Imposts, laid by any State on Imports or Exports, shall be for the Use of the Treasury of the United States; and all such Laws shall be subject to the Revision and Controul of the Congress.

No State shall, without the Consent of Congress, lay any Duty of Tonnage, keep Troops, or Ships of War in time of Peace, enter into any Agreement or Compact with another State, or with a foreign Power, or engage in War, unless actually invaded, or in such imminent Danger as will not admit of delay.

Article II.

SECTION 1. The executive Power shall be vested in a President of the United States of America. He shall hold his Office during the Term of four Years, and, together with the Vice President, chosen for the same Term, be elected, as follows:

Each State shall appoint, in such Manner as the Legislature thereof may direct, a Number of Electors, equal to the whole Number of Senators and Representatives to which the State may be entitled in the Congress: but no Senator or Representative, or Person holding an Office of Trust or Profit under the United States, shall be appointed an Elector.

The Electors shall meet in their respective States, and vote by Ballot for two Persons, of whom one at least shall not be an Inhabitant of the same State with themselves. And they shall make a List of all the Persons voted for, and of the Number of Votes for each; which List they shall sign and certify, and transmit sealed to the Seat of the Government of the United States, directed to the President of the Senate. The President of the Senate shall, in the Presence of the Senate and House of Representatives, open all the Certificates, and the Votes shall then be counted. The Person having the greatest Number of Votes shall be the President, if such Number be a Majority of the whole Number of Electors appointed; and if there be more than one who have such Majority, and have an equal Number of Votes, then the House of Representatives shall immediately chuse by

Ballot one of them for President; and if no Person have a Majority, then from the five highest on the List the said House shall in like Manner chuse the President. But in chusing the President, the Votes shall be taken by States, the Representation from each State having one Vote; a quorum for this Purpose shall consist of a Member or Members from two thirds of the States, and a Majority of all the States shall be necessary to a Choice. In every Case, after the Choice of the President, the Person having the greatest Number of Votes of the Electors shall be the Vice President. But if there should remain two or more who have equal Votes, the Senate shall chuse from them by Ballot the Vice President.

The Congress may determine the Time of chusing the Electors, and the Day on which they shall give their Votes; which Day shall be the same throughout the United States.

No Person except a natural born Citizen, or a Citizen of the United States, at the time of the Adoption of this Constitution, shall be eligible to the Office of President; neither shall any Person be eligible to that Office who shall not have attained to the Age of thirty five Years, and been fourteen Years a Resident within the United States.

In Case of the Removal of the President from Office, or of his Death, Resignation, or Inability to discharge the Powers and Duties of the said Office, the Same shall devolve on the Vice President, and the Congress may by Law provide for the Case of Removal, Death, Resignation or Inability, both of the President and Vice President, declaring what Officer shall then act as President, and such Officer shall act accordingly, until the Disability be removed, or a President shall be elected.

The President shall, at stated Times, receive for his Services, a Compensation, which shall neither be increased nor diminished during the Period for which he shall have been elected, and he shall not receive within that Period any other Emolument from the United States, or any of them.

Before he enter on the Execution of his Office, he shall take the following Oath or Affirmation: "I do solemnly swear (or affirm) that I will faithfully execute the Office of President of the United States, and will to the best of my Ability, preserve, protect and defend the Constitution of the United States."

SECTION 2. The President shall be Commander in Chief of the Army and Navy of the United States, and of the Militia of the several States, when called into the actual Service of the United States; he may require the Opinion, in writing, of the principal Officer in each of the executive Departments, upon any Subject relating to the Duties of their respective Offices, and he shall have Power to grant Reprieves and Pardons for Offences against the United States, except in Cases of Impeachment.

He shall have Power, by and with the Advice and Consent of the Senate, to make Treaties, provided two thirds of the Senators present concur; and he shall nominate, and by and with the Advice and Consent of the Senate, shall appoint Ambassadors, other public Ministers and Consuls, Judges of the Supreme Court, and all other Officers of the United States, whose Appointments are not herein otherwise provided for, and which shall be established by Law: but the Congress may by Law vest the Appointment of such inferior Officers, as they think proper, in the President alone, in the Courts of Law, or in the Heads of Departments.

The President shall have Power to fill up all Vacancies that may happen during the Recess of the Senate, by granting Commissions which shall expire at the End of their next Session.

SECTION 3. He shall from time to time give to the Congress Information of the State of the Union, and recommend to their Consideration such Measures as he shall judge necessary and expedient; he may, on extraordinary Occasions, convene both Houses, or either of them, and in Case of Disagreement between them, with Respect to the Time of Adjournment, he may adjourn them to such Time as he shall think proper; he shall receive Ambassadors and other public Ministers; he shall take Care that the Laws be faithfully executed, and shall Commission all the Officers of the United States.

SECTION 4. The President, Vice President and all civil Officers of the United States, shall be removed from Office on Impeachment for, and Conviction of, Treason, Bribery, or other high Crimes and Misdemeanors.

Article III.

SECTION 1. The judicial Power of the United States shall be vested in one Supreme Court, and in such inferior Courts as the Congress may from time to time ordain and establish. The Judges, both of the supreme and inferior Courts, shall hold their Offices during good Behaviour, and shall, at stated Times, receive for their Services a Compensation, which shall not be diminished during their Continuance in Office.

SECTION 2. The judicial Power shall extend to all Cases, in Law and Equity, arising under this Constitution, the Laws of the United States, and Treaties made, or which shall be made, under their Authority; –to all Cases affecting Ambassadors, other public Ministers and Consuls; –to all Cases of admiralty and maritime Jurisdiction; –to Controversies to which the United States shall be a Party; –to Controversies between two or more States; – between a State and Citizens of another State; –between Citizens of different States; –between Citizens of the same State claiming Lands under Grants of different States, and between a State, or the Citizens thereof, and foreign States, Citizens or Subjects.

In all Cases affecting Ambassadors, other public Ministers and Consuls, and those in which a State shall be Party, the Supreme Court shall have original Jurisdiction. In all the other Cases before mentioned, the Supreme Court shall have appellate Jurisdiction, both as to Law and Fact, with such Exceptions, and under such Regulations as the Congress shall make.

The Trial of all Crimes, except in Cases of Impeachment, shall be by Jury; and such Trial shall be held in the State where the said Crimes shall have been committed; but when not committed within any State, the Trial shall be at such Place or Places as the Congress may by Law have directed.

SECTION 3. Treason against the United States shall consist only in levying War against them, or in adhering to their Enemies, giving them Aid and Comfort. No Person shall be convicted of Treason unless on the Testimony of two Witnesses to the same overt Act, or on Confession in open Court.

The Congress shall have Power to declare the Punishment of Treason, but no Attainder of Treason shall work Corruption of Blood, or Forfeiture except during the Life of the Person attainted.

Article IV.

SECTION 1. Full Faith and Credit shall be given in each State to the public Acts, Records, and judicial Proceedings of every other State. And the Congress may by general Laws prescribe the

Manner in which such Acts, Records and Proceedings shall be proved, and the Effect thereof.

SECTION 2. The Citizens of each State shall be entitled to all Privileges and Immunities of Citizens in the several States.

A Person charged in any State with Treason, Felony, or other Crime, who shall flee from Justice, and be found in another State, shall on Demand of the executive Authority of the State from which he fled, be delivered up, to be removed to the State having Jurisdiction of the Crime.

No Person held to Service or Labour in one State, under the Laws thereof, escaping into another, shall, in Consequence of any Law or Regulation therein, be discharged from such Service or Labour, but shall be delivered up on Claim of the Party to whom such Service or Labour may be due.

SECTION 3. New States may be admitted by the Congress into this Union; but no new State shall be formed or erected within the Jurisdiction of any other State; nor any State be formed by the Junction of two or more States, or Parts of States, without the Consent of the Legislatures of the States concerned as well as of the Congress.

The Congress shall have Power to dispose of and make all needful Rules and Regulations respecting the Territory or other Property belonging to the United States; and nothing in this Constitution shall be so construed as to Prejudice any Claims of the United States, or of any particular State.

SECTION 4. The United States shall guarantee to every State in this Union a Republican Form of Government, and shall protect each of them against Invasion; and on Application of the Legislature, or of the Executive (when the Legislature cannot be convened), against domestic Violence.

Article V.

The Congress, whenever two thirds of both Houses shall deem it necessary, shall propose Amendments to this Constitution, or, on the Application of the Legislatures of two thirds of the several States, shall call a Convention for proposing Amendments, which, in either Case, shall be valid to all Intents and Purposes, as Part of this Constitution, when ratified by the Legislatures of three fourths of the several States, or by

Conventions in three fourths thereof, as the one or the other Mode of Ratification may be proposed by the Congress; Provided that no Amendment which may be made prior to the Year One thousand eight hundred and eight shall in any Manner affect the first and fourth Clauses in the Ninth Section of the first Article; and that no State, without its Consent, shall be deprived of its equal Suffrage in the Senate.

Article VI.

All Debts contracted and Engagements entered into, before the Adoption of this Constitution, shall be as valid against the United States under this Constitution, as under the Confederation.

This Constitution, and the Laws of the United States which shall be made in Pursuance thereof; and all Treaties made, or which shall be made, under the Authority of the United States, shall be the supreme Law of the Land; and the Judges in every State shall be bound thereby, any Thing in the Constitution or Laws of any State to the Contrary notwithstanding.

The Senators and Representatives before mentioned, and the Members of the several State Legislatures, and all executive and judicial Officers, both of the United States and of the several States, shall be bound by Oath or Affirmation, to support this Constitution; but no religious Test shall ever be required as a Qualification to any Office or public Trust under the United States.

Article VII.

The Ratification of the Conventions of nine States, shall be sufficient for the Establishment of this Constitution between the States so ratifying the Same.

The Word, "the," being interlined between the seventh and eighth Lines of the first Page, The Word "Thirty" being partly written on an Erazure in the fifteenth Line of the first Page, The Words "is tried" being interlined between the thirty second and thirty third Lines of the first Page and the Word "the" being interlined between the forty third and forty fourth Lines of the second Page.

Attest William Jackson Secretary

done in Convention by the Unanimous Consent of the States present the Seventeenth Day of September in the Year of our Lord one thousand seven hundred and Eighty seven and of the Independence of the United States of America the Twelfth In witness whereof We have hereunto subscribed our Names,

Go. WASHINGTON, Presidt. and deputy from Virginia

NEW HAMPSHIRE: John Langdon, Nicholas Gilman

MASSACHUSETTS: Nathaniel Gorham, Rufus King

CONNECTICUT: Wm. Saml. Johnson, Roger Sherman

NEW YORK: Alexander Hamilton

NEW JERSEY: Wil. Livingston, David Brearley, Wm. Paterson, Jona. Dayton

PENSYLVANIA [sic]: B. Franklin, Thomas Mifflin, Robt. Morris, Geo. Clymer, Thos. FitzSimons, Jared Ingersoll, James Wilson, Gouv. Morris

DELAWARE: Geo. Read, Gunning Bedford jun., John Dickinson, Richard Bassett, Jaco. Broom

MARYLAND: James McHenry, Dan of St. Thos. Jenifer, Danl. Carroll

VIRGINIA: John Blair, James Madison Jr.

NORTH CAROLINA: Wm. Blount, Richd. Dobbs Spaight, Hu. Williamson

SOUTH CAROLINA: J. Rutledge, Charles Cotesworth Pinckney, Charles Pinckney, Pierce Butler

GEORGIA: William Few, Abr. Baldwin

Attest: William Jackson, Secretary.

In Convention Monday, September 17th, 1787. Present The States of New Hampshire, Massachusetts, Connecticut, MR. Hamilton from New York, New Jersey, Pennsylvania, Delaware, Maryland, Virginia, North Carolina, South Carolina and Georgia.

Resolved,

That the preceeding Constitution be laid before the United States in Congress assembled, and that it is the Opinion of this Convention, that it should afterwards be submitted to a Convention of Delegates, chosen in each State by the People thereof, under the Recommendation of its Legislature, for their Assent and Ratification; and that each Convention assenting to, and ratifying the Same, should give Notice thereof to the United States in Congress assembled.

Resolved, That it is the Opinion of this Convention, that as soon as the Conventions of nine States shall have ratified this Constitution, the United States in Congress assembled should fix a Day on which Electors should be appointed by the States which have ratified the same, and a Day on which the Electors should assemble to vote for the President, and the Time and Place for commencing Proceedings under this Constitution. That after such Publication the Electors should be appointed, and the Senators and Representatives elected: That the Electors should meet on the Day fixed for the Election of the President, and should transmit their Votes certified, signed, sealed and directed, as the Constitution requires, to the Secretary of the United States in Congress assembled, that the Senators and Representatives should convene at the Time and Place assigned; that the Senators should appoint a President of the Senate, for the sole purpose of receiving, opening and counting the Votes for President; and, that after he shall be chosen, the Congress, together with the President, should, without Delay, proceed to execute this Constitution.

By the Unanimous Order of the Convention

Go. WASHINGTON–Presidt. W. JACKSON Secretary.

AMENDMENTS

Articles in Addition to, and Amendment of, the Constitution of the United States of America, Proposed by Congress, and Ratified by the Legislatures of the Several States, Pursuant to the Fifth Article of the Original Constitution.

Article I.

Congress shall make no law respecting an establishment of religion, or prohibiting the free exercise thereof; or abridging the freedom of speech, or of the press, or the right of the people peaceably to assemble, and to petition the Government for a redress of grievances.

Article II.

A well regulated Militia, being necessary to the security of a free State, the right of the people to keep and bear Arms, shall not be infringed.

Article III.

No Soldier shall, in time of peace be quartered in any house, without the consent of the Owner, nor in time of war, but in a manner to be prescribed by law.

Article IV.

The right of the people to be secure in their persons, houses, papers, and effects, against unreasonable searches and seizures, shall not be violated, and no Warrants shall issue, but upon probable cause, supported by Oath or affirmation, and particularly describing the place to be searched, and the persons or things to be seized.

Article V.

No person shall be held to answer for a capital, or otherwise infamous crime, unless on a presentment or indictment of a Grand Jury, except in cases arising in the land or naval forces, or in the Militia, when in actual service in time of War or public danger; nor shall any person be subject for the same offence to be twice put in jeopardy of life or limb, nor shall be compelled in any criminal case to be a witness against himself, nor be deprived of life, liberty, or property, without due process of law; nor shall private property be taken for public use without just compensation.

Article VI.

In all criminal prosecutions, the accused shall enjoy the right to a speedy and public trial, by an impartial jury of the State and district wherein the crime shall have been committed; which district shall have been previously ascertained by law, and to be informed of the nature and cause of the accusation; to be confronted with the witnesses against him; to have compulsory process for obtaining witnesses in his favor, and to have the assistance of counsel for his defence.

Article VII.

In Suits at common law, where the value in controversy shall exceed twenty dollars, the right of trial by jury shall be preserved, and no fact tried by a jury shall be otherwise re-examined in any Court of the United States, than according to the rules of the common law.

Article VIII.

Excessive bail shall not be required, nor excessive fines imposed, nor cruel and unusual punishments inflicted.

Article IX.

The enumeration in the Constitution of certain rights shall not be construed to deny or disparage others retained by the people.

Article X.

The powers not delegated to the United States by the Constitution, nor prohibited by it to the States, are reserved to the States respectively, or to the people.

Article XI.

The Judicial power of the United States shall not be construed to extend to any suit in law or equity, commenced or prosecuted against one of the United States by Citizens of another State, or by Citizens or Subjects of any Foreign State.

Article XII.

The Electors shall meet in their respective states, and vote by ballot for President and Vice President, one of whom, at least, shall not be an inhabitant of the same state with themselves; they shall name in their ballots the person voted for as President, and in distinct ballots the person voted for as Vice-President, and they shall make distinct lists of all persons voted for as President, and of all persons voted for as Vice-President, and of the number of votes for each, which lists they shall sign and certify, and transmit sealed to the seat of the government of the United States, directed to the President of the Senate;

The President of the Senate shall, in the presence of the Senate and House of Representatives, open all the certificates and the votes shall then be counted;

The person having the greatest number of votes for President, shall be the President, if such number be a majority of the whole number of Electors appointed; and if no person have such majority, then from the persons having the highest numbers not exceeding three on the list of those voted for as President, the House of Representatives shall choose immediately, by ballot, the President. But in choosing the President, the votes shall be taken by states, the representation from each state having one vote; a quorum for this purpose shall consist of a member or members from two-thirds of the states, and a majority of all the states shall be necessary to a choice.

And if the House of Representatives shall not choose a President whenever the right of choice shall devolve upon them, before the fourth day of March next following, then the Vice-President shall act as President, as in the case of the death or other constitutional disability of the President. The person having the greatest number of votes as Vice-President, shall be the Vice-President, if such number be a majority of the whole number of Electors appointed, and if no person have a majority, then from the two highest numbers on the list, the Senate shall choose the Vice-President; a quorum for the purpose shall consist of two-thirds of the whole number of Senators, and a majority of the whole number shall be necessary to a choice. But no person constitutionally ineligible to the office of President shall be eligible to that of Vice-President of the United States.

Article XIII.

SECTION 1. Neither slavery nor involuntary servitude, except as a punishment for crime whereof the party shall have been duly convicted, shall exist within the United States, or any place subject to their jurisdiction.

SECTION 2. Congress shall have power to enforce this article by appropriate legislation.

Article XIV.

SECTION 1. All persons born or naturalized in the United States and subject to the jurisdiction thereof, are citizens of the United

States and of the State wherein they reside. No State shall make or enforce any law which shall abridge the privileges or immunities of citizens of the United States; nor shall any State deprive any person of life, liberty, or property, without due process of law; nor deny to any person within its jurisdiction the equal protection of the laws.

SECTION 2. Representatives shall be apportioned among the several States according to their respective numbers, counting the whole number of persons in each State, excluding Indians not taxed. But when the right to vote at any election for the choice of electors for President and Vice President of the United States, Representatives in Congress, the Executive and Judicial officers of a State, or the members of the Legislature thereof, is denied to any of the male inhabitants of such State, being twenty-one years of age, and citizens of the United States, or in any way abridged, except for participation in rebellion, or other crime, the basis of representation therein shall be reduced in the proportion which the number of such male citizens shall bear to the whole number of male citizens twenty-one years of age in such State.

SECTION 3. No person shall be a Senator or Representative in Congress, or elector of President and Vice President, or hold any office, civil or military, under the United States, or under any State, who, having previously taken an oath, as a member of Congress, or as an officer of the United States, or as a member of any State legislature, or as an executive or judicial officer of any State, to support the Constitution of the United States, shall have engaged in insurrection or rebellion against the same, or given aid or comfort to the enemies thereof. But Congress may by a vote of two-thirds of each House, remove such disability.

SECTION 4. The validity of the public debt of the United States, authorized by law, including debts incurred for payment of pensions and bounties for services in suppressing insurrection or rebellion, shall not be questioned. But neither the United States nor any State shall assume or pay any debt or obligation incurred in aid of insurrection or rebellion against the United States, or any claim for the loss or emancipation of any slave; but all such debts, obligations and claims shall be held illegal and void.

SECTION 5. The Congress shall have power to enforce, by appropriate legislation, the provisions of this article.

Article XV.

SECTION 1. The right of citizens of the United States to vote shall not be denied or abridged by the United States or by any State on account of race, color, or previous condition of servitude.

SECTION 2. The Congress shall have power to enforce this article by appropriate legislation.

Article XVI.

The Congress shall have power to lay and collect taxes on incomes, from whatever source derived, without apportionment among the several States, and without regard to any census or enumeration.

Article XVII.

The Senate of the United States shall be composed of two Senators from each State, elected by the people thereof, for six years; and each Senator shall have one vote. The electors in each State shall have the qualifications requisite for electors of the most numerous branch of the State legislatures.

When vacancies happen in the representation of any State in the Senate, the executive authority of such State shall issue writs of election to fill such vacancies: Provided, That the legislature of any State may empower the executive thereof to make temporary appointments until the people fill the vacancies by election as the legislature may direct.

This amendment shall not be so construed as to affect the election or term of any Senator chosen before it becomes valid as part of the Constitution.

Article XVIII.

SECTION 1. After one year from the ratification of this article the manufacture, sale, or transportation of intoxicating liquors within, the importation thereof into, or the exportation thereof from the United States and all territory subject to the jurisdiction thereof for beverage purposes is hereby prohibited.

SECTION 2. The Congress and the several States shall have concurrent power to enforce this article by appropriate legislation.

SECTION 3. This article shall be inoperative unless it shall have been ratified as an amendment to the Constitution by the legislatures of the several States, as provided in the Constitution, within seven years from the date of the submission hereof to the States by the Congress.

Article XIX.

The right of citizens of the United States to vote shall not be denied or abridged by the United States or by any State on account of sex.

Congress shall have power to enforce this article by appropriate legislation.

Article XX.

SECTION 1. The terms of the President and Vice President shall end at noon the 20th day of January, and the terms of Senators and Representatives at noon on the 3d day of January, of the years in which such terms would have ended if this article had not been ratified; and the terms of their successors shall then begin.

SECTION 2. The Congress shall assemble at least once in every year, and such meeting shall begin at noon on the 3d day of January, unless they shall by law appoint a different day.

SECTION 3. If, at the time fixed for the beginning of the term of the President, the President elect shall have died, the Vice President elect shall become President. If a President shall not have been chosen before the time fixed for the beginning of his term, or if the President elect shall have failed to qualify, then the Vice President elect shall act as President until a President shall have qualified; and the Congress may by law provide for the case wherein neither a President elect nor a Vice President elect shall have qualified, declaring who shall then act as President, or the manner in which one who is to act shall be selected, and such person shall act accordingly until a President or Vice President shall have qualified.

SECTION 4. The Congress may by law provide for the case of the death of any of the persons from whom the House of Representatives may choose a President whenever the right of choice shall have devolved upon them, and for the case of the death of any of the persons from whom the Senate may choose a Vice President whenever the right of choice shall have devolved upon them.

SECTION 5. Sections 1 and 2 shall take effect on the 15th day of October following the ratification of this article.

SECTION 6. This article shall be inoperative unless it shall have been ratified as an amendment to the Constitution by the legislatures of three-fourths of the several States within seven years from the date of its submission.

Article XXI.

SECTION 1. The eighteenth article of amendment to the Constitution of the United States is hereby repealed.

SECTION 2. The transportation or importation into any State, Territory, or possession of the United States for delivery or use therein of intoxicating liquors, in violation of the laws thereof, is hereby prohibited.

SECTION 3. This article shall be inoperative unless it shall have been ratified as an amendment to the Constitution by conventions in the several States, as provided in the Constitution, within seven years from the date of the submission hereof to the States by the Congress.

Article XXII.

SECTION 1. No person shall be elected to the office of the President more than twice, and no person who has held the office of President, or acted as President, for more than two years of a term to which some other person was elected President shall be elected to the office of President more than once. But this Article shall not apply to any person holding the office of President when this Article was proposed by the Congress, and shall not prevent any person who may be holding the office of President, or acting as President, during the term within which this Article becomes operative from holding the office of President or acting as President during the remainder of such term.

SECTION 2. This article shall be inoperative unless it shall have been ratified as an amendment to the Constitution by the legislatures of three-fourths of the several States within seven years from the date of its submission to the States by the Congress.

Article XXIII.

SECTION 1. The District constituting the seat of Government of the United States shall appoint in such manner as the Congress may direct:

A number of electors of President and Vice President equal to the whole number of Senators and Representatives in Congress to which the District would be entitled if it were a State, but in no event more than the least populous State; they shall be in addition to those appointed by the States, but they shall be considered, for the purposes of the election of President and Vice President, to be electors appointed by a State; and they shall meet in the District and perform such duties as provided by the twelfth article of amendment.

SECTION 2. The Congress shall have power to enforce this article by appropriate legislation.

Article XXIV.

SECTION 1. The right of citizens of the United States to vote in any primary or other election for President or Vice President, for electors for President or Vice President, or for Senator or Representative in Congress, shall not be denied or abridged by the United States or any State by reason of failure to pay any poll tax or other tax.

SECTION 2. The Congress shall have power to enforce this article by appropriate legislation.

Article XXV.

SECTION 1. In case of the removal of the President from office or of his death or resignation, the Vice President shall become President.

SECTION 2. Whenever there is a vacancy in the office of the Vice President, the President shall nominate a Vice President who shall take office upon confirmation by a majority vote of both Houses of Congress.

SECTION 3. Whenever the President transmits to the President pro tempore of the Senate and the Speaker of the House of Representatives his written declaration that he is unable to discharge the powers and duties of his office, and until he transmits to them a written declaration to the contrary, such powers and duties shall be discharged by the Vice President as Acting President.

SECTION 4. Whenever the Vice President and a majority of either the principal officers of the executive departments or of such other body as Congress may by law provide, transmit to the President pro tempore of the Senate and the Speaker of the House of Representatives their written declaration that the President is unable to discharge the powers and duties of his office, the Vice President shall immediately assume the powers and duties of the office as Acting President.

Thereafter, when the President transmits to the President pro tempore of the Senate and the Speaker of the House of Representatives his written declaration that no inability exists, he shall resume the powers and duties of his office unless the Vice President and a majority of either the principal officers of the executive department or of such other body as Congress may by law provide, transmit within four days to the President pro tempore of the Senate and the Speaker of the House of Representatives their written declaration that the President is unable to discharge the powers and duties of his office. Thereupon Congress shall decide the issue, assembling within forty-eight hours for that purpose if not in session. If the Congress, within twenty-one days after receipt of the latter written declaration, or, if Congress is not in session, within twenty-one days after Congress is required to assemble, determines by two-thirds vote of both Houses that the President is unable to discharge the powers and duties of his office, the Vice President shall continue to discharge the same as Acting President; otherwise, the President shall resume the powers and duties of his office.

Article XXVI.

SECTION 1. The right of citizens of the United States, who are eighteen years of age or older, to vote shall not be denied or abridged by the United States or by any State on account of age.

SECTION 2. The Congress shall have power to enforce this article by appropriate legislation.

Article XXVII.

No law, varying the compensation for the services of the Senators and Representatives, shall take effect, until an election of Representatives shall have intervened.

Where to Learn More

Books

Abraham, Henry J. *Justices, Presidents, and Senators.* Lanham, MD: Rowman & Littlefield Publishers, 1999.

Baum, Lawrence. *The Supreme Court.* Washington, DC: Congressional Quarterly Inc., 1998.

Beard, Charles A. *American Government and Politics.* 10th ed. New York: Macmillan Co., 1949.

Beard, Charles A. *An Economic Interpretation of the Constitution of the United States.* New York: Macmillan, 1935.

Biskupic, Joan, and Elder Witt. *The Supreme Court & the Powers of the American Government.* Washington, DC: Congressional Quarterly Inc., 1997.

Biskupic, Joan, and Elder Witt. *The Supreme Court at Work.* Washington, DC: Congressional Quarterly Inc., 1997.

Brannen, Daniel E., and Richard Clay Hanes. *Supreme Court Drama: Cases That Changed America.* Detroit: UXL, 2001.

Burnham, James. *Congress and the American Tradition.* New Brunswick, NJ: Transaction Publishers, 2003.

Carp, Robert A., and Ronald Stidham. *The Federal Courts.* 2nd ed. Washington, DC: Congressional Quarterly Inc., 1991.

Charleton, James H., Robert G. Ferris, and Mary C. Ryan, eds. *Framers of the Constitution.* Washington, DC: National Archives and Records Administration, 1976.

Choper, Jesse H., ed. *The Supreme Court and Its Justices.* 2nd ed. Chicago: American Bar Association, 2001.

Clark, J. C. D. *The Language of Liberty, 1660–1832.* Cambridge, Eng.: Cambridge University Press, 1994.

Congressional Quarterly Inc. *Guide to the Congress of the United States.* 1st ed. Washington, DC: Congressional Quarterly Service, 1971.

Congressional Quarterly Inc. *Powers of the Presidency.* 2nd ed. Washington, DC: Congressional Quarterly Inc., 1997.

Cronin, Thomas E. *Inventing the American Presidency.* Lawrence: University Press of Kansas, 1989.

DiClerico, Robert E. *The American President.* 5th ed. Upper Saddle River, NJ: Prentice Hall, 2000.

Dougherty, J. Hampden. *Power of Federal Judiciary over Legislation.* New York: Putnam's Sons, 1912. Reprint, Clark, NJ: Lawbook Exchange, 2004.

Fisher, Louis. *Constitutional Conflicts between Congress and the President.* 3rd ed. Lawrence: University Press of Kansas, 1991.

Fisher, Louis. *The Politics of Shared Power: Congress and the Executive.* 4th ed. College Station: Texas A&M University Press, 1998.

Goebel, Julius, Jr. *Antecedents and Beginnings to 1801.* Vol. I. New York: Macmillan, 1971.

Green, Mark. *Who Runs Congress?* 3rd ed. New York: The Viking Press, 1979.

Hart, John. *The Presidential Branch.* 2nd ed. Chatham, NJ: Chatham House Publishers, 1995.

Irons, Peter. *A People's History of the Supreme Court.* New York: Penguin Books, 1999.

Janda, Kenneth, Jeffrey M. Berry, and Jerry Goldman. *The Challenge of Democracy.* 5th ed. Boston: Houghton Mifflin Company, 1997.

Kelly, Alfred H., and Winfred A. Harbison. *The American Constitution: Its Origins and Development.* 5th ed. New York: W. W. Norton & Co., 1976.

Kurland, Philip B., and Ralph Lerner. *The Founders' Constitution.* 5 vols. Indianapolis: Liberty Fund, 1987.

Lazarus, Edward P. *Closed Chambers.* New York: Times Books, 1998.

Levy, Leonard W. *Original Intent and the Framers' Constitution.* New York: Macmillan, 1988.

Lintcott, Andrew. *The Constitution of the Roman Republic.* Oxford: Clarendon Press, 1999.

Loomis, Burdett A. *The Contemporary Congress.* 3rd ed. Boston: Bedford/St. Martin's, 2000.

MacNeil, Neil. *Forge of Democracy: The House of Representatives.* New York: David MacKay Co., 1963.

McClenaghan, William A. *Magruder's American Government 2003.* Needham, MA: Prentice Hall School Group, 2002.

McDonald, Forrest. *The American Presidency.* Lawrence: University Press of Kansas, 1994.

Milkis, Sidney M., and Michael Nelson. *The American Presidency: Origins & Development.* 3rd ed. Washington, DC: Congressional Quarterly Inc., 1999.

Millar, Fergus. *The Roman Republic in Political Thought*. Hanover and London: Brandeis University Press and Historical Society of Israel, 2002.

Moran, Thomas Francis. *The Rise and Development of the Bicameral System in America*. Baltimore: The Johns Hopkins Press, 1895.

Nelson, Michael, ed. *The Evolving Presidency*. Washington, DC: Congressional Quarterly Inc., 1999.

Nelson, Michael, ed. *The Presidency and the Political System*. 7th ed. Washington, DC: CQ Press, 2003.

Parenti, Michael. *Democracy for the Few*. 6th ed. New York: St. Martin's Press, 1995.

Pole, J. R. *Political Representation in England and the Origins of the American Republic*. London: Macmillan, 1966.

Ripley, Randall B. *Party Leaders in the House of Representatives*. Washington, DC: Brookings Institution, 1967.

Roelofs, H. Mark. *The Poverty of American Politics*. 2nd ed. Philadelphia: Temple University Press, 1998.

Rozell, Mark J. *Executive Privilege*. Lawrence: University Press of Kansas, 2002.

Rozell, Mark J., William D. Pederson, and Frank J. Williams. *George Washington and the Origins of the American Presidency*. Westport, CT: Praeger, 2000.

Schwartz, Bernard. *A History of the Supreme Court*. New York: Oxford University Press, 1993.

Shelley, Mack C., II. *American Government and Politics Today*. 2004–2005 ed. Belmont, CA: Wadsworth Publishing, 2003.

Surrency, Erwin C. *History of the Federal Courts*. 2nd ed. Dobbs Ferry, NY: Oceana Publications, 2002.

Volkomer, Walter E. *American Government*. 8th ed. Upper Saddle River, NJ: Prentice Hall, 1998.

Wasby, Stephen L. *The Supreme Court in the Federal Judicial System*. 2nd ed. New York: Holt, Rinehart and Winston, 1984.

Wheeler, Russell R., and Cynthia Harrison. *Creating the Federal Judicial System*. Washington, DC: Federal Judicial Center, 1994.

Wilson, Woodrow. *Congressional Government*. Houghton Mifflin Co., 1885. Reprint, New Brunswick, NJ: Transaction Publishers, 2002.

Wolfensberger, Donald R. *Congress and the People*. Washington, DC, and Baltimore: Woodrow Wilson Center Press and Johns Hopkins University Press, 2000.

Woll, Peter. *American Government: Readings and Cases*. 15th ed. New York: Longman, 2003.

Young, Roland. *American Law and Politics: The Creation of Public Order*. New York: Harper & Row, 1967.

Zinn, Howard. *A People's History of the United States*. New York: HarperCollins, 2003.

CD-ROMs

21st Century Complete Guide to U.S. Courts. Progressive Management, 2003.

Web Sites

Federal Judicial Center. http://www.fjc.gov/ (accessed on March 31, 2005).

Federal Judiciary. http://www.uscourts.gov (accessed on February 18, 2005).

Library of Congress. http://www.loc.gov (accessed on March 15, 2005).

O'Hara, James B. "Court History Quizzes." *Supreme Court Historical Society.* http://www.supremecourthistory.org/02_history/subs_
history/02_f.html (accessed on March 30, 2005).

Supreme Court of the United States. http://www.supremecourtus.gov (accessed on February 18, 2005).

United States Department of Justice. http://www.usdoj.gov/ (accessed on February 12, 2005).

United States House of Representatives. http://www.house.gov (accessed on March 14, 2005).

United States Senate. http://www.senate.gov (accessed on March 14, 2005).

U.S. Census Bureau. http://www.census.gov (accessed on February 16, 2005).

U.S. Courts: The Federal Judiciary. http://www.uscourts.gov (accessed on March 23, 2005).

U.S. Term Limits. http://www.termlimits.org/ (accessed on March 11, 2005).

The White House. http://www.whitehouse.gov (accessed on February 16, 2005).

Index

Italic *type indicates volume number; illustrations are marked by (ill.).*

abolitionism, *3:* 430. *See also* slavery

Abraham, Spencer, *1:* 8 (ill.)

Abrams, Elliot, *1:* 153

Ackerman, Gary, *2:* 303

Act for Establishing Religious Freedom, *3:* 389

Act to Establish the Federal Courts of the United States. *See* Judiciary Act of 1789

Adams, Abigail, *1:* 93

Adams, John, *2:* 230 (ill.)
    appointment power of, *1:* 161–63; *3:* 475
    on class, *2:* 210–11, 228–29
    on democracy, *2:* 206
    election of, *1:* 93
    executive orders of, *1:* 76
    Library of Congress and, *2:* 305
    Marbury v. Madison and, *2:* 342; *3:* 424, 497
    Sedition Act of 1798 and, *2:* 244
    on separation of powers, *2:* 220–21
    as vice president, *1:* 93; *2:* 277, 278
    White House and, *2:* 221

Adams, John Quincy, *1:* 69, 69 (ill.), 87; *3:* 442

Adams, Samuel, *2:* 206, 210–11

Administration for Children and Families, *1:* 100

Administration on Aging, *1:* 100

administrative law, *1:* 124–25, 127–28, 169–71; *3:* 481–82. *See also* executive agencies; executive departments; independent regulatory commissions

administrative law judges, *1:* 128

Administrative Office of the United States Courts, *3:* 440, 469

admiralty
cases concerning, *2:* 346; *3:* 403, 415, 418, 501
Court of Appeals for, *3:* 391–93
federal district courts and, *3:* 417
advice and consent
agency appointments and, *1:* 109, 124, 125
ambassador appointments and, *1:* 56
checks and balances and, *1:* 143–46, 173; *2:* 323–27, 349–50, 352–53; *3:* 485–86, 506
department appointments and, *1:* 95; *3:* 418
independent regulatory commission appointments and, *1:* 109, 127
judicial appointments and, *1:* 17, 173; *2:* 195; *3:* 375–76, 433, 437, 439, 485–86
overview of, *1:* 5, 11, 143–46; *2:* 184, 190, 277, 323–27; *3:* 364, 369
vice president and, *2:* 352
African Americans, *3:* 500–501. *See also* discrimination; race
Age of Enlightenment, *1:* 26; *2:* 202–3
agencies. *See* executive agencies
Agency for Healthcare Research and Quality, *1:* 100
Agency for International Development, *1:* 105
Agnew, Spiro T., *1:* 96; *3:* 368 (ill.)
Agriculture, Department of, *1:* 95–98
agriculture, secretary of, *1:* 95–97
Air Force, Department of the, *1:* 98
Akerman, Amos Tappan, *3:* 419 (ill.)
Albert, Carl, *3:* 368 (ill.)
Albright, Madeleine, *1:* 85
alcohol, *2:* 258–59
Aldrich, Nelson W., *2:* 255
Allen, Richard, *1:* 105 (ill.)
ambassadors
appointment of, *2:* 277
cases concerning, *1:* 14, 15; *2:* 192, 193, 346; *3:* 373, 403–4, 415, 417, 501
in Constitution, *1:* 55–56
president and, *1:* 11; *2:* 189; *3:* 369
work of, *1:* 106

amendments, constitutional. *See also* specific amendments
checks and balances and, *1:* 17; *2:* 195, 348–49; *3:* 375, 500–501, 504–5
executive branch and, *1:* 61–62
judicial interpretation and, *3:* 500–501
judicial power and, *2:* 348–49; *3:* 504–5
overview of, *1:* 1, 3; *3:* 504–5
ratification of, *2:* 236, 255, 257–58, 258–59
term limits and, *2:* 259–61
time limit for, *2:* 257–58
American Association for Retired Persons, *2:* 285 (ill.)
American Civil War
amnesty after, *1:* 52–53
taxation during, *2:* 254, 350
war powers and, *3:* 425
writs of habeas corpus and, *2:* 355; *3:* 510
American Declaration of Independence, *1:* 34 (ill.); *3:* 431 (ill.). *See also* American Revolutionary War
Constitution and, *3:* 430–31
Fourteenth Amendment and, *3:* 431
George III in, *2:* 208
government under, *1:* 4; *2:* 182; *3:* 362
grievances in, *1:* 30, 32–34
inalienable rights in, *3:* 430–31, 500
military in, *2:* 234
Parliament in, *2:* 208
signing of, *1:* 30, 39
American Revolutionary War, *2:* 220, 233, 235. *See also* American Declaration of Independence
amnesty, *1:* 52–53. *See also* pardon power
Annapolis Convention, *1:* 41; *3:* 396
Antiballistic Missile Treaty, *1:* 57
Anti-federalists
Bill of Rights and, *2:* 241–43; *3:* 418
Constitution and, *2:* 240–42; *3:* 418
judicial branch and, *3:* 416–17
judicial review and, *3:* 418
Necessary and Proper Clause and, *2:* 246

state power and, *3:* 423–24

Anti-Saloon League, *2:* 258

appeals

admiralty, *3:* 392

in American colonies, *3:* 386

to circuit courts, *3:* 417, 428–29

to circuit courts of appeals, *3:* 435, 443–45, 446, 447, 458, 460–62

civil law and, *3:* 418

criminal law and, *3:* 418

in Great Britain, *3:* 385

judicial interpretation and, *3:* 409–11

overview of, *1:* 13–14; *2:* 191–92; *3:* 371–72, 379–80, 404, 407–9

purpose of, *3:* 461

regulatory, *1:* 125

in Schiavo case, *3:* 381

in state cases, *3:* 418

to Supreme Court, *1:* 15; *2:* 193; *3:* 373, 403, 404–5, 415, 417–18, 429, 432–33, 435, 440–43, 462–68

appearance of impropriety, *3:* 476–77

appellate jurisdiction, *3:* 407–8, 415, 417–18, 432–33, 435. *See also* appeals

appointment power. *See also* advice and consent

agency appointments and, *1:* 109

ambassador appointments and, *1:* 56

bureau appointments and, *1:* 109

checks and balances and, *1:* 11, 17, 143–46, 173; *2:* 190, 195, 323–27, 351–52; *3:* 369, 375–76, 485–86, 506

department appointments and, *1:* 95, 145–46; *2:* 325; *3:* 418

independent regulatory commission appointments and, *1:* 109, 127

judicial appointments and, *1:* 173, 174–75; *3:* 413, 425, 433, 437, 439, 440, 443–44, 445, 447, 458, 485–86

overview of, *1:* 11, 17, 127; *2:* 195, 349, 351–52; *3:* 369, 375–76, 506

apportionment, *1:* 3; *2:* 181; *3:* 361

appropriations power

checks and balances and, *1:* 140–43; *2:* 320–23

debate and, *2:* 293

federal budget and, *2:* 301

first bill for, *2:* 288–89

historic roots of, *1:* 29

impoundment and, *1:* 141; *2:* 320–22

line item veto and, *2:* 316

reprogramming and, *1:* 142–43; *2:* 322–23

veto power and, *1:* 141; *2:* 321

Arago, 3: 466–67

arbitrators, *3:* 384

Architect of the Capitol, *2:* 305

Aristotle, *2:* 201–2, 202 (ill.)

arms, right to bear, *1:* 6; *2:* 185, 243–45, 268; *3:* 364

Army, Department of the, *1:* 98

Arnold, Benedict, *3:* 407 (ill.)

arraignment, *3:* 457

arrest. *See* search and seizure

Articles of Confederation

commerce under, *1:* 40–41; *2:* 215, 230–31, 249; *3:* 395

executive power and, *1:* 31–35, 39

government under, *1:* 4; *2:* 182, 197, 215; *3:* 362

judiciary in, *3:* 390–93, 395, 396

law enforcement under, *1:* 48; *2:* 221

legislation under, *2:* 215, 221

military under, *1:* 32–35, 40; *2:* 215

president under, *1:* 39

problems under, *1:* 31–35, 37–41, 42–43, 48; *2:* 215, 217, 230–31, 235, 249; *3:* 395–97

states under, *2:* 217, 235

taxation under, *1:* 31–32, 39–40; *2:* 215, 217, 235; *3:* 395

Ashcroft, John, *1:* 8 (ill.), 123

assemblies, Roman, *1:* 20–21; *2:* 199, 200

assistant to the president for national security affairs, *1:* 108–9

assistant U.S. attorneys, *1:* 120, 121; *3:* 418, 450

associate attorney general, *1:* 102, 120, 121–22

associate justices, *3:* 439, 440, 441–43, 462, 467. *See also* justices, Supreme court

Attlee, Clement, *1:* 148 (ill.)

attorney general
  appointment of, *3:* 418
  associate attorney general, *1:* 102, 120, 121–22
  creation of, *1:* 50, 73; *3:* 418
  deputy attorney general, *1:* 102, 120, 121–22
  as head of department, *1:* 95, 102, 119–20
  work of, *1:* 121–22

attorneys, *1:* 66; *3:* 450–51. *See also* specific posts

bail, *3:* 423

Bailey, Joseph W., *2:* 255

balanced budget amendment, *2:* 261–62, 272

Bank of the United States, *2:* 247–49

bankruptcy, *3:* 432, 460

bench trials, *3:* 379, 409, 446–47, 459, 460

bicameralism
  checks and balances and, *2:* 209–10
  class and, *2:* 212–15, 312
  in colonies, American, *2:* 212–15
  Constitution and, *2:* 197, 223–24
  Federal Convention and, *2:* 198–99, 223–24
  Madison, James, on, *2:* 312
  states and, *2:* 212–15

Bill of Rights, *2:* 242 (ill.). *See also* specific amendments
  Anti-federalists and, *2:* 241–43; *3:* 418
  civil liberties in, *1:* 16; *2:* 194, 243–46; *3:* 374–75, 430
  Federal Convention and, *2:* 239–40
  Federalist Party and, *2:* 241–43; *3:* 418
  judicial power and, *3:* 418–23
  legislative power and, *1:* 6; *2:* 185, 239–46; *3:* 364

Madison, James, and, *1:* 63; *2:* 242–43; *3:* 418, 430
  Magna Carta and, *1:* 24
  ratification of, *1:* 6; *2:* 185, 242–43, 257; *3:* 364, 418–19
  ratification of Constitution and, *1:* 62–63; *2:* 240–43; *3:* 418
  states and, *3:* 430

bills. *See* legislation

bills of attainder
  legislative power and, *1:* 6; *2:* 184, 355; *3:* 364, 510
  liberty and, *2:* 205

Black Codes, *3:* 427, 428 (ill.), 500–501

Black, Hugo L., *1:* 166; *3:* 439 (ill.)

Black, Jeremiah, *2:* 187 (ill.)

Black, Shirley Temple, *1:* 56 (ill.)

Blackmun, Harry A., *3:* 372 (ill.), 463 (ill.)

Blackstone, Sir William, *1:* 25; *2:* 210

Blount, William, *1:* 155, 155 (ill.); *2:* 333

Blumenthal, Richard, *3:* 451 (ill.)

Board of Trade, *3:* 387

Board of Veterans Appeals, *3:* 458

Body of Civil Law, *3:* 383

Boies, David, *3:* 451 (ill.)

Boland Amendment, *1:* 153

bootlegging, *2:* 258

Bork, Robert H., *1:* 17; *2:* 195, 326 (ill.), 352; *3:* 376

Boston Gazette, *2:* 302

Boston Tea Party, *1:* 39

breach of the peace, *1:* 131–32; *2:* 309–10, 337; *3:* 493

Brennan, William J., Jr., *3:* 372 (ill.), 439 (ill.), 463 (ill.)

bribery
  as impeachable offense, *1:* 5, 91, 153–54; *2:* 182–84, 333, 353–54; *3:* 437, 508
  impeachments for, *3:* 363

briefs, *3:* 441, 444, 448, 461, 465

British Empire. *See* Great Britain

Broom, Jacob, *1:* 46

Brown, Henry B., *3:* 466–67, 467 (ill.)

Brown v. Board of Education of Topeka, 2: 345; *3:* 499–500

Brutus, *2:* 236, 237

Buchanan, James, *2:* 187 (ill.)

budget. *See* federal budget

Budget and Accounting Act of 1921, *1:* 72–73; *2:* 299

Budget and Impoundment Control Act of 1974, *1:* 141; *2:* 299–301, 321–22

Bureau of Competition, *1:* 127

Bureau of Consumer Protection, *1:* 127

Bureau of Indian Affairs, *1:* 102

Bureau of Labor Statistics, *1:* 103

Bureau of Land Management, *1:* 102

Bureau of Reclamation, *1:* 102

Bureau of the Budget, *1:* 72; *2:* 299. *See also* Office of Management and Budget

bureaus, *1:* 109. *See also* specific bureaus

Burger, Warren, *3:* 372 (ill.), 463 (ill.), 486 (ill.), 488–89

Burr, Aaron, *1:* 48, 66–67, 68–69

Bursey, Brett A., *1:* 122–23

Bush, Barbara, *1:* 119 (ill.)

Bush, George (forty-first president), *1:* 10 (ill.), 119 (ill.)
    appointment power of, *2:* 352
    debate by, *1:* 86
    Iran-Contra scandal and, *1:* 153
    Noriega, Manuel, and, *1:* 82
    pardons by, *1:* 52, 153, 176; *3:* 490
    as vice president, *1:* 104–5, 118
    War Powers Resolution and, *1:* 82

Bush, George W. (forty-third president), *1:* 8 (ill.), 145 (ill.); *2:* 189 (ill.), 260 (ill.), 318 (ill.); *3:* 370 (ill.)
    appointment power of, *1:* 144, 145; *2:* 324–25
    cabinet of, *1:* 8 (ill.), 107
    congressional messages of, *1:* 10; *2:* 188; *3:* 368
    election of, *1:* 13–14, 66, 84, 87; *2:* 191–92; *3:* 371–72, 464–65
    Iraq and, *1:* 122–23

Office of Faith-Based and Community Initiatives and, *1:* 75–76

Office of Homeland Security and, *1:* 100

reprogramming by, *1:* 142; *2:* 322

Schiavo case and, *3:* 381

State of the Union address of, *1:* 51–52

treaties made by, *1:* 11, 57; *2:* 190; *3:* 369

vetoes by, *1:* 136; *2:* 315

Bush, Laura, *1:* 103; *3:* 370 (ill.)

Bush v. Gore, 3: 464–65

business. *See* commerce

Butler, Pierce, *1:* 174

Butterfield, Alexander, *3:* 488

Byrd, Robert, *2:* 189 (ill.), 280

Byrne, James F., *3:* 442

Byrns, Joseph, *2:* 188 (ill.)

cabinet
    appointment power and, *1:* 145–46; *2:* 325
    of Buchanan, James, *2:* 187 (ill.)
    of Bush, George W., *1:* 8 (ill.)
    chief of staff in, *1:* 8; *2:* 186; *3:* 366
    composition of, *1:* 7–8, 95, 107; *2:* 186; *3:* 366
    executive heads in, *1:* 7–8; *2:* 186; *3:* 366
    of Lincoln, Abraham, *3:* 366 (ill.)
    of Monroe, James, *1:* 98 (ill.)
    vice president in, *1:* 8, 94, 115; *2:* 186; *3:* 366
    of Washington, George, *1:* 74 (ill.), 77

calendars, *2:* 293

campaign finance reform, *1:* 85; *2:* 288

campaigning, *2:* 268, 303–5. *See also* elections

Cannon, Joseph G., *2:* 268 (ill.), 270, 270 (ill.), 271

capital crime, *1:* 65, 165; *3:* 422, 479–80

capital punishment, *2:* 245–46

capitalism, *1:* 152

Card, Andrew, *1:* 8 (ill.)

Carrington, Edward, *1:* 44

Carswell, G. Harrold, *1:* 17; *2:* 195; *3:* 376, 508 (ill.)

Carter, Jimmy, *1:* 52, 53, 96

"case of the mutinous mariner," *3:* 391

cases and controversies. *See also* jurisdiction
  checks and balances and, *2:* 346–47; *3:* 501–3
  friendly suits and, *2:* 346–47; *3:* 503
  historic roots of, *3:* 390–93
  judicial power and, *2:* 339; *3:* 495
  mootness and, *2:* 347; *3:* 503–4
  overview of, *1:* 14–15; *2:* 192–93; *3:* 373, 402–5
  ripeness and, *2:* 347; *3:* 503–4
  test cases and, *2:* 346–47; *3:* 503

casework, *2:* 267, 275, 276, 301–3

Cass, Lewis, *2:* 187 (ill.)

Catron, John, *3:* 426

ceilings, personnel, *1:* 143; *2:* 323

Center on Budget and Policy Priorities, *2:* 262

Centers for Disease Control and Protection, *1:* 100

Centers for Medicare and Medicaid Services, *1:* 100

Centinel, *1:* 41; *2:* 237

Central Intelligence Agency, *1:* 109, 124, 152–53

centuriate assembly, *1:* 21; *2:* 199

Chamber of Commerce, *1:* 116

Chamorro, Edgar, *1:* 152

chancellors, *3:* 385

chancery courts, *3:* 386

Chao, Elaine, *1:* 8 (ill.)

Chase, Salmon P., *3:* 440, 442, 484 (ill.)

Chase, Samuel, *2:* 354 (ill.); *3:* 438 (ill.), 511 (ill.)
  impeachment of, *1:* 18; *2:* 196, 354; *3:* 376, 438, 510, 511

checks and balances
  advice and consent and, *1:* 143–46, 173; *2:* 323–27, 349–50, 352–53; *3:* 485–86, 506
  amendment power and, *1:* 17; *2:* 195, 348–49; *3:* 375, 500–501, 504–5
  appointment power and, *1:* 11, 17, 143–46, 173; *2:* 190, 195, 323–27, 351–52; *3:* 369, 375–76, 485–86, 506

appropriations power and, *1:* 140–43; *2:* 320–23

bicameralism and, *2:* 209–10

bills of attainder and, *2:* 355; *3:* 510

in British Empire, *1:* 31

cases and controversies and, *2:* 346–47; *3:* 501–3

class and, *2:* 201–2, 312–13

commander in chief and, *1:* 6; *2:* 185; *3:* 364

in Constitution, *1:* 1; *2:* 179, 222–23, 339; *3:* 359, 495

Democratic Party and, *2:* 313

executive branch and, *1:* 133; *2:* 222, 310–14

executive power and, *1:* 45–46

executive privilege and, *1:* 173–76; *3:* 486–87

Federal Convention and, *1:* 45–46, 133, 160–61; *2:* 217–18, 222–23, 310–14, 339; *3:* 474–75, 495

Federalist on, *2:* 222

Fifth Amendment and, *1:* 165–68; *3:* 479–81

Founding Fathers and, *2:* 312

Fourth Amendment and, *1:* 163–65; *3:* 478–79

historic roots of, *1:* 21–22

House of Representatives and, *2:* 312–13

impeachment and, *1:* 11–12, 17–18, 151–55, 172–73; *2:* 190, 195–96, 332–33, 353–54; *3:* 369, 376, 483–85, 508–10

income tax and, *2:* 350–51

Iran-Contra scandal and, *1:* 152–53

judicial branch and, *2:* 222, 339; *3:* 495

judicial interpretation and, *1:* 169–71; *2:* 344–45; *3:* 481–82, 498–501

judicial power and, *2:* 348–54, 354–55; *3:* 369–70, 504–10, 510–12

judicial review and, *1:* 6–7, 15–16, 161–69; *2:* 185, 193–94, 339–44; *3:* 364–65, 374–75, 412, 475–78, 495–98

law enforcement and, *1:* 6, 12; *2:* 185, 190; *3:* 364, 369

legislation and, *1:* 16–17, 51–54; *2:* 194–95, 349; *3:* 375, 506

legislative branch and, *1:* 6–7, 133; *2:* 185, 209–10, 222–23, 310–14, 339; *3:* 364–65, 495 legislative oversight and, *1:* 150–51; *2:* 331

legislative power and, *1:* 6–7; *2:* 185, 354–55; *3:* 364, 510–12

Madison, James, on, *2:* 222

Marbury v. Madison and, *1:* 6–7; *2:* 185, 341–44; *3:* 365, 497–98

overview of, *1:* 133, 160–61; *2:* 310–14, 339; *3:* 474–75, 495

pardon power and, *1:* 176; *3:* 487–90

Parliament and, *2:* 209–10

political parties and, *2:* 313

political question doctrine and, *2:* 347–48; *3:* 504

prosecution and, *1:* 165–68; *3:* 479–81

Republican Party and, *2:* 313

in Roman Republic, *1:* 21–22

search and seizure and, *1:* 163–65; *3:* 478–79

Senate and, *2:* 312–13

Sixth Amendment and, *1:* 168–69; *3:* 481

special interest groups and, *2:* 313

treaties and, *1:* 11, 146–47; *2:* 190, 327–28; *3:* 369

veto power and, *1:* 11, 133–39; *2:* 189–90, 222, 314–19; *3:* 369

war powers and, *1:* 147–49; *2:* 329–31

writs of habeas corpus and, *1:* 171; *2:* 354–55; *3:* 482–86, 510

writs of mandamus and, *1:* 171–72; *3:* 483

writs of prohibition and, *1:* 171–72; *3:* 483

Cheney, Dick, *1:* 8 (ill.); *2:* 279 (ill.); *3:* 476–77

chief judges, *3:* 443

chief justice

administrative duties of, *3:* 440, 469–70

appointment of, *3:* 440

compensation for, *3:* 440

impeachment trials and, *1:* 151–52, 152–53, 172–73; *2:* 332–33; *3:* 413, 440, 483–85

Marshall, John, appointed to, *2:* 342; *3:* 497

removal of, *3:* 440

role of, *3:* 417, 439–40, 443, 462, 466–67

chief of staff

in cabinet, *1:* 8, 107; *2:* 186; *3:* 366

work of, *1:* 75, 107–8

chief of state, *1:* 90, 113

Chipman, Nathaniel, *3:* 397–400

Chipman, Norton P., *2:* 286

Chisholm v. Georgia, *3:* 423

Choate, Joseph, *2:* 254

Christianity, *3:* 388–89

Church of England, *3:* 388

Cicero, Marcus Tillius, *3:* 382, 382 (ill.)

circuit courts, *3:* 416–17, 425, 428–29. *See also* circuit courts of appeals

circuit courts of appeals. *See also* circuit courts

appeals to, *3:* 444–45, 446, 447, 458, 460–62

clerk of the court of, *3:* 449–50

creation of, *3:* 429

decision-making by, *3:* 461–62

judges of, *3:* 443–44, 448

Judicial Conference of the United States and, *3:* 469

judicial interpretation in, *3:* 462

judicial review in, *3:* 462

law clerks at, *3:* 448–49

opinions of, *3:* 461–62

oral argument in, *3:* 461

organization of, *3:* 435, 443, 444, 460–61

overview of, *1:* 13; *2:* 191; *3:* 371, 379–80, 432, 435

Schiavo case and, *3:* 381

summary judgment and, *3:* 446

Circuit Courts of Appeals Act of 1891, *3:* 429

citizens

African Americans as, *3:* 500–501

cases concerning, *1:* 14; *2:* 192; *3:* 373, 403, 415, 417, 418, 432

Citizens for Term Limits, *2:* 261

civil cases

in American colonies, *3:* 386–87

appeals concerning, *3:* 418

in circuit courts, *3:* 417

in Constitution, *3:* 406–7

in federal district courts, *1:* 13; *2:* 191; *3:* 371, 379, 417, 432, 435, 445–47, 459–60

in Great Britain, *3:* 384–85

Justice, Department of, and, *1:* 64–65, 122

magistrate judges and, *3:* 448

civil liberties. *See also* inalienable rights; liberty

in Bill of Rights, *2:* 243–46

Fourteenth Amendment and, *2:* 252–53; *3:* 430–31

Interstate Commerce Clause and, *2:* 251–53

judicial branch and, *1:* 16; *2:* 194; *3:* 374–75

judicial review and, *3:* 427–28

Magna Carta and, *1:* 23–24

Civil Rights Act of 1875, *2:* 251

Civil Rights Act of 1964, *2:* 251–53

Civil War. *See* American Civil War

civilians, *1:* 8–9, 78–79; *2:* 186, 234–35; *3:* 366–67

Claiborne, Harry, *2:* 354; *3:* 510

Clark, Tom C., *3:* 421

Clarridge, Duane R., *1:* 153

class. *See also* property

Adams, John, on, *2:* 228–29

Aristotle on, *2:* 201–2

bicameralism and, *2:* 212–15, 312

checks and balances and, *2:* 201–2, 312–13

Constitution and, *2:* 226–29

democracy and, *1:* 133; *2:* 311

elections and, *2:* 226–29, 255–57

Federal Convention and, *1:* 133; *2:* 198–99, 217–19, 226–29, 311

House of Lords and, *2:* 210

House of Representatives and, *2:* 226–28, 312–13

income tax and, *2:* 254–55

legislation and, *2:* 202

legislative branch and, *2:* 198–99, 201–2, 206, 214, 226–29, 312–13

liberty and, *2:* 210–11

monarchy and, *2:* 202

Parliament and, *2:* 208–9

representatives, *2:* 202

Senate and, *2:* 202, 210–11, 228–29, 312–13

senators and, *2:* 202

separation of powers and, *2:* 201–2; *3:* 400–402

unicameralism, *2:* 312

voting rights and, *2:* 226–29, 255–57

war and, *2:* 245

Clay, Henry, *1:* 69

Clean Air Act, *1:* 169; *2:* 251; *3:* 482

Clean Water Act, *1:* 125, 169; *3:* 482

clerk of the court, *3:* 449–50

Cleveland, Grover, *1:* 78–79

Clifford, Nathan, *3:* 442

Clinton, Bill, *1:* 59 (ill.), 76 (ill.); *2:* 296 (ill.), 313 (ill.), 317 (ill.)

Clinton, Hillary, and, *1:* 103

Contract with America and, *2:* 272

election of, *1:* 86; *2:* 272

executive privilege of, *1:* 79

impeachment of, *1:* 5, 59, 91, 154, 173; *2:* 184, 333; *3:* 363, 440, 485

line item veto and, *2:* 316

State of the Union address of, *2:* 316

vetoes by, *1:* 11; *2:* 190, 272, 296 (ill.), 297; *3:* 369

Clinton, Hillary, *1:* 85, 103, 103 (ill.); *2:* 304 (ill.)

Clinton v. City of New York, *2:* 316

closing argument, *3:* 457, 459, 460

cloture rule, *2:* 294

Coard, Bernard, *1:* 149; *2:* 331

Coast Guard, U.S., *1:* 98

Coats, Dan, *2:* 316

Cobb, Howell, *2:* 187 (ill.)

Cold War, *1:* 99

Coleman, William T., Jr., *1:* 116

Colfax, Schuyler, *3:* 431

colonies, American, *1:* 28–29; *2:* 211–15; *3:* 386–87, 388–89. *See also* states

commander in chief

checks and balances and, *1:* 6, 147–49; *2:* 185, 329–31; *3:* 364

    role of, *1:* 6, 8–9, 54–55, 80–82, 113; *2:* 185, 186; *3:* 364, 366–67

    steel seizure case and, *1:* 166

Commentaries on the Constitution, 3: 398–99

Commentaries on the Laws of England, 1: 25; *2:* 210

commerce. *See also* economy

    under Articles of Confederation, *1:* 40–41; *2:* 215, 230–31, 249; *3:* 395

    Constitution and, *2:* 230–32, 239, 241

    executive power and, *1:* 38–39

    Federal Convention and, *2:* 218–19, 230–32, 239

    Federalist on, *2:* 232

    Federalist Party and, *2:* 241

    Great Britain and, *1:* 38–39; *2:* 231, 249

    Hamilton, Alexander, on, *2:* 229–30, 231, 247

    Interstate Commerce Clause and, *2:* 249–53

    legislative branch and, *1:* 2; *2:* 180, 205, 215, 239; *3:* 360

    legislative power and, *2:* 230–32

    lobbying and, *2:* 284–85

    Madison, James, on, *2:* 230–31, 232

    military and, *2:* 232

    with Native Americans, *2:* 232

    Sherman Antitrust Act and, *2:* 344–45; *3:* 499

    taxation and, *2:* 231–32, 249

    Washington, George, on, *2:* 231

Commerce, Chamber of, *1:* 116

Commerce, Department of, *1:* 97

commerce, secretary of, *1:* 97

commissioners, *1:* 109, 127, 144; *2:* 324

Committee of Detail, *3:* 398

Committee of the States, *1:* 39

committees, congressional. *See also* political action committees; specific committees

    composition of, *2:* 291

    conference, *2:* 276, 295–96

    federal budget and, *2:* 299–301

    iron triangles and, *2:* 292

    issue networks and, *2:* 292

    joint, *2:* 270, 276, 299

    legislation and, *2:* 266–67, 270, 271, 276, 290–93, 295–96, 299

    legislative oversight by, *2:* 297

    lobbying and, *2:* 286

    majority party and, *2:* 291

    minority party and, *2:* 291

    select, *2:* 298–99

    Senate, *2:* 276, 281

    Speaker of the House and, *2:* 270, 295

    staff for, *2:* 275, 281

    standing, *2:* 266–67, 290, 291, 297, 299–301

    Washington, D.C., and, *2:* 286

    work of, *2:* 266–67

common law

    American colonies and, *3:* 386

    in Great Britain, *3:* 384–85

    infamous crimes under, *1:* 166–68; *3:* 480

    judicial interpretation and, *3:* 410

    reception provisions and, *3:* 387–90

    Seventh Amendment and, *3:* 422–23

Common Sense, 1: 31

communism, *1:* 52

compensation

    in American Revolutionary War, *2:* 220, 233

    in Congress, *2:* 257–58

    of judges, *2:* 338; *3:* 413, 437, 440, 443, 445, 447, 458, 494

    of president, *1:* 132; *2:* 310

competition, *1:* 127

"Completing the Constitution," *3:* 431

Concord Coalition, *2:* 262

concurring opinions, *3:* 442, 448, 462, 467

conference committees, *2:* 276, 295–96. *See also* joint committees

confirmation power. *See* advice and consent

Confrontation Clause, *1:* 168–69; *3:* 481

Congress, *2:* 313 (ill.), 321 (ill.); *3:* 367 (ill.). *See also* Congress (under Articles of Confederation); Continental Congress; House of Representatives; legislative branch; Senate

bicameralism and, *2:* 223–24

checks and balances on, *1:* 6–7, 133; *2:* 185; *3:* 495

checks and balances within, *2:* 209–10, 312–13

class and, *2:* 198–99, 201–2, 226–29, 312–13

commerce and, *1:* 2; *2:* 180, 205, 215, 239; *3:* 360

composition of, *2:* 197, 223–24, 265, 283, 312–13

in Constitution, *1:* 1, 3–5; *2:* 179, 181–85, 283; *3:* 359–65

economy and, *1:* 82

election to, *1:* 131; *2:* 223–24, 226–29, 309, 312, 337; *3:* 493

federal budget and, *1:* 72–73, 108; *2:* 316

Federal Convention and, *2:* 197–99, 312

Founding Fathers and, *2:* 312

historic roots of, *1:* 24–25; *2:* 197–215

introduction of a bill in, *2:* 289

Iran-Contra scandal and, *1:* 152–53

iron triangles and, *2:* 292

issue networks and, *2:* 292

judicial branch and, *3:* 429

judicial interpretation and, *2:* 344–45; *3:* 498–500

judicial review and, *2:* 339–44; *3:* 424–25, 495–98

judicial system created by, *1:* 12–13; *2:* 190–91; *3:* 370–71

legislative courts of, *3:* 458

liberty and, *2:* 203–6

military and, *1:* 2, 54–55; *2:* 180, 215, 239; *3:* 360

money and, *1:* 2; *2:* 180; *3:* 360

naturalization and, *1:* 2; *2:* 180; *3:* 360

oversight by, *1:* 150–51; *2:* 331

overview of, *1:* 1–7; *2:* 179–85; *3:* 359–65

Parliament and, *2:* 208–11

political philosophers and, *2:* 201–8

property and, *2:* 203–6, 239

qualifications to serve in, *1:* 131; *2:* 309

Reconstruction and, *3:* 425–26

representation and, *2:* 210–11, 223–26

republicanism and, *2:* 206–8

Roman Republic and, *2:* 199–200

Schiavo case and, *3:* 381

Senate minority leader and, *2:* 280–81

separation of powers and, *1:* 131–32; *2:* 203, 209, 219–22, 309–10, 337–38; *3:* 397–400, 400–402, 493–94

slavery and, *2:* 225–26

special interest groups and, *2:* 313

State of the Union address and, *1:* 9–10; *2:* 187–88; *3:* 367–68

Supreme Court and, *3:* 425–26

taxation and, *1:* 2; *2:* 180, 215; *3:* 360

terms in, *2:* 272

veto power and, *1:* 136–38; *2:* 316–19

voting in, *1:* 133–34; *2:* 314

war powers and, *1:* 22, 54–55, 80–82, 147–49; *2:* 329–31

in Washington, D.C., *2:* 221

Congress (under the Articles of Confederation). *See also* Continental Congress

executive power of, *1:* 31–33, 39–40; *2:* 221

invasion of, *2:* 220

judicial power of, *3:* 395, 396

legislative power of, *2:* 215, 221

problems with, *2:* 217

Congressional Budget Office, *2:* 300

congressional districts

constituents in, *2:* 267, 301, 305

gerrymandering and, *2:* 302

organization of, *2:* 265, 267, 283

congressional staff, *2:* 275–76, 281, 301–3

Conklin, Scott, *2:* 267

Connecticut Compromise, *2:* 224

constituents, *2:* 267, 301–3

Constitution, *1:* 4 (ill.), xxxvii–l; *2:* 183 (ill.), 242 (ill.), xxxvii–l; *3:* xxxvii–l. *See also* amendments, constitutional; Federal Convention; specific amendments and clauses

  ambassadors in, *1:* 55–56

  American Declaration of Independence and, *3:* 430–31

  Anti-federalists and, *2:* 240–42; *3:* 418

  avoiding questions concerning, *2:* 347; *3:* 504

  bicameralism and, *2:* 223–24

  Bill of Rights and, *1:* 62–63, 240–43; *3:* 418

  cases concerning, *1:* 14–15; *2:* 192–93, 346; *3:* 373, 402, 415, 417–18, 424, 501

  checks and balances in, *1:* 1; *2:* 179, 222–23, 339; *3:* 359, 495

  class and, *2:* 226–29

  commerce and, *2:* 230–32, 239, 241

  Congress in, *1:* 1, 3–5; *2:* 179, 181–85, 283; *3:* 359–65

  on criminal trials, *3:* 406

  duration of, *3:* 420

  elections under, *2:* 226–29

  executive departments in, *1:* 7, 50; *2:* 186; *3:* 365–66

  executive power in, *1:* 48–49

  executive privilege in, *3:* 488

  Federalist Party and, *2:* 240–42; *3:* 418

  House of Representatives in, *1:* 1, 3–5; *2:* 179, 181–85, 223–24, 265; *3:* 359, 361–64

  inalienable rights in, *3:* 430–31

  interpretation of, *3:* 410, 420, 462

  Interstate Commerce Clause in, *1:* 2; *2:* 180; *3:* 360

  Jefferson, Thomas, on, *3:* 420

  judicial branch in, *3:* 395

  judicial power in, *2:* 339; *3:* 495

  judicial review and, *1:* 6; *2:* 185, 340, 342–44; *3:* 365, 411–12, 424, 495–96, 498

  law enforcement and, *1:* 49–50

  legislative power in, *1:* 2–3; *2:* 180–81; *3:* 360–61

  Madison, James, and, *2:* 241–43

  military in, *1:* 2, 54–55; *2:* 180, 232–35, 239; *3:* 360

  money in, *1:* 2; *2:* 180; *3:* 360

  naturalization in, *1:* 2; *2:* 180; *3:* 360

  original intent of, *3:* 410

  overview of, *1:* 1; *2:* 179; *3:* 359

  preamble of, *3:* 398–99, 430

  property and, *2:* 239

  ratification of, *1:* 1, 4, 62–63; *2:* 179, 182, 220, 234, 236, 237, 239, 240–43; *3:* 359, 362, 417, 418, 430

  representation and, *2:* 223–26

  Senate in, *1:* 1, 3–5; *2:* 179, 181–85, 223–24, 276; *3:* 359, 361–64

  separation of powers in, *1:* 1, 131–32; *2:* 179, 219–22, 309–10, 337–38; *3:* 359, 415, 493–94

  slavery and, *2:* 225–26, 232; *3:* 430

  Speaker of the House in, *2:* 269

  states and, *2:* 240–42

  Supreme Court in, *1:* 12; *2:* 190–91; *3:* 370, 402, 415, 417–18, 462

  taxation and, *1:* 2; *2:* 180, 231–32, 235–36, 253–55; *3:* 360

  voting rights and, *2:* 226–29

Constitution of England, *1:* 27–28

constitutional amendments. *See* amendments, constitutional

Constitutional Convention of 1787. *See* Federal Convention

constitutional courts, *3:* 458

consuls

  cases concerning, *3:* 403–4, 415, 417

  in Roman Republic, *1:* 20–21; *2:* 199

consumers, *1:* 127

Continental Congress. *See also* Congress (under Articles of Confederation)

  executive power of, *1:* 31, 37–39

  government under, *1:* 4; *2:* 182; *3:* 362

  judicial power of, *3:* 390

Continentalist, 2: 231

Contract with America, *2:* 261, 272–73, 273 (ill.)

Contras, *1:* 152–53

Coolidge, Calvin, *1:* 9, 135 (ill.); *2:* 187; *3:* 367

Corpus Juris Civilus, 3: 383

Council of Economic Advisors, *1:* 75

counsel, right to, *3:* 422

Court of Appeals (prize cases), *3:* 392–93

Court of Appeals for the Armed Services, *3:* 458

Court of Appeals for the Federal Circuit, *3:* 443, 444, 458, 460, 468

Court of Appeals for Veterans Claims, *3:* 458

Court of Common Pleas, *3:* 384–85

Court of Exchequer, *3:* 384–85

Court of Federal Claims, *3:* 443, 468

Court of International Trade, *3:* 432, 443, 460, 468, 469

Court of King's Bench, *3:* 384–85

Court of Queen's Bench, *3:* 384–85

court stenographers, *3:* 450

court-martial, *3:* 458

court-packing plans, *1:* 174–75; *3:* 425

courts. *See* judicial branch; specific courts

Cox, Archibald, *3:* 488

Crawford, William H., *1:* 69

criminal cases. *See also* prosecution

    in American colonies, *3:* 386

    appeals concerning, *3:* 418

    arraignment, *3:* 457

    in circuit courts, *3:* 417

    in Constitution, *3:* 406

    Eighth Amendment and, *3:* 423

    in federal district courts, *1:* 13; *2:* 191; *3:* 371, 379, 417, 432, 435, 445–47, 456–59

    Fifth Amendment and, *1:* 64–65; *3:* 422

    in Great Britain, *3:* 384–85

    Interstate Commerce Clause and, *2:* 251

    Justice, Department of, and, *1:* 122

    magistrate judges and, *3:* 447

sentencing, *3:* 459

    Sixth Amendment and, *1:* 65–66; *3:* 422

Cromwell, Oliver, *2:* 235

cross-examination, *1:* 65; *3:* 422

Cushing, William, *3:* 425, 425 (ill.)

Daniels, Mitch, *1:* 8 (ill.)

Daschle, Tom, *2:* 294 (ill.)

death penalty, *2:* 245–46

debate

    appropriations power and, *2:* 293

    filibuster and, *2:* 293–94

    in House of Representatives, *2:* 271, 293–95

    in Senate, *2:* 278, 279, 280, 281, 293–95

    Speech and Debate Clause, *1:* 131–32; *2:* 309–10, 337; *3:* 493

Debs, Eugene, *2:* 245, 245 (ill.)

Declaration of Independence. *See* American Declaration of Independence

declarations of war. *See also* military; war powers

    by Congress, *1:* 54–55, 149; *2:* 329–31

    separation of powers and, *1:* 22, 147, 149; *2:* 234–35, 329

    War Powers Resolution and, *1:* 80–82

Defence of the Constitutions of Government of the United States, 2: 220–21, 228–29, 230

defense. *See* military

Defense, Department of, *1:* 50, 97–99, 142; *2:* 323. *See also* War, Department of

defense, secretary of, *1:* 97–99, 108–9

DeLay, Tom, *2:* 274 (ill.), 288

Delolme, Jean Louis, *1:* 25, 27–28

democracy

    class and, *1:* 133; *2:* 206, 311

    elections and, *1:* 46; *2:* 255–57

    Federal Convention and, *1:* 133; *2:* 255–56, 311

    French Revolution and, *2:* 256

Montesquieu, Charles, on, *2:* 206–8

representation and, *2:* 206, 255–57

voting rights and, *2:* 226, 255–57

war and, *2:* 245

Democratic Caucus, *2:* 269, 271, 273, 274–75

Democratic Conference, *2:* 281

Democratic Federalist, *2:* 234

Democratic National Committee, *3:* 488

Democratic Party

  checks and balances and, *2:* 313

  elections and, *2:* 267

  income tax and, *2:* 254

  presidency and, *1:* 84, 85–86

  prohibition and, *2:* 258

Democratic-Republican Party

  election of 1800 and, *1:* 48, 66–67

  gerrymandering and, *2:* 302

  Marbury v. Madison and, *2:* 341–44; *3:* 497–98

  Sedition Act of 1798 and, *2:* 244

Department of Agriculture, *1:* 95–98

Department of Commerce, *1:* 97

Department of Defense, *1:* 50, 97–99, 142; *2:* 323. *See also* Department of War

Department of Education, *1:* 99

Department of Energy, *1:* 99

Department of Health & Human Services, *1:* 99–100

Department of Homeland Security, *1:* 100–101

Department of Housing & Urban Development, *1:* 101–2

Department of Justice. *See* Justice, Department of

Department of Labor, *1:* 102–3, 119

Department of State, *1:* 31, 50, 56, 73, 104–6

Department of the Interior, *1:* 102

Department of the Navy, *1:* 31, 98

Department of the Treasury. *See* Treasury, Department of the

Department of Transportation, *1:* 98, 106

Department of Veterans Affairs, *1:* 107

Department of War, *1:* 31, 97. *See also* Department of Defense

deputy attorney general, *1:* 102, 120, 121–22

Dickinson, John, *1:* 46

Discourses on the First Ten Books of Titus Livius, *2:* 200

discovery, *3:* 445–46, 447, 459

discretionary acts, *1:* 172; *2:* 347–48; *3:* 483, 504

discrimination. *See also* African Americans; race

  by Black Codes, *3:* 427

  in education, *1:* 99

  Fifteenth Amendment and, *2:* 256

  Fourteenth Amendment and, *2:* 345; *3:* 499–500, 500–501

  gerrymandering and, *2:* 302

  in housing, *1:* 101

  Interstate Commerce Clause and, *2:* 251–53

  in jury selection, *3:* 446

  in voting, *1:* 70–71; *3:* 427

dissenting opinions, *3:* 442, 448, 462, 467

Dissertation on the First Principles of Government, *2:* 226

District of Columbia. *See* Washington, D.C.

Double Jeopardy Clause, *1:* 65, 168; *3:* 422, 480

Douglas, William O., *1:* 166; *2:* 252; *3:* 439 (ill.), 511

Drug Enforcement Agency, *1:* 123–24

drugs, *1:* 75, 100, 107, 123–24

dual service, *3:* 442

Due Process Clause

  in Fifth Amendment, *1:* 65, 168; *3:* 422, 430, 480–81

  in Fourteenth Amendment, *3:* 427, 430–31

East India Company, *1:* 39

Eckhardt, Christopher, *3:* 408–9

economy, *1:* 75, 82–83, 91; *2:* 299. *See also* commerce

Edmunds, George, *2:* 254

education, *2:* 201

Education, Department of, *1:* 99

education, secretary of, *1:* 99

Eighteenth Amendment, *1:* lv–lvi; *2:* 258–59, lv–lvi; *3:* lv–lvi

Eighth Amendment, *1:* lii; *2:* lii; *3:* lii
   civil liberties and, *1:* 16; *2:* 194; *3:* 375
   criminal law and, *3:* 423
   judicial power and, *3:* 423
   legislative power and, *1:* 6; *2:* 185, 245–46; *3:* 364

elections. *See also* electoral system; voting rights
   campaign finance reform and, *1:* 85; *2:* 288
   campaigning for, *2:* 268, 303–5
   casework and, *2:* 303
   class and, *2:* 226–29, 255–57
   congressional, *1:* 131; *2:* 223–24, 226–29, 255–57, 265–66, 267–68, 276–77, 303–5, 309, 312–13, 337; *3:* 493
   under Constitution, *2:* 226–29
   democracy and, *1:* 46; *2:* 255–57
   Democratic Party and, *2:* 267
   Federal Convention and, *1:* 46; *2:* 226–29
   First Amendment and, *1:* 85
   gender and, *1:* 84–85
   House of Representatives and, *2:* 202, 208
   incumbency and, *2:* 268
   instant runoff, *1:* 87
   judicial, *3:* 433
   legislative branch and, *2:* 226–29
   lobbying and, *2:* 268
   monarchy and, *1:* 46–47
   money and, *1:* 85
   political parties and, *1:* 85–86, 87; *2:* 267
   popular, *1:* 87
   presidential, *1:* 13–14, 46–48, 66–69, 91; *2:* 191–92, 257, 286; *3:* 371–72
   property and, *2:* 256
   proportional representation and, *2:* 267
   representation and, *2:* 226–29
   Republican Party and, *2:* 267

   Senate and, *2:* 202
   Seventeenth Amendment and, *2:* 255–57
   of 2000, *1:* 13–14; *2:* 191–92; *3:* 371–72, 464–65
   vice presidential, *1:* 47–48, 58, 66–69, 93–94

electoral system, *1:* 47–48, 66–69, 87; *3:* 464–65. *See also* elections

Eleventh Amendment, *1:* lii; *2:* 348, lii; *3:* 403, 423–24, 505, lii

Elk Grove Unified School District v. Newdow, 1: 15–16; *2:* 193–94; *3:* 374

Ellsworth, Oliver, *2:* 236

Emerson, John, *3:* 500

Employee Standards Administration, *1:* 103

en banc review, *3:* 445, 461

Energy, Department of, *1:* 99

energy policy, *3:* 476–77

energy, secretary of, *1:* 99

English Bill of Rights, *1:* 24–25

Environmental Hearings Board, *1:* 125

environmental law, *2:* 251

Environmental Protection Agency, *1:* 107, 124–25, 169–70; *3:* 482

Equal Protection Clause, *2:* 345; *3:* 427, 430–31, 464–65, 499–500

equity, *3:* 385, 386, 402

espionage, *1:* 124

Espionage Act of 1917, *2:* 244–45

Establishment Clause, *1:* 15–16, 76; *2:* 193–94; *3:* 374

Evans, Donald, *1:* 8 (ill.)

evidence, *3:* 446, 457, 460

ex post facto laws, *1:* 6; *2:* 184–85, 205; *3:* 364

Excellencie of a Free-State, 2: 199

exclusionary rule
   Fourteenth Amendment and, *3:* 457
   search and seizure and, *1:* 165; *3:* 421–22, 457, 479
   self-incrimination and, *1:* 168; *3:* 480

executive agencies. *See also* administrative law; executive departments; specific agencies

appointment to, *1:* 109, 124, 125, 144; *2:* 323–24

growth of, *1:* 73–74

heads of, *1:* 144; *2:* 324

judicial interpretation and, *1:* 169–71; *3:* 481–82

law enforcement by, *1:* 7–8, 169–71; *2:* 186; *3:* 365–66, 482

legislative veto and, *1:* 139; *2:* 319

oversight of, *2:* 297

overview of, *1:* 109, 124

regulatory power of, *1:* 7; *2:* 186; *3:* 365–66

executive agreements, *1:* 147; *2:* 328

executive branch. *See also* executive agencies; executive departments; executive power; president; specific departments and agencies; vice president

checks and balances and, *2:* 222

in Constitution, *1:* 1; *2:* 179; *3:* 359

constitutional amendments and, *1:* 61–62

future of, *1:* 83–87

historic roots of, *1:* 19–35, 39

iron triangles and, *2:* 292

issue networks and, *2:* 292

law enforcement by, *3:* 419–22

oversight of, *1:* 150–51; *2:* 331

overview of, *1:* 7–12, 19, 37, 61–62; *2:* 185–90; *3:* 365–70

separation of powers and, *1:* 131–32, 159–60; *2:* 199–200, 203, 209, 309–10; *3:* 473–74, 488–89

executive bureaus, *1:* 109

executive departments. *See also* administrative law; executive agencies; specific departments

appointment to, *1:* 95, 144; *2:* 323–24

in Constitution, *1:* 7, 50; *2:* 186; *3:* 365–66

growth of, *1:* 73–74

heads of, *1:* 7–8, 95, 144; *2:* 186, 324; *3:* 366

historic roots of, *1:* 31

law enforcement by, *1:* 7–8, 119; *2:* 186; *3:* 365–66

oversight of, *2:* 297

overview of, *1:* 7, 37, 95; *2:* 186; *3:* 365–66

regulatory power of, *1:* 7; *2:* 186; *3:* 365–66

removal from, *1:* 146; *2:* 325–26

Executive Office of the President, *1:* 72, 74–75, 107–9

executive orders, *1:* 75–77, 114

executive power. *See also* executive branch; specific powers

in American colonies, *1:* 28–29

Articles of Confederation and, *1:* 31–35, 39

checks and balances and, *1:* 45–46

commerce and, *1:* 38–39

in Constitution, *1:* 48–49

Continental Congress and, *1:* 37–39

Delolme, Jean Louis, on, *1:* 27–28

Federal Convention and, *1:* 41–45

foreign relations and, *1:* 11, 55–57; *2:* 190; *3:* 369

in Great Britain, *1:* 22–25, 45–46

Hamilton, Alexander, on, *1:* 49

historic roots of, *1:* 21–22; *2:* 199

judicial interpretation and, *1:* 169–71; *3:* 481–82

judicial review and, *1:* 161–69; *3:* 475–78

limits on, *1:* 11–12; *2:* 189–90; *3:* 369–70

Locke, John, on, *1:* 49

military and, *1:* 54–55

overview of, *1:* 7–12, 89–91; *2:* 185–90; *3:* 365–70

political philosophers on, *1:* 25–28

in Roman Republic, *1:* 21–22

search and seizure and, *3:* 419–22

separation of powers and, *3:* 397–400

executive privilege, *2:* 321 (ill.)

checks and balances and, *1:* 173–76; *3:* 486–87

Cheney, Dick, and, *3:* 476–77

in Constitution, *3:* 488

judicial branch and, *1:* 173–76; *3:* 486–87

judicial review and, *3:* 488–89

legislative oversight and, *1:* 151; *2:* 331

military and, *3:* 488–89

national security and, *3:* 488–89

Nixon, Richard M., and, *1:* 78–79; *3:* 488–89

overview of, *1:* 77–79

separation of powers and, *3:* 476–77, 488–89

Fauntroy, Walter E., *2:* 286

Federal Aviation Administration, *1:* 73, 106

federal budget

    appropriations power and, *2:* 301

    balanced budget amendment, *2:* 261–62, 272

    committees and, *2:* 299–301

    impoundment and, *1:* 141; *2:* 320–22

    legislative branch and, *1:* 72–73, 108; *2:* 316

    legislative power and, *2:* 299–301

    line item veto and, *2:* 316

    Office of Management and Budget and, *1:* 72–73, 75, 108; *2:* 300

    president and, *1:* 11, 72–73, 114; *2:* 188–89, 299–301, 316; *3:* 368

    reprogramming and, *1:* 142–43; *2:* 322–23

Federal Bureau of Investigation, *1:* 50, 64, 120

Federal Convention, *1:* 43 (ill.); *3:* 362 (ill.). *See also* Constitution; Founding Fathers

    bicameralism and, *2:* 198–99, 223–24

    Bill of Rights and, *2:* 239–40

    checks and balances and, *1:* 45–46, 133, 160–61; *2:* 217–18, 222–23, 310–14, 339; *3:* 474–75, 495

    class and, *1:* 133; *2:* 198–99, 217–19, 226–29, 311

    commerce and, *2:* 218–19, 230–32, 239

    Committee of Detail of, *3:* 398

    Congress and, *2:* 197–99, 312

    Connecticut Compromise, *2:* 224

    democracy and, *1:* 133; *2:* 206, 255–56, 311

    elections and, *1:* 46; *2:* 226–29

    executive branch and, *1:* 41–45

    judicial review and, *1:* 6; *2:* 185, 340; *3:* 365, 411–12, 496

    legality of, *1:* 42–43

    military and, *2:* 232–35, 239

    monarchy and, *1:* 19–20

    original intent of, *3:* 410

    overview of, *1:* 4; *2:* 182; *3:* 362

    pardon power and, *1:* 51

    political philosophers and, *1:* 25–28; *2:* 201–8

    preamble and, *3:* 398–99

    property and, *2:* 239

    purpose of, *2:* 197–98, 217–19; *3:* 396–97

    representation and, *2:* 223–26

    resolution for, *1:* 35, 41; *3:* 396

    seat of government and, *2:* 220

    separation of powers and, *1:* 41–45; *2:* 219–22; *3:* 397–402

    Shays's Rebellion and, *1:* 41

    slavery and, *2:* 218–19, 225–26

    states at, *1:* 4; *2:* 182, 197–98, 223–24; *3:* 361, 362

    taxation and, *2:* 231–32, 235–36

    vice president and, *2:* 277

    Virginia Plan, *1:* 47; *2:* 223–24

    voting rights and, *2:* 226–29

    war powers and, *1:* 148–49; *2:* 329

federal district courts

    admiralty and, *3:* 417

    bankruptcy and, *3:* 432, 460

    civil cases in, *3:* 417, 432, 435, 459–60

    clerk of the court of, *3:* 449–50

    creation of, *3:* 416–17

    criminal cases in, *3:* 417, 432, 435, 456–59

    error in, *3:* 461

    growth of, *3:* 425, 428–29

    historic roots of, *3:* 387

    judges of, *3:* 445–47, 448

    Judicial Conference of the United States and, *3:* 469

law clerks at, *3:* 448–49

magistrate judges of, *3:* 447–48

motions in, *3:* 449

organization of, *3:* 432, 435, 445, 455–56

overview of, *1:* 13; *2:* 191; *3:* 371, 379, 435, 455–56

Schiavo case and, *3:* 381

trials in, *3:* 416–17, 428–29, 432, 435, 445–47, 455–60

work of, *3:* 429–32

Federal Highway Administration, *1:* 106

Federal Housing Administration, *1:* 101

Federal Judicial Center, *3:* 440, 469–70

Federal Magistrates Act, *3:* 447

Federal Motor Carrier Safety Administration, *1:* 106

federal public defenders, *3:* 450

federal question jurisdiction, *2:* 355; *3:* 512

Federal Railroad Administration, *1:* 106

Federal Reporter, 3: 451

Federal Supplement, 3: 451–52

Federal Trade Commission, *1:* 127–28

Federal Transit Administration, *1:* 106

Federalist, 3: 401 (ill.)

    on checks and balances, *2:* 222

    on commerce, *2:* 232

    on elections, *2:* 228

    on federal government, *2:* 229–30

    on foreign relations, *2:* 229–30

    on high crimes and misdemeanors, *1:* 154; *2:* 333

    on judicial branch, *3:* 400–402

    on judicial review, *2:* 340; *3:* 412, 496

    on military, *2:* 234

    on Necessary and Proper Clause, *2:* 237

    purpose of, *2:* 219

    on representation, *2:* 228

    on separation of powers, *1:* 43–44; *2:* 219–20; *3:* 400–402

Federalist Party

    Bill of Rights and, *2:* 241–43; *3:* 418

    commerce and, *2:* 241

    Constitution and, *2:* 240–42; *3:* 418

    election of 1800 and, *1:* 48, 66–67, 68–69

    gerrymandering and, *2:* 302

    judicial branch and, *3:* 416–17

    Marbury v. Madison and, *2:* 341–44; *3:* 497–98

    Sedition Act of 1798 and, *2:* 244

    state power and, *3:* 423–24

    Supreme Court and, *3:* 425

felonies

    congresspersons and, *1:* 131–32; *2:* 309–10

    as infamous crime, *1:* 166–67; *3:* 480

    Speech and Debate Clause and, *2:* 337; *3:* 493

Ferraro, Geraldine, *1:* 84

Field, Stephen J., *2:* 254–55; *3:* 425, 426 (ill.)

Fiers, Alan, *1:* 153

Fifteenth Amendment, *1:* 70, lv; *2:* 256, lv; *3:* 426–28, lv

Fifth Amendment, *1:* 64–65, 165–68, li; *2:* li; *3:* 422, 479–81, li

filibuster, *1:* 145; *2:* 293–94, 325

fines, *3:* 423

First Amendment, *1:* l–li; *2:* l–li; *3:* l–li

    campaign finance and, *2:* 288

    civil liberties and, *1:* 16; *2:* 194; *3:* 374

    elections and, *1:* 85

    Espionage Act of 1917 and, *2:* 244–45

    freedom of religion under, *3:* 388

    freedom of speech under, *1:* 122–23

    judicial review and, *1:* 15–16; *2:* 193–94; *3:* 374

    legislative power and, *1:* 6; *2:* 185, 243; *3:* 364

    Office of Faith-Based and Community Initiatives and, *1:* 76

    prosecution and, *1:* 165–68; *3:* 479–81

    protest and, *3:* 408–9

    Sedition Act of 1798 and, *2:* 244

first lady, *1:* 103

Fish and Wildlife Service, *1:* 102

floor procedure, *2:* 293–95

floors, personnel, *1:* 143; *2:* 323

Floyd, John B., *2:* 187 (ill.)

Food and Drug Administration, *1:* 73, 74, 100

Ford, Betty, *1:* 116

Ford, Gerald, *1:* 53 (ill.), 56 (ill.), 96 (ill.), 117 (ill.)
    pardons by, *1:* 52, 53, 96
    as president, *1:* 96, 116–17
    Rockefeller, Nelson, and, *1:* 95
    as vice president, *1:* 96

foreign relations. *See also* treaties
    executive privilege and, *1:* 77
    Federalist on, *2:* 229–30
    Hamilton, Alexander, on, *2:* 229–30
    president in, *1:* 11, 55–57, 113; *2:* 189; *3:* 369
    Senate and, *2:* 280
    State, Department of, and, *1:* 56, 104–6
    vice president and, *1:* 94, 118

formulary system, *3:* 384

Fortas, Abe, *3:* 408–9, 439 (ill.), 511

Founding Fathers, *3:* 362 (ill.), 431 (ill.). *See also* Federal Convention
    checks and balances and, *2:* 312
    Congress and, *2:* 312
    democracy and, *2:* 206, 255–56
    education of, *2:* 201
    original intent of, *3:* 410
    separation of powers and, *3:* 397–402
    vice president and, *2:* 277

Fourteenth Amendment, *1:* liii–liv; *2:* liii–liv; *3:* liii–liv
    American Declaration of Independence and, *3:* 431
    civil liberties and, *2:* 252–53; *3:* 430–31
    Civil Rights Act of 1875 and, *2:* 251
    Civil Rights Act of 1964 and, *2:* 252–53
    discrimination and, *2:* 345; *3:* 499–500, 500–501
    exclusionary rule and, *3:* 457
    freedom of religion under, *3:* 388
    inalienable rights in, *3:* 430–31

judicial interpretation and, *2:* 345; *3:* 499–500
    judicial power and, *3:* 426–28
    ratification of, *2:* 348; *3:* 427, 505

Fourth Amendment, *1:* li; *2:* li; *3:* li
    checks and balances and, *1:* 163–65; *3:* 478–79
    civil liberties and, *1:* 16; *2:* 194; *3:* 374–75
    judicial power and, *3:* 419–22
    judicial review and, *1:* 163–65; *3:* 478–79
    law enforcement and, *1:* 64, 163–65; *3:* 478–79
    search and seizure and, *1:* 63–64; *3:* 419–22

Frank, Barney, *1:* 123

Franklin, Benjamin, *1:* 29; *2:* 214, 214 (ill.); *3:* 388, 389 (ill.)

free speech. *See* freedom of speech

freedom of assembly
    civil liberties and, *1:* 16; *2:* 194; *3:* 374
    legislative power and, *1:* 6; *2:* 185; *3:* 364

Freedom of Information Act, *1:* 173–74; *3:* 486–87

freedom of religion
    civil liberties and, *1:* 16; *2:* 194; *3:* 374
    history of, *3:* 388–89
    judicial review and, *1:* 15–16; *2:* 193–94; *3:* 374
    legislative power and, *1:* 6; *2:* 185, 243; *3:* 364

freedom of speech
    campaign finance and, *2:* 288
    civil liberties and, *1:* 16; *2:* 194; *3:* 374
    Espionage Act of 1917 and, *2:* 244–45
    legislative power and, *1:* 6; *2:* 185, 243; *3:* 364
    protest and, *1:* 122–23; *3:* 408–9
    regulation of, *2:* 243
    Sedition Act of 1798 and, *2:* 244

French Revolution, *2:* 244, 256

friendly suits, *2:* 346–47; *3:* 503

Frist, Bill, *2:* 294 (ill.)

Gandhi, Indira, *1:* 84

Garfield, James A., *1:* 136; *2:* 315–16

Garner, John Nance, *1:* 93; *2:* 188 (ill.)

gender, *1:* 84–85. *See also* women

George, Clair, *1:* 153

George III, *1:* 30 (ill.)

    American Declaration of Independence and, *1:* 22, 30, 32–34; *2:* 208

    executive power and, *1:* 38

    military of, *2:* 234

    presidency and, *1:* 47

Gerry, Elbridge, *1:* 55 (ill.); *3:* 411 (ill.)

    Bill of Rights and, *2:* 239–40

    in Continental Congress, *2:* 217

    gerrymandering by, *2:* 302

    on judicial review, *3:* 411–12

    military power and, *1:* 54

gerrymandering, *2:* 302, 302 (ill.)

Gibbons v. Ogden, 2: 250

Gingrich, Newt, *2:* 272–73, 273 (ill.)

Ginsburg, Douglas H., *2:* 352, 353 (ill.)

Ginsburg, Ruth Bader, *1:* 84

Glorious Revolution, *1:* 24, 26

Goldberg, Arthur J., *2:* 252–53

Gonzalez, Henry, *1:* 153

Gore, Al, *2:* 279 (ill.)

    election of 2000 and, *1:* 13–14, 66; *2:* 191–92; *3:* 371–72, 464–65

    as vice president, *1:* 103

Gore, Tipper, *2:* 279 (ill.)

Government Printing Office, *2:* 305

grand juries, *1:* 65, 165–68; *3:* 422, 457, 479–80. *See also* juries

Grant, Ulysses S., *3:* 426

Great Britain

American colonies and, *3:* 386–87

    checks and balances in, *1:* 31

    commerce and, *1:* 38–39; *2:* 231, 249

    executive power in, *1:* 22–25, 45–46

    freedom of religion in, *3:* 389

    judiciary in, *3:* 384–85

    legislative power in, *2:* 208–11

    military of, *2:* 234

    monarchy in, *1:* 22–25, 45–46

    separation of powers in, *1:* 22–23

    tyrants in, *1:* 22–25

Great Depression, *1:* 82, 174; *2:* 258

Grenada, *1:* 149; *2:* 331

Guam, *2:* 236

Guarantee Clause, *1:* 22

Haig, Alexander, *1:* 104–5, 105 (ill.), 119 (ill.)

Haig, Patricia, *1:* 119 (ill.)

Halonen, Tarja, *1:* 84

Hamilton, Alexander, *1:* 74 (ill.); *2:* 229 (ill.)

    Bank of the United States and, *2:* 247

    on commerce, *2:* 229–30, 231, 247

    Constitution and, *2:* 241

    Delolme, Jean Louis, and, *1:* 27

    on elections, *1:* 46

    on executive power, *1:* 49

    on federal government, *2:* 229–30

    Federalist and, *2:* 219; *3:* 400

    on foreign relations, *2:* 229–30

    on high crimes and misdemeanors, *1:* 154; *2:* 333

    on judicial branch, *3:* 400–402

    on judicial review, *2:* 340; *3:* 412, 496

    on military, *2:* 229, 234

    on Necessary and Proper Clause, *2:* 237, 246–47

    on pardon power, *1:* 51

    on representation, *2:* 224

as secretary of the treasury, *2:* 247

on separation of powers, *3:* 400–402

on taxation, *2:* 231–32

Hancock, John, *1:* 39

happiness, *3:* 430

Harding, Warren G., *2:* 245

Harlan, John Marshall, *3:* 439 (ill.), 467, 467 (ill.)

Harrison, Benjamin, *1:* 87

Harrison, William Henry, *1:* 75, 92

Hartzok, Alanna, *2:* 267

Hastert, Dennis, *2:* 189 (ill.), 274 (ill.)

Hastings, Alcee L., *2:* 354; *3:* 509 (ill.), 510

Hawaii, *2:* 355; *3:* 510

Hayes, George, *3:* 502 (ill.)

Hayes, Rutherford B., *1:* 87

Haynsworth, Clement, Jr., *1:* 17; *2:* 195, 349 (ill.); *3:* 376

Health & Human Services, Department of, *1:* 99–100

health & human services, secretary of, *1:* 99–100

Health Resources and Services Administration, *1:* 100

Heart of Atlanta Motel v. United States, *2:* 251–53, 252 (ill.)

Henry, Patrick, *2:* 232; *3:* 389

Heston, Charlton, *2:* 269 (ill.)

high crimes and misdemeanors
Federalist on, *1:* 154; *2:* 333
as impeachable offense, *1:* 5, 91, 154; *2:* 182–84, 333, 353–54; *3:* 363, 437, 508–9

Hill, Anita F., *2:* 352–53

Hinckley, John, *1:* 104

Holt, Joseph, *2:* 187 (ill.)

Homeland Security, Department of, *1:* 100–101, 144; *2:* 324–25

homeland security, secretary of, *1:* 100

Hoover, Herbert, *2:* 258

Hoover, J. Edgar, *1:* 121 (ill.)

House Appropriations Committee, *2:* 286, 293, 301

House Committee on Homeland Security, *2:* 298–99

House Government Reform Committee, *2:* 286

House of Commons, *1:* 22; *2:* 208–9, 284

House of Lords, *1:* 22; *2:* 208–9, 210

House of Representatives, *2:* 268 (ill.). *See also* Congress; legislative branch; legislative power; representatives

apportionment of, *1:* 3; *2:* 181; *3:* 361

calendars of, *2:* 293

campaigning and, *2:* 268

casework in, *2:* 267, 275, 301–3

checks and balances and, *2:* 312–13

class and, *2:* 226–28, 312–13

committees of, *2:* 266–67, 270, 271, 275, 286, 290–93, 297–99, 299–301

composition of, *1:* 3; *2:* 181, 265–76; *3:* 361

in Constitution, *1:* 1, 3–5; *2:* 179, 181–85, 223–24, 265; *3:* 359, 361–64

debate in, *2:* 271, 293–95, 337; *3:* 493

Democratic Caucus in, *2:* 269, 271, 273, 274–75

districts covered by, *2:* 265, 267, 283, 301, 302, 305

election to, *1:* 131; *2:* 202, 208, 223–24, 226–28, 256, 265–66, 267–68, 303–5, 309, 312, 337; *3:* 493

electoral system and, *1:* 48, 67, 68–69

executive privilege and, *1:* 77

floor procedure in, *2:* 293, 295

impeachment by, *1:* 5, 58–59, 91, 151–55, 172; *2:* 182–84, 332–33, 354; *3:* 363, 412, 437, 484, 509–10, 511

legislation and, *2:* 266, 289

lobbying and, *2:* 268, 275, 283–88

majority leader of, *2:* 270–71, 274, 293

majority party in, *2:* 269–70, 271, 272–73, 291

minority leader of, *2:* 271–72, 274

minority party in, *2:* 291

powers exclusive to, *1:* 5; *2:* 182–84; *3:* 363

powers shared with Senate, *1:* 4–5; *2:* 181–82; *3:* 361–63

proportional representation in, *2:* 267

qualifications to serve in, *2:* 228, 265–66, 337; *3:* 493

redistricting for, *1:* 3; *2:* 181; *3:* 361

removal from, *1:* 154–55; *2:* 333

Republican Conference in, *2:* 269, 271, 273, 274–75

rules of, *1:* 131, 155; *2:* 309, 333, 337; *3:* 493

slavery and, *2:* 226

Speaker of the House in, *2:* 269–70, 270–71, 293

staff for, *2:* 275–76, 301–3

terms in, *2:* 228, 259–61, 272, 303

treaties and, *1:* 147; *2:* 327

voting in, *1:* 133–34; *2:* 265, 271, 314

whips in, *2:* 273–74

work of, *2:* 265–76

House Rules Committee, *2:* 270, 293

House Ways and Means Committee, *2:* 301

Housing & Urban Development, Department of, *1:* 101–2

housing & urban development, secretary of, *1:* 101

Houston, E. & W. Tex. Ry. v. United States, 2: 251

Houston, Thomas, *3:* 391

Hughes, Charles Evans, *3:* 462, 462 (ill.)

Hume, David, *2:* 206, 207 (ill.)

Humphreys, West H., *1:* 5; *2:* 183–84; *3:* 363

hung jury, *3:* 459

Hussein, Saddam, *1:* 122

Ickes, Harold, *1:* 175, 175 (ill.)

immigration. *See* naturalization

impeachment

    checks and balances and, *1:* 11–12, 17–18, 151–55, 172–73; *2:* 190, 195–96, 332–33, 353–54; *3:* 369, 376, 483–85, 508–10

    chief justice role in, *1:* 151–52, 152–53, 172–73; *2:* 332–33; *3:* 413, 440, 483–85

    of congresspersons, *1:* 154–55; *2:* 333

    federal courts and, *1:* 159–60; *3:* 473

    House of Representatives and, *1:* 91

    of judges, *1:* 17–18, 146, 159, 173; *2:* 195–96, 327, 338, 353–54; *3:* 376, 413, 433, 437–38, 444, 445, 473, 485, 494, 508–10, 511

    judicial power and, *3:* 412–13

    offenses covered by, *1:* 5, 51, 91, 153–54, 159; *2:* 182–84, 333, 353–54; *3:* 363, 437, 473, 508–9

    overview of, *1:* 5, 58–59, 172; *2:* 182–84; *3:* 363, 483–85

    pardon power and, *1:* 51

    of president, *1:* 5, 11–12, 58–59, 91, 138, 159–60, 172–73; *2:* 184, 190, 318; *3:* 363, 369, 412–13, 440, 473–74, 484–85

    Senate and, *1:* 91

    vice president role in, *1:* 152–53, 172; *2:* 332; *3:* 413, 484–85

    Watergate scandal and, *1:* 52

imports, *2:* 253–54, 255. *See also* commerce

impoundment, *1:* 141; *2:* 320–22, 321 (ill.)

inalienable rights, *3:* 430–31, 500. *See also* civil liberties

income tax, *2:* 253–55, 346–47, 350–51, 351 (ill.); *3:* 503. *See also* taxation

incumbency, *2:* 268

independent regulatory commissions. *See also* regulatory power; specific commissions

    appointment to, *1:* 127, 144; *2:* 324

    removal from, *1:* 146; *2:* 326–27

    work of, *1:* 73–74, 109, 127

Independents, *2:* 275

Indian Health Service, *1:* 100

indictments, *3:* 457

Industrial Revolution, *2:* 250, 254

infamous crimes, *1:* 65, 165–68; *3:* 422, 479–80

INS v. Chadha, 1: 139, 141, 142; *2:* 319, 322, 323

instant runoff voting, *1:* 87

Interior, Department of the, *1:* 102

interior, secretary of the, *1:* 102

Internal Revenue Code, *3:* 458

Internal Revenue Service, *1:* 107, 119

International Space Station, *1:* 126

Interstate Commerce Clause, *1:* 2; *2:* 180, 249–53; *3:* 360

involuntary servitude, *3:* 466–67. *See also* slavery

Iran-Contra scandal, *1:* 52, 152–53, 176; *2:* 298; *3:* 490

Iraq, *1:* 122–23

iron triangles, *2:* 292

issue networks, *2:* 292

Istook, Ernest, *2:* 262

Jackson, Andrew, *1:* 69, 137; *2:* 311 (ill.)

Jacobson, Henning, *3:* 399

Jacobson v. Massachusetts, *3:* 399

James II, *1:* 23, 24–25

Jaworski, Leon, *3:* 488

Jay, John, *2:* 219, 231; *3:* 400

Jefferson, Thomas, *1:* 44 (ill.), 74 (ill.); *2:* 248 (ill.); *3:* 389 (ill.), 421 (ill.)

   American Declaration of Independence and, *1:* 30, 32; *3:* 430

   appointment power of, *3:* 425

   Bank of the United States and, *2:* 247

   Bill of Rights and, *2:* 242

   Chase, Samuel, and, *1:* 18; *2:* 196; *3:* 376, 511

   on Constitution, *3:* 420

   election of, *1:* 48, 66–67, 68–69, 93

   executive orders of, *1:* 76

   on freedom of religion, *3:* 388, 389

   Library of Congress and, *2:* 305

   Marbury v. Madison and, *1:* 162; *2:* 341–42; *3:* 476–77, 497

   Necessary and Proper Clause and, *2:* 247

   Sedition Act of 1798 and, *2:* 244

   on separation of powers, *1:* 44–45

   slavery and, *2:* 232

   State of the Union address of, *1:* 9; *2:* 187; *3:* 367

Jet Propulsion Laboratory, *1:* 126

John, king of England, *1:* 23 (ill.), 23–24

Johnson, Andrew

   appointment power of, *3:* 425–26

   impeachment of, *1:* 5, 59, 91, 138, 173; *2:* 184, 318; *3:* 363, 440, 485

   pardons by, *1:* 52–53

   Reconstruction and, *3:* 425–26

   as senator, *3:* 442

   veto power and, *1:* 72, 138; *2:* 318

Johnson, Lyndon B., *1:* 149, 150 (ill.); *2:* 329

Johnson Space Center, *1:* 126

Joint Chiefs of Staff, Office of, *1:* 98, 109

Joint Committee on Taxation, *2:* 299

joint committees, *2:* 270, 299. *See also* conference committees

Joint Economic Committee, *2:* 299

judex, *3:* 384

judges. *See also* justices, Supreme Court

   appearance of impropriety of, *3:* 476–77

   appointment of, *2:* 277, 349–50; *3:* 413, 425, 433, 439, 443, 445, 458, 506

   of circuit courts of appeals, *3:* 443, 448

   compensation of, *2:* 338; *3:* 413, 437, 440, 443, 445, 447, 458, 494

   decision-making by, *3:* 444–45, 461–62

   election of, *3:* 433

   fairness of, *3:* 382

   of federal district courts, *3:* 445–47, 448

   good behavior of, *2:* 338; *3:* 413, 437, 443, 445, 494

   historic roots of, *3:* 383–84

   impeachment of, *1:* 173; *2:* 353–54; *3:* 413, 433, 437–38, 444, 445, 485, 508–10, 511

   law clerks for, *3:* 448–49

   of legislative courts, *3:* 458

   magistrate, *3:* 447–48

   recusal of, *3:* 476–77

   removal of, *3:* 413, 433, 444, 445, 458, 462

   term limits for, *3:* 433

   work of, *3:* 444–45, 445–47, 455–62

judgment, *3:* 445–46, 447. *See also* verdicts

judicial branch. *See also* specific courts

administration of, *3:* 440, 468–70

in American colonies, *3:* 386–87

Anti-federalists and, *3:* 416–17

appeals in, *1:* 13; *2:* 191–92; *3:* 371–72

appointment to, *1:* 173, 174–75; *2:* 277; *3:* 485–86

Articles of Confederation and, *3:* 390–93, 395, 396

cases and controversies heard by, *1:* 14–15; *2:* 192–93; *3:* 373, 402–3

checks and balances and, *2:* 222, 339; *3:* 412, 495

Circuit Courts of Appeals Act of 1891 and, *3:* 429

composition of, *1:* 12–14; *2:* 190–92; *3:* 370–73, 379–81, 429–33, 435

in Constitution, *1:* 1; *2:* 179; *3:* 359, 395

Continental Congress and, *3:* 390

executive privilege and, *1:* 173–76; *3:* 486–87

Federalist on, *3:* 400–402

Federalist Party and, *3:* 416–17

Great Britain and, *3:* 384–85

Hamilton, Alexander, on, *3:* 400–402

historic roots of, *3:* 379–93, 395–97

judicial interpretation and, *1:* 15; *2:* 193; *3:* 373–74

judicial review and, *1:* 15; *2:* 193–94; *3:* 374–75

Judiciary Act of 1789 and, *3:* 416–18

Judiciary Act of 1869 and, *3:* 428–29

Judiciary Act of 1875 and, *3:* 429

legislative branch and, *3:* 424–25, 429

legislative power over, *3:* 402, 404–5, 415–18

limits on, *1:* 16–18; *2:* 194–96; *3:* 375–76

overview of, *1:* 12–18; *2:* 190–96; *3:* 370–76, 379–81, 455

pardon power and, *1:* 176; *3:* 487–90

powers of, *1:* 14–16; *2:* 192–94; *3:* 370–76

Roman Republic and, *3:* 382–84

separation of powers and, *1:* 159–60; *2:* 337–38; *3:* 397–402, 413, 473–74, 488–89, 493–94

in states, *3:* 387–90, 418, 424

trials in, *1:* 13; *2:* 191; *3:* 371

Judicial Conference of the United States, *3:* 440, 469

judicial interpretation. *See also* judicial review

administrative law and, *1:* 169–71; *3:* 481–82

checks and balances and, *1:* 169–71; *2:* 344–45; *3:* 481–82, 498–500

in circuit courts of appeals, *3:* 462

constitutional amendment and, *3:* 500–501

executive agencies and, *1:* 169–71; *3:* 481–82

executive power and, *1:* 169–71; *3:* 481–82

Fourteenth Amendment and, *2:* 345; *3:* 499–500

legislative branch and, *2:* 344–45; *3:* 498–500

limits on, *2:* 345–48; *3:* 500–504

original intent and, *3:* 410

overview of, *1:* 15; *2:* 193; *3:* 373–74, 409–11

judicial power. *See also* cases and controversies; judicial interpretation; judicial review

appeals, *3:* 407–9

Bill of Rights and, *3:* 418–23

checks and balances and, *2:* 348–54, 354–55; *3:* 369–70, 504–10, 510–12

in Constitution, *2:* 339; *3:* 495

constitutional amendments and, *2:* 348–49; *3:* 504–5

Eighth Amendment and, *3:* 423

Eleventh Amendment and, *3:* 423–24

Fifteenth Amendment and, *3:* 426–28

Fifth Amendment and, *3:* 422

Fourteenth Amendment and, *3:* 426–28

Fourth Amendment and, *3:* 419–22

impeachment and, *3:* 412–13

Judiciary Act of 1789 and, *3:* 416–19

Judiciary Act of 1869 and, *3:* 428–29

Judiciary Act of 1875 and, *3:* 429

legislation and, *2:* 349; *3:* 506

limits on, *1:* 16–18; *2:* 194–96, 345–48; *3:* 375–76, 500–504

overview of, *1:* 14–16; *2:* 192–94; *3:* 370–76, 405–13

Seventh Amendment and, *3:* 422–23

Sixth Amendment and, *3:* 422

Thirteenth Amendment and, *3:* 426–28

trials, *3:* 406–7

writs of habeas corpus and, *3:* 409

judicial review. *See also* judicial interpretation

Anti-federalists and, *3:* 418

checks and balances and, *1:* 6–7, 15–16, 161–69; *2:* 185, 193–94, 339–44; *3:* 364–65, 374–75, 475–78, 495–98

in circuit courts of appeals, *3:* 462

civil liberties and, *3:* 427–28

Constitution and, *1:* 6; *2:* 185, 340, 342–44; *3:* 365, 411–12, 424, 495–96, 498

creation of, *1:* 161–63; *3:* 475–78

executive power and, *1:* 161–69; *3:* 475–78

executive privilege and, *3:* 488–89

Federal Convention and, *1:* 6; *2:* 185, 340; *3:* 365, 411–12, 496

Fourth Amendment and, *1:* 163–65; *3:* 478–79

Hamilton, Alexander, on, *2:* 340; *3:* 496

historic roots of, *3:* 386–87, 387–90

Judiciary Act of 1789 and, *3:* 424

legislative branch and, *2:* 339–44; *3:* 495–98

limits on, *2:* 345–48; *3:* 500–504

Marbury v. Madison and, *2:* 341–44; *3:* 424–25, 462, 497–98

overview of, *1:* 15; *2:* 193–94; *3:* 374–75, 411–12, 424–25

states and, *3:* 418, 424

Supremacy Clause and, *3:* 411, 412, 424

Judicial Watch, *3:* 476–77

Judiciary Act of 1789

judicial power and, *3:* 416–18

judicial review and, *3:* 424

Marbury v. Madison and, *1:* 162–63; *2:* 342–44; *3:* 424–25, 477–78, 497–98

overview of, *3:* 416–18

Supreme Court justices in, *2:* 351; *3:* 425, 437, 506

Judiciary Act of 1869, *3:* 428–29

Judiciary Act of 1875, *3:* 429

juries. *See also* grand juries

fairness of, *1:* 65, 168–69; *2:* 355; *3:* 382, 446, 481, 512

historic roots of, *3:* 384

selection of, *3:* 446, 457, 460

Sixth Amendment and, *1:* 16; *2:* 194; *3:* 375

trial by, *2:* 205, 355; *3:* 379, 406, 409, 422, 446–47, 457–59, 460, 510–12

jurisdiction. *See also* cases and controversies

appellate, *1:* 15; *2:* 193; *3:* 403, 404–5, 407–8, 415, 417–18, 432–33, 435

federal question, *2:* 355; *3:* 512

Marbury v. Madison and, *2:* 342–44; *3:* 497–98

original, *1:* 15; *2:* 193; *3:* 373, 403–4, 417, 424–25

overview of, *3:* 373

Justice, Department of

creation of, *1:* 50; *3:* 418

Federal Trade Commission and, *1:* 128

head of, *1:* 95, 119–20; *3:* 418

investigation by, *1:* 120

law enforcement by, *1:* 50, 64–65, 102, 119–24

U.S. attorneys in, *3:* 450

justices, Supreme Court, *3:* 372 (ill.), 439 (ill.), 463 (ill.). *See also* chief justice; judges; Supreme Court

appearance of impropriety of, *3:* 476–77

appointment of, *1:* 144–45; *2:* 324, 325, 349, 352–53; *3:* 413, 425, 433, 437, 439, 506

associate justices, *3:* 439, 440, 441–43, 462, 467

circuit court duties of, *3:* 417, 425, 429

compensation of, *3:* 413, 437, 440, 494

decision-making by, *2:* 352; *3:* 440–43, 448, 465–68, 507

election of, *3:* 433

good behavior of, *2:* 338; *3:* 413, 437, 494

impeachment of, *1:* 146, 173; *2:* 327, 338, 353–54; *3:* 413, 433, 437–38, 485, 494, 508–10, 511

law clerks for, *3:* 448

number of, *1:* 16, 174–75; *2:* 194, 351–52; *3:* 375, 417, 425–26, 436–37, 462, 506–7

opinions of, *3:* 441–43, 448, 451–52, 466–68

overview of, *3:* 436–43

recusal of, *3:* 476–77

removal of, *1:* 146; *2:* 327, 338; *3:* 413, 433, 437, 494

term limits for, *3:* 433

work of, *3:* 439–43

Justinian I, *3:* 383

Katzenbach v. McClung, 2: 251–53

Kennedy, Edward M., *2:* 281

Kennedy Space Center, *1:* 125, 126 (ill.)

Kensinger, John, II, *2:* 267

Kerik, Bernard, *1:* 144, 145 (ill.); *2:* 324–25

King, Rufus, *2:* 217; *3:* 411–12, 412 (ill.)

Kissinger, Henry A., *1:* 116

Klein, Joel, *3:* 451 (ill.)

Knox, Henry, *1:* 34, 42–43, 74 (ill.)

Korean War, *1:* 55

labor, *1:* 78–79, 166–67; *2:* 345; *3:* 466–67, 499

Labor, Department of, *1:* 102–3, 119

labor, secretary of, *1:* 102

Lamar, Lucius Q., *3:* 442

law clerks, *3:* 448–49

law enforcement

under Articles of Confederation, *1:* 48; *2:* 221

checks and balances and, *1:* 6, 12; *2:* 185, 190; *3:* 364, 369

by Congress (under the Articles of Confederation), *2:* 221

Constitution and, *1:* 49–50

Drug Enforcement Agency and, *1:* 123–24

by executive agencies, *1:* 7–8, 169–71; *2:* 186; *3:* 365–66, 482

by executive branch generally, *1:* 6, 7, 49–50; *2:* 185–86; *3:* 364, 365–66

by executive departments, *1:* 7–8; *2:* 186; *3:* 365–66

Fourth Amendment and, *1:* 64, 163–65; *3:* 419–22, 478–79

Justice, Department of, and, *1:* 50, 64–65, 102, 119–24

Magna Carta and, *1:* 24

ripeness and, *2:* 347; *3:* 503

Law of the Twelve Tables, *3:* 382–83

lawmaking. *See* legislation

lawsuits. *See* cases and controversies; trials

lawyers. *See* attorneys

Lazio, Rick, *1:* 103

League of Nations, *1:* 147; *2:* 290 (ill.), 327

legislation

under Articles of Confederation, *2:* 221

bills of attainder, *1:* 6; *2:* 184; *3:* 364

calendars for, *2:* 293

cases concerning, *2:* 346; *3:* 402, 415, 417–18, 501

checks and balances and, *1:* 16–17, 51–54; *2:* 194–95, 349; *3:* 375, 506

class and, *2:* 202

committees and, *2:* 266–67, 270, 271, 276, 290–93, 295–96, 299

Congress (under the Articles of Confederation) and, *2:* 221

congressional staff and, *2:* 275

debate on, *2:* 293–95

ex post facto laws, *1:* 6; *2:* 184–85; *3:* 364
filibuster and, *2:* 293–94
in Great Britain, *3:* 385
historic roots of, *3:* 382–83
House of Representatives and, *2:* 266, 289
introduction of, *2:* 289
judicial interpretation of, *3:* 409–11, 462
judicial power and, *2:* 349; *3:* 506
legislative oversight and, *2:* 297
lobbying and, *2:* 283–88
majority leader and, *2:* 271
minority leader and, *2:* 271
Montesquieu, Charles, on, *2:* 203–6
overview of, *1:* 4–5; *2:* 182, 265, 288–97; *3:* 363
reception provisions and, *3:* 387–90
recommendation power and, *1:* 11, 114; *2:* 189; *3:* 368–69
representatives and, *2:* 266
Senate and, *2:* 276, 289
Senate majority leader and, *2:* 280
senators and, *2:* 276
separation of powers and, *1:* 26, 28; *2:* 209; *3:* 400–402
Speaker of the House and, *2:* 270, 296
State of the Union address and, *1:* 51–52; *2:* 289
veto power and, *1:* 5, 52–54, 72, 114, 133–39; *2:* 182, 314–19; *3:* 363
vice president and, *1:* 115, 133–34; *2:* 277–78, 295, 296, 314
voting on, *2:* 295
whips and, *2:* 273–74, 281
legislative branch. *See also* Congress; legislative power
in American colonies, *2:* 211–15
checks and balances and, *2:* 209–10
class and, *2:* 201–2, 206, 214
democracy and, *2:* 206
separation of powers and, *2:* 199–200, 202–3
legislative courts, *3:* 458
legislative oversight, *1:* 150–51; *2:* 297, 331

legislative power. *See also* legislative branch; specific powers
Bill of Rights and, *1:* 6; *2:* 185, 239–46; *3:* 364
checks and balances and, *1:* 6–7; *2:* 185, 354–55; *3:* 364, 510–12
commerce and, *2:* 230–32
compensation and, *2:* 257–58
in Constitution, *1:* 2–3; *2:* 180–81; *3:* 360–61
constitutional amendments, *2:* 258–59
Eighteenth Amendment and, *2:* 258–59
Eighth Amendment and, *2:* 245–46
federal budget and, *2:* 261–62, 299–301
First Amendment and, *2:* 243
historic roots of, *1:* 21–22
Interstate Commerce Clause and, *2:* 249–53
judicial branch and, *3:* 402, 404–5, 415–18
legislative veto, *1:* 138–39, 141, 142–43; *2:* 318–19, 322, 323
liberty and, *2:* 205–6
life and, *2:* 205
limits on, *1:* 6–7; *2:* 185; *3:* 364–65
military and, *1:* 2; *2:* 180, 232–35; *3:* 360
money and, *1:* 2; *2:* 180, 232; *3:* 360
naturalization and, *1:* 2; *2:* 180; *3:* 360
Necessary and Proper Clause and, *1:* 2–3; *2:* 180–81, 236–37, 246–49; *3:* 360–61
overview of, *2:* 219, 229–37
of president, *1:* 51–54, 90, 114, 137; *2:* 276, 289
prohibition and, *2:* 258–59
property and, *2:* 205
resolutions, *1:* 138; *2:* 319
Second Amendment and, *2:* 243–45
Sixteenth Amendment and, *2:* 253–55
slavery and, *2:* 232
taxation and, *1:* 2; *2:* 180, 231–32, 235–36; *3:* 360
Tenth Amendment and, *2:* 246
treaty power, *1:* 5, 11; *2:* 184, 190; *3:* 363–64, 369
Twenty-seventh Amendment and, *2:* 257–58

veto override, *1:* 5, 11; *2:* 182, 189–90, 265; *3:* 363, 369

writs of habeas corpus and, *1:* 171; *3:* 483

legislative veto

impoundment and, *1:* 141; *2:* 322

overview of, *1:* 138–39; *2:* 318–19

reprogramming and, *1:* 142–43; *2:* 323

letters of marque, *3:* 391–93

Lever Act, *2:* 258

Lewinsky, Monica, *1:* 79, 154; *2:* 333

liberty. *See also* civil liberties

in American Declaration of Independence, *3:* 430

bills of attainder and, *2:* 205

class and, *2:* 210–11

in Constitution, *3:* 430

in Due Process Clause, *3:* 422, 427, 430

ex post facto laws and, *2:* 205

legislative branch and, *2:* 203–6

property as, *2:* 230

representation and, *2:* 225–26

slavery and, *2:* 205–6

writs of habeas corpus and, *2:* 205

Library of Congress, *2:* 305

Lieberman, Joseph, *2:* 286

life, *2:* 205; *3:* 422, 427, 430

Lincoln, Abraham, *3:* 366 (ill.)

Agriculture, Department of, and, *1:* 95

cabinet of, *3:* 366 (ill.)

executive orders of, *1:* 76

pardons by, *1:* 52–53

vetoes by, *1:* 71

war powers of, *3:* 425

Lincoln Memorial, *2:* 287 (ill.)

line item veto, *1:* 141; *2:* 272, 316–17, 321

lobbying, *2:* 268, 275, 276, 283–88, 292

local courts, *3:* 384

Locke, John, *1:* 26 (ill.)

on executive power, *1:* 49

on property, *2:* 205

on separation of powers, *1:* 25–26; *2:* 202–3, 209

Lomen, Lucille, *3:* 449 (ill.)

Long, Russell B., *2:* 281

Love Fellowship Tabernacle, *2:* 304 (ill.)

Lyons, Lisa, *1:* 116

Machiavelli, Niccolò, *2:* 200, 201 (ill.)

Maddox, Lester, *2:* 253 (ill.)

Madison, James, *1:* 46 (ill.), 162 (ill.), 164 (ill.); *2:* 222 (ill.); *3:* 421 (ill.), 424 (ill.)

on bicameralism, *2:* 312

Bill of Rights and, *1:* 63; *2:* 242–43; *3:* 418, 430

on checks and balances, *2:* 222

on commerce, *2:* 230–31, 232

Constitution and, *2:* 241–43

executive power and, *1:* 19

Federalist and, *2:* 219–20; *3:* 400

on humanity, *2:* 219

on judicial interpretation, *3:* 410

Marbury v. Madison and, *1:* 162–63; *2:* 341–44; *3:* 424–25, 476–77, 497–98

military power and, *1:* 54

on representation, *2:* 224, 228

on seat of government, *2:* 220

on separation of powers, *1:* 43–44

on taxation, *2:* 235

Twenty-seventh Amendment and, *2:* 257

Virginia Plan and, *1:* 47

on war powers, *1:* 148–49; *2:* 329

magistrate judges, *3:* 447–48

Magna Carta, *1:* 23 (ill.), 23–24

majority leader, *2:* 270–71, 279–80, 293, 295

majority party

committees and, *2:* 291

in House of Representatives, *2:* 269–70, 271, 272–73

in Senate, *2:* 280

whips and, *2:* 274

manorial courts, *3:* 384

Mansfield, Mike, *2:* 281

Mapp, Dollree, *3:* 420–22

Mapp v. Ohio, 3: 420–22

Marbury v. Madison, 1: 162 (ill.)

    checks and balances and, *1:* 6–7; *2:* 185, 341–44; *3:* 365, 497–98

    judicial review and, *1:* 161–63; *2:* 341–44; *3:* 424–25, 462, 475–78, 497–98

Marbury, William, *2:* 342–44, 343 (ill.); *3:* 424–25, 497–98

Marine Corps, U.S., *1:* 98

maritime. *See* admiralty

Marshall, John, *2:* 250 (ill.), 341 (ill.)

    as chief justice, *2:* 342; *3:* 497–98

    federal service of, *3:* 442

    Gibbons v. Ogden and, *2:* 250

    Interstate Commerce Clause and, *2:* 250

    Marbury v. Madison and, *1:* 161–63; *2:* 341–44; *3:* 424–25, 475–78, 497–98

    McCulloch v. Maryland and, *2:* 249

Marshall, Thurgood, *2:* 352; *3:* 372 (ill.), 439 (ill.), 463 (ill.), 502 (ill.)

Martinez, Mel, *1:* 8 (ill.)

Marxism, *1:* 152

Mary II, *1:* 24

Maryland, *2:* 248–49

Mason, George, *2:* 220, 239–40

Massachusetts

    legislature in, *2:* 211–12

    ratification and, *2:* 241, 242

    religion in, *2:* 243; *3:* 388–89

    voting rights in, *2:* 228

McAleese, Mary, *1:* 84

McClurg, James, *1:* 46

McCord, James W., Jr., *3:* 488

McCulloch, James W., *2:* 249

McCulloch v. Maryland, 2: 247–49

McFarlane, Robert, *1:* 153

McGovern, George, *3:* 488

McReynolds, James C., *1:* 174

Meese, Edwin, III, *1:* 104

Meir, Golda, *1:* 84

Mercer, John Francis, *1:* 46

Mexican-American War, *1:* 54, 80, 149; *2:* 329

Middle Ages, *3:* 384

military. *See also* declarations of war; war powers

    in American Declaration of Independence, *2:* 234

    under Articles of Confederation, *1:* 32–35, 40; *2:* 215

    civilians and, *1:* 8–9, 78–79; *2:* 186, 234–35; *3:* 366–67

    commerce and, *2:* 232

    Congress and, *2:* 215

    in Constitution, *1:* 2, 54–55; *2:* 180, 232–35, 239; *3:* 360

    Court of Appeals for the Armed Services, *3:* 458

    executive power and, *1:* 54–55

    Federal Convention and, *2:* 232–35, 239

    Federalist on, *2:* 234

    of Great Britain, *2:* 234

    Hamilton, Alexander, on, *2:* 229, 234

    labor strikes and, *1:* 78–79

    legislative branch and, *1:* 2, 54–55; *2:* 180, 239; *3:* 360

    legislative power and, *2:* 232–35

    overview of, *1:* 8–9; *2:* 186; *3:* 366–67

    president and, *1:* 54–55

    quartering soldiers, *1:* 62–63

    separation of powers and, *2:* 234–35

    Shays's Rebellion and, *2:* 232–34

Militia Clause, *1:* 78

Minerals Management Service, *1:* 102

Mineta, Norman, *1:* 8 (ill.)

ministerial acts, *1:* 171–72; *3:* 483

minor parties, *2:* 267, 275

minority leader, *2:* 271–72, 274, 280–81, 293

minority party, *2:* 280–81, 291

Minton, Sherman, *3:* 442

Mitchell, John N., *3:* 488

monarchy

  class and, *2:* 202

  elections and, *1:* 46–47

  Federal Convention and, *1:* 19–20

  French Revolution and, *2:* 256

  in Great Britain, *1:* 22–25, 45–46

  president and, *1:* 19–20

Mondale, Walter, *1:* 84, 95

money

  in Constitution, *1:* 2; *2:* 180; *3:* 360

  legislative power and, *1:* 2; *2:* 180, 232; *3:* 360

  paper, *2:* 233

  presidency and, *1:* 84, 85

Monroe, James, *1:* 98 (ill.); *3:* 397 (ill.), 398

Montesquieu, Charles, *1:* 27 (ill.)

  on democracy, *2:* 206–8

  influence of, *1:* 25

  on legislation, *2:* 203–6

  on republicanism, *2:* 206–8

  on separation of powers, *1:* 27

mootness, *2:* 347; *3:* 503 4

Morris, Gouverneur, *1:* 46

Moscow Treaty on Strategic Offensive Reductions, *1:* 11, 57; *2:* 190; *3:* 369

motions, *3:* 446–47, 449, 459

n

Nabrit, James M., *3:* 502 (ill.)

Nader, Ralph, *1:* 86 (ill.)

National Aeronautics and Space Administration, *1:* 125–27

National Economic Council, *1:* 75, 108

National Energy Policy Development Group, *3:* 476–77

National Guard, U.S., *1:* 98

National Highway System, *1:* 106

National Highway Traffic Safety Administration, *1:* 106

National Institutes of Health, *1:* 100

National Military Establishment, *1:* 50

National Parks Service, *1:* 102

National Prohibition Act of 1919, *2:* 258

National Reserve, U.S., *1:* 98

National Rifle Association, *2:* 268, 269 (ill.)

national security

  executive privilege and, *1:* 77; *3:* 488–89

  legislative oversight and, *1:* 151; *2:* 331

  National Security Council and, *1:* 75, 94, 108–9, 115, 116, 124

  vice president and, *1:* 94

national security advisor, *1:* 108–9

National Security Council

  Central Intelligence Agency in, *1:* 124

  in Executive Office of the President, *1:* 75

  Ford, Gerald, and, *1:* 116

  vice president in, *1:* 94, 115

  work of, *1:* 108–9

National Union of Christian Schools, *1:* 116

Native Americans, *1:* 100, 102; *2:* 232

natural law, *3:* 382, 399

naturalization, *1:* 2; *2:* 180; *3:* 360, 427

navigable waters. *See* admiralty

Navigation Acts, *3:* 386–87

Navy, Department of the, *1:* 31, 98

Nebraska, *2:* 197

Necessary and Proper Clause

  in Constitution, *1:* 2–3; *2:* 180–81; *3:* 360–61

  Hamilton, Alexander, on, *2:* 237, 246–47

  legislative power and, *2:* 246–49

  overview of, *2:* 236–37

New Deal, *1:* 174

New Hampshire, *2:* 241

New Haven, *3:* 388

New Jersey, *2:* 212–15

New York, *2:* 241

Newdow, Michael, *1:* 15–16; *2:* 193–94; *3:* 374

Nicaragua, *1:* 152–53

Nineteenth Amendment, *1:* 70, 71 (ill.), lvi; *2:* 257, 349, lvi; *3:* 505, lvi

Ninth Amendment, *1:* lii; *2:* lii; *3:* 430, lii

Nixon, Richard M., *1:* 170 (ill.); *2:* 278 (ill.), 321 (ill.), 330 (ill.); *3:* 368 (ill.), 489 (ill.)

   appointment power of, *1:* 17; *2:* 195; *3:* 376

   executive privilege of, *1:* 78–79, 176; *3:* 487, 488–89

   Ford, Gerald, and, *1:* 96

   impeachment discussions surrounding, *1:* 52, 91, 96

   impoundment by, *1:* 141; *2:* 320–21

   Office of Management and Budget and, *1:* 72

   pardon of, *1:* 52, 96

   vetoes by, *1:* 80

   as vice president, *2:* 277

   Vietnam War and, *1:* 149; *2:* 329

   War Powers Resolution and, *1:* 80

   Watergate scandal and, *1:* 52, 78–79, 96, 176; *3:* 487

Nixon, Walter L., Jr., *2:* 354; *3:* 510

No Taxation Without Representation Act, *2:* 286

nobility, *2:* 210–11

nominations. *See* appointment power

Noriega, Manuel, *1:* 81 (ill.)

Norman dynasty, *3:* 384

North Carolina, *2:* 241; *3:* 417

North Korea, *1:* 166

North, Oliver, *2:* 298 (ill.)

Norton, Eleanor Holmes, *2:* 286

Norton, Gale, *1:* 8 (ill.)

Notes on the State of Virginia, 3: 388

notice, *3:* 422

Observations on the Government of Pennsylvania, 2: 226–27

Observations upon the Proposed Plan of Federal Government, 3: 398

Occupational Safety and Health Administration, *1:* 73–74, 103

O'Connor, John J., *3:* 486 (ill.)

O'Connor, Sandra Day, *1:* 84; *3:* 372 (ill.), 463 (ill.), 486 (ill.)

Office of Administration, *1:* 75

Office of Chief of Staff. *See* chief of staff

Office of Faith-Based and Community Initiatives, *1:* 75–76

Office of Homeland Security, *1:* 100

Office of Management and Budget, *1:* 72–73, 75. *See also* Bureau of the Budget

   in cabinet, *1:* 107

   creation of, *2:* 299

   director of, *1:* 107, 108

   federal budget and, *1:* 108, 114; *2:* 300

   overview of, *1:* 108

   personnel ceilings and, *1:* 143; *2:* 323

Office of National Drug Control Policy, *1:* 75, 107

Office of Surface Mining Reclamation and Enforcement, *1:* 102

Office of the Attorney General, *1:* 50, 73. *See also* attorney general

Office of the Solicitor General, *1:* 102. *See also* solicitor general

Old Whig, *2:* 237

Olmstead, Gideon, *3:* 391

O'Neill, Paul, *1:* 8 (ill.)

O'Neill, Tip, *1:* 10 (ill.), 140 (ill.); *2:* 288

opening statement, *3:* 457, 459, 460

opinions, *3:* 441–43, 448, 461–62, 466–68

oral argument, *3:* 441, 444, 448, 461, 465

original intent, *3:* 410

original jurisdiction, *3:* 403–4, 417, 424–25

oversight, legislative, *1:* 150–51; *2:* 297, 331

Paige, Roderick, *1:* 8 (ill.)

Paine, Thomas, *1:* 31; *2:* 226

Panama, *1:* 82

pardon power

    checks and balances and, *1:* 176; *3:* 487–90

    examples of, *1:* 52–53, 96, 153

    judicial branch and, *1:* 176; *3:* 487–90

    overview of, *1:* 50–51

Parliament

    American colonies and, *3:* 386–87

    American Declaration of Independence and, *1:* 32–34; *2:* 208

    checks and balances and, *2:* 209–10

    class and, *2:* 208–9

    composition of, *1:* 22; *2:* 208–11

    English Bill of Rights and, *1:* 24–25

    lobbying in, *2:* 284

    representation and, *2:* 210–11

    separation of powers and, *1:* 22

    whips in, *2:* 273

patents, *2:* 232; *3:* 460

Pearl Harbor, *1:* 108

Pelosi, Nancy, *2:* 274 (ill.)

Pennsylvania, *2:* 214; *3:* 388

perjury, *1:* 167, 168; *3:* 479, 480

Permanent Representative to the United Nations, *1:* 105

Perot, H. Ross, *1:* 86

Persian Gulf Wars, *1:* 55

personnel ceilings, *1:* 143; *2:* 323

personnel floors, *1:* 143; *2:* 323

Peterson, David A., *1:* 116

Philippines, *2:* 355; *3:* 510

Pickering, John, *1:* 17–18; *2:* 195–96; *3:* 376

Pierce, Franklin, *1:* 83, 137

Pitts, Lewis, *1:* 123

pleadings, *3:* 384, 445, 459

Plessy v. Ferguson, *2:* 345; *3:* 499–500

pocket vetoes, *1:* 54, 134–35, 136, 138; *2:* 315, 318

political action committees, *2:* 288, 304

political parties. *See also* specific parties

    checks and balances and, *2:* 313

    elections and, *1:* 85–86; *2:* 267

    independents, *2:* 275

    presidency and, *1:* 84, 87

    third parties, *2:* 267, 275

    veto power and, *1:* 138; *2:* 318

    vice president and, *1:* 93–94

political philosophers, *1:* 25–28; *2:* 201–8; *3:* 382. *See also* specific philosophers

political question doctrine, *2:* 347–48; *3:* 504

poll taxes, *2:* 228, 256, 257

Pollock, Charles, *2:* 350

Pollock v. Farmers' Loan and Trust Co., *2:* 346–47, 350–51; *3:* 503

post-trial motions, *3:* 446–47

Potsdam Conference, *1:* 148 (ill.)

Powell, Colin, *1:* 8 (ill.)

Powell, Lewis F., Jr., *2:* 352; *3:* 372 (ill.), 463 (ill.)

praetors, *3:* 383

preamble, *3:* 398–99, 430

president. *See also* executive branch; specific powers

    appropriations power and, *1:* 140–43; *2:* 320–23

    under Articles of Confederation, *1:* 39

    checks and balances and, *1:* 133; *2:* 310–14

    as chief of state, *1:* 90, 113

    compensation of, *1:* 132; *2:* 310

    day in the life of, *1:* 113–14, 116–17

    economy and, *1:* 75, 82–83, 91

    election of, *1:* 13–14, 46–48, 66–69, 83–87, 91; *2:* 191–92, 257, 286; *3:* 371–72

    executive powers of, *1:* 7–11, 48–51, 61, 89–91, 113–14; *2:* 185–89; *3:* 365–69 federal budget and, *1:* 11, 72–73, 114; *2:* 188–89, 299–301, 316; *3:* 368

foreign relations and, *1:* 11, 55–57, 113; *2:* 189; *3:* 369

future of, *1:* 83–87

historic roots of, *1:* 21, 24–25, 28–29, 30–31; *2:* 199

impeachment of, *1:* 5, 11–12, 58–59, 91, 138, 159–60, 172–73; *2:* 184, 190, 318; *3:* 363, 369, 412–13, 473–74, 484–85

impoundment by, *1:* 141; *2:* 320–22

law enforcement by, *1:* 6, 7, 49–50; *2:* 185–86; *3:* 364, 365–66

legislative power of, *1:* 51–54, 90, 114, 137; *2:* 276, 289, 296–97

limits on, *1:* 11–12; *2:* 189–90; *3:* 369–70

monarchy and, *1:* 19–20

money and, *1:* 84, 85

pardon power and, *1:* 50–51

qualifications to be, *1:* 47, 89

recommendation power of, *1:* 9, 11; *2:* 187–89, 289, 319–20; *3:* 367, 368–69

replacement of, *1:* 58, 61, 92–93, 104–5, 115; *2:* 278; *3:* 413

reprogramming by, *1:* 142–43; *2:* 322–23

State of the Union address of, *1:* 9, 51–52, 139–40; *2:* 187–88, 289, 316, 319–20; *3:* 367–68

terms of, *1:* 19, 37, 58, 66, 67–68, 91; *2:* 260

title of, *1:* 47

treaty power of, *1:* 56–57; *2:* 277

veto power of, *1:* 5, 11, 71–72, 133–36; *2:* 182, 189, 296–97, 314–19; *3:* 363, 368–69

vice president and, *1:* 93–95, 104–5

president *pro tempore*, *1:* 115; *2:* 278–79, 280

Principi, Anthony, *1:* 8 (ill.)

Private Securities Litigation Reform Act, *1:* 11; *2:* 190; *3:* 369

Privileges and Immunities Clause, *3:* 427, 430–31

Privy Council, *3:* 386

prize cases, *3:* 391–93, 396

probable cause, *1:* 64, 120, 164; *3:* 419–22, 478–79

Progressive Party, *2:* 275

Prohibition, *2:* 258–59, 259 (ill.)

Prohibition Party, *2:* 275

Project Exile, *2:* 269 (ill.)

property. *See also* class

    Constitution and, *2:* 239

    in Due Process Clause, *3:* 422, 427, 430

    elections and, *2:* 256

    Federal Convention and, *2:* 239

    legislative branch and, *2:* 203–6, 239

    legislative power and, *2:* 205

    as liberty, *2:* 230

    Locke, John, on, *2:* 205

    republicanism and, *2:* 230

    taking of, *3:* 422

    voting rights and, *2:* 202, 228, 229, 233, 256

proportional representation, *2:* 267

prosecution, *1:* 64–65, 121–22, 165–69; *3:* 479–81. *See also* criminal cases; trials

Protection Clause, *1:* 78

protest, *1:* 122–23; *3:* 408–9

Protestants, *3:* 388–89

public ministers, *3:* 403–4, 415, 417

Puerto Rico, *1:* 3–4; *2:* 181–82, 236; *3:* 361

Pullman Palace Car Company, *1:* 78

Pullman Strike of 1894, *1:* 78–79, 79 (ill.)

punishment, capital, *2:* 245–46

punishment, cruel and unusual

    civil liberties and, *1:* 16; *2:* 194; *3:* 375

    legislative power and, *1:* 6; *2:* 185, 245–46; *3:* 364

    Supreme Court on, *3:* 423

Puritans, *3:* 388

Putin, Lyumilla, *3:* 370 (ill.)

Putin, Vladimir, *1:* 11, 57; *2:* 190; *3:* 369, 370 (ill.)

quaestors, *3:* 383

Quakers, *3:* 388

quartering soldiers, *1:* 62–63

Queries and Remarks Respecting Alterations in the Constitution of Pennsylvania, 2: 214

quorum, *1:* 138; *2:* 318

race, *1:* 70; *2:* 267, 302. *See also* African Americans; discrimination

Randolph, Edmund, *1:* 22, 47, 74 (ill.); *2:* 223

Reagan, Nancy, *1:* 119 (ill.)

Reagan, Ronald, *1:* 140 (ill.); *2:* 300 (ill.), 317 (ill.), 353 (ill.)

    appointment power of, *1:* 17; *2:* 195, 352; *3:* 376

    assassination attempt on, *1:* 104–5

    election of, *1:* 84

    impeachment of threatened, *1:* 153

    Iran-Contra scandal and, *1:* 52, 152–53; *2:* 298

    line item veto and, *2:* 316

    recommendation power of, *1:* 139–40; *2:* 320

    State of the Union address of, *1:* 10 (ill.); *2:* 316

    on Twenty-second Amendment, *1:* 68

reception provisions, *3:* 387–90

recommendation power

    legislation and, *2:* 289

    legislative power and, *1:* 51–52; *2:* 319–20

    overview of, *1:* 9–11, 139–40; *2:* 187–89; *3:* 367–69

Reconstruction

    Supreme Court and, *3:* 404–5, 425–26

    veto override and, *1:* 138; *2:* 318

    writs of habeas corpus and, *2:* 355; *3:* 510

Records of the Federal Convention, 1: 22, 29

recusal, *3:* 476–77

redistricting, *1:* 3; *2:* 181, 302; *3:* 361

regulatory commissions. *See* independent regulatory commissions

regulatory power, *1:* 7, 125; *2:* 186; *3:* 365–66. *See also* independent regulatory commissions

Rehnquist, William, *1:* 154 (ill.); *3:* 372 (ill.), 440, 441 (ill.), 463 (ill.)

Reid, Harry, *2:* 294 (ill.)

religion, *1:* 75–76, 84. *See also* freedom of religion

Religious Tolerance, 3: 389

removal power. *See also* impeachment

    from executive branch, *1:* 146; *2:* 325–27

    from judicial branch, *3:* 413, 437, 440, 444, 445, 447, 458, 462

    from legislative branch, *1:* 154–55; *2:* 333

Reno, Janet, *3:* 451 (ill.)

reporter of decisions, *3:* 451–52

representation. *See also* republicanism

    Constitution and, *2:* 223–26

    democracy and, *2:* 255–57

    elections and, *2:* 226–29

    Federal Convention and, *2:* 223–26

    Federalist on, *2:* 228

    Hamilton, Alexander, on, *2:* 224

    legislative branch and, *2:* 223–26

    liberty and, *2:* 225–26

    Madison, James, on, *2:* 224, 228

    Montesquieu, Charles, on, *2:* 206–8

    in Parliament, *2:* 210–11

    proportional, *2:* 267

    Sherman, Roger, on, *2:* 224

    slavery and, *2:* 225–26

    voting rights and, *2:* 226–29

    Washington, D.C., and, *2:* 286–87

representatives

    campaigning by, *2:* 268, 303–5

    casework of, *2:* 267, 275, 301–3

    class and, *2:* 202

    committee work of, *2:* 266–67, 270, 275

    compensation of, *2:* 257–58

criminal liability of, *1:* 131–32; *2:* 309–10, 337; *3:* 493

election of, *2:* 226–28, 267–68, 303–5, 312, 337; *3:* 493

impeachment of, *1:* 154–55; *2:* 333

legislation and, *2:* 266

lobbying and, *2:* 268, 275

qualifications to be, *2:* 228, 265–66

staff for, *2:* 275–76

terms of, *2:* 228, 259–61, 303

votes of, *2:* 265, 271

whips for, *2:* 273–74

work of, *2:* 265–76

reprieves. *See* pardon power

reprogramming, *1:* 142–43; *2:* 322–23

Republican Conference (House), *2:* 269, 271, 273, 274–75

Republican Conference (Senate), *2:* 281

Republican Party

  checks and balances and, *2:* 313

  Contract with America and, *2:* 261

  elections and, *2:* 267

  presidency and, *1:* 84, 85–86

  Republican Revolution of 1994 and, *2:* 272

  Twenty-second Amendment and, *1:* 67–68

  Watergate scandal and, *1:* 78–79, 91, 96

Republican Revolution of 1994, *2:* 272–73

republicanism

  Guarantee Clause and, *1:* 22

  property and, *2:* 230

  representation and, *2:* 206–8

  in Roman Republic, *1:* 20; *2:* 199; *3:* 382

requisitions, *2:* 235. *See also* taxation

resolutions, *1:* 138; *2:* 319

restraint of trade, *2:* 344–45; *3:* 499

return vetoes

  number of, *1:* 136, 138; *2:* 318

  override of, *1:* 138; *2:* 296–97, 318

  overview of, *1:* 53–54, 134; *2:* 314–15

Revolutionary War. *See* American Revolutionary War

Rhode Island, *2:* 197, 241; *3:* 417

Rice, Condoleezza, *1:* 85

Ridge, Tom, *1:* 101 (ill.)

right to bear arms, *1:* 6; *2:* 185, 243–45, 268; *3:* 364

ripeness, *2:* 347; *3:* 503–4

Robertson v. Baldwin, 3: 466–67

Robinson, Mary, *1:* 84

Rockefeller, Nelson, *1:* 95, 116

Roe v. Wade, 1: 16–17; *2:* 195; *3:* 375

Rolleston, Morton, *2:* 252 (ill.)

Roman codes, *3:* 382–83

Roman Empire, *3:* 382, 383. *See also* Roman Republic

Roman Forum, *3:* 382–83

Roman Republic. *See also* Roman Empire

  assemblies in, *1:* 20–21; *2:* 199, 200

  checks and balances in, *1:* 21–22

  codes of law in, *3:* 382–83

  consuls in, *1:* 20–21; *2:* 199

  democracy in, *2:* 206

  executive power in, *1:* 21–22

  formulary system in, *3:* 384

  judiciary in, *3:* 382–84

  legislature in, *2:* 199–200

  republicanism and, *2:* 199

  Senate in, *2:* 199–200

  separation of powers in, *2:* 199–200

Roosevelt, Franklin D., *1:* 70 (ill.), 83 (ill.), 94 (ill.), 175 (ill.); *2:* 188 (ill.)

  Bureau of the Budget and, *1:* 72

  court-packing plan of, *1:* 174–75

  death of, *1:* 115–18

  executive agreements and, *1:* 147; *2:* 328

  Executive Office of the President and, *1:* 74, 107

  New Deal of, *1:* 82, 174

  prohibition and, *2:* 258

  terms of, *1:* 58, 67, 91

  vetoes by, *1:* 72, 136, 137; *2:* 315

  vice president of, *1:* 93

Roosevelt, Theodore, *1:* 76

Ross, George, *3:* 391

Rother, John, *2:* 285 (ill.)

royal courts, *3:* 384

Ruckelshaus, William D., *1:* 170 (ill.)

Rumsfeld, Donald, *1:* 8 (ill.)

Rush, Benjamin, *2:* 226–27, 227 (ill.)

St. Clair, Arthur, *1:* 77

salaries. *See* compensation

Sanders, Bernard, *2:* 275

Sandinista National Liberation Front, *1:* 152

Sanford, John F. A., *3:* 500

Sawyer, Charles, *1:* 166

Scalia, Antonin, *3:* 476–77, 477 (ill.)

Schiavo, Michael, *3:* 381

Schiavo, Terri, *3:* 381

Schindler, Mary, *3:* 381

Schindler, Robert, *3:* 381

Schlesinger, James R., *1:* 116

Scott, Dred, *3:* 500, 501 (ill.)

Scott v. Sandford, 3: 500

Scowcroft, Brent, *1:* 116

search and seizure

    checks and balances and, *1:* 163–65; *3:* 478–79

    civil liberties and, *1:* 16; *2:* 194; *3:* 374–75

    exclusionary rule and, *3:* 457

    executive power and, *3:* 419–22

    by Federal Bureau of Investigation, *1:* 120

    Fourth Amendment and, *1:* 63–64; *3:* 419–22

    law enforcement and, *3:* 419–22

    probable cause and, *3:* 419–22

search warrants, *1:* 64, 120, 163–64; *3:* 419–22, 478–79. *See also* search and seizure

Second Amendment, *1:* 6, li; *2:* 185, 243–45, li; *3:* 364, li

Secret Service, *1:* 122–23

Sedition Act of 1798, *2:* 244

seizure. *See* search and seizure

select committees, *2:* 298–99

self-incrimination, privilege against, *1:* 65, 168; *3:* 422, 480

Senate. *See also* Congress; legislative branch; legislative power; senators

    calendars of, *2:* 293

    campaigning for, *2:* 276

    casework in, *2:* 276, 301–3

    checks and balances and, *2:* 312–13

    class and, *2:* 202, 210–11, 228–29, 312–13

    cloture rule in, *2:* 294

    committees of, *2:* 270, 276, 277, 281, 286, 290–93, 297–99, 299–301

    composition of, *1:* 3; *2:* 181, 276–81; *3:* 361

    in Constitution, *1:* 1, 3–5; *2:* 179, 181–85, 223–24, 276; *3:* 359, 361–64

    debate in, *2:* 276, 278, 279, 280, 281, 293–95, 337; *3:* 493

    Democratic Conference in, *2:* 281

    election to, *1:* 131; *2:* 202, 223–24, 228–29, 255–57, 276–77, 303–5, 309, 312–13, 337; *3:* 493

    electoral system and, *1:* 48, 68–69

    executive privilege and, *1:* 78–79

    filibuster in, *1:* 145; *2:* 293–94, 325

    floor procedure in, *2:* 293–95

    foreign relations and, *2:* 280

    historic roots of, *1:* 21–22; *2:* 210–11

    impeachment trials by, *1:* 5, 58–59, 91, 151–55, 172–73; *2:* 184, 332–33, 354; *3:* 363, 437–38, 484–85, 509–10, 511

    legislation and, *2:* 276, 289

    lobbying and, *2:* 276, 283–88

    majority leader of, *2:* 279–80, 293, 295

    majority party in, *2:* 280, 291

    minority leader of, *2:* 280–81, 293

    minority party in, *2:* 280–81, 291

    powers exclusive to, *1:* 5, 11; *2:* 184, 190, 277; *3:* 363–64, 369 powers shared with House of Representatives, *1:* 4–5; *2:* 181–82; *3:* 361–63

president of, *1:* 58, 61, 92, 115, 133–34, 152–53, 172; *2:* 277–78, 280, 295, 314, 332, 352; *3:* 413, 484–85

president *pro tempore* of, *1:* 115; *2:* 278–79

qualifications to serve in, *2:* 229, 276, 337; *3:* 493

removal from, *1:* 154–55; *2:* 333

Republican Conference in, *2:* 281

rules of, *1:* 131, 155; *2:* 309, 333, 337; *3:* 493

staff for, *2:* 281, 301–3

terms in, *2:* 259–61, 303

treaty power of, *1:* 5, 11, 57; *2:* 184, 190, 277; *3:* 363–64, 369

unanimous consent in, *2:* 280, 293

vice president in, *1:* 58, 61, 92, 115, 133–34, 152–53, 172; *2:* 277–78, 280, 295, 314, 332, 352; *3:* 413, 484–85

voting in, *1:* 133–34; *2:* 265, 314

whips in, *2:* 281

work of, *2:* 276–81

Senate Appropriations Committee, *2:* 286, 301

Senate Finance Committee, *2:* 301

Senate Foreign Relations Committee, *1:* 146; *2:* 277, 327

Senate Governmental Affairs Committee, *2:* 286

Senate Judiciary Committee, *1:* 144–45; *2:* 277, 325, 352; *3:* 437

Senate, Roman, *1:* 21; *2:* 199–200

senatorial courtesy, *1:* 146; *2:* 325

senators

campaigning by, *2:* 276–77, 303–5

casework of, *2:* 276, 301–3

class and, *2:* 202

committee work of, *2:* 277

compensation of, *2:* 257–58

criminal liability of, *1:* 131–32; *2:* 309–10, 337; *3:* 493

debate by, *2:* 276

election of, *2:* 228–29, 276, 303–5, 312–13, 337; *3:* 493

impeachment of, *1:* 154–55; *2:* 333

legislation and, *2:* 276

lobbying and, *2:* 276

qualifications to be, *2:* 229, 276

terms of, *2:* 229, 259–61, 303

votes of, *2:* 265

work of, *2:* 276–81

sentencing, *3:* 447, 458, 459

separation of powers

Adams, John, on, *2:* 220–21

Cheney, Dick, and, *3:* 476–77

class and, *2:* 201–2; *3:* 400–402

in Constitution, *1:* 1, 131–32; *2:* 179, 219–22, 309–10, 337–38; *3:* 359, 415, 493–94

declarations of war and, *2:* 234–35

dual service and, *3:* 442

executive branch and, *1:* 131–32, 159–60; *2:* 199–200, 203, 209, 309–10; *3:* 397–400, 473–74, 488–89

executive privilege and, *3:* 476–77, 488–89

Federal Convention and, *1:* 41–45; *2:* 219–22; *3:* 397–402

Founding Fathers and, *3:* 397–402

in Great Britain, *1:* 22–23

Hamilton, Alexander, on, *3:* 400–402

Jefferson, Thomas, on, *1:* 44–45

judicial branch and, *1:* 159–60; *2:* 337–38; *3:* 397–402, 413, 473–74, 488–89, 493–94

legislation and, *1:* 26, 28; *2:* 209; *3:* 400–402

legislative branch and, *1:* 131–32; *2:* 199–200, 202–3, 209, 219–22, 309–10, 337–38; *3:* 397–400, 400–402, 493–94

Locke, John, on, *1:* 26; *2:* 202–3, 209

Madison, James, on, *1:* 43–44; *2:* 219–20

military and, *2:* 234–35

Montesquieu, Charles, on, *1:* 27

Parliament and, *2:* 209

political question doctrine and, *2:* 347–48; *3:* 504

in Roman Republic, *2:* 199–200

Scalia, Antonin, and, *3:* 476–77

tyranny and, *2:* 337; *3:* 493

veto power and, *2:* 209

war powers and, *1:* 22, 54–55, 80–82

Washington, George, on, *2:* 221–22

September 11, 2001, terrorist attacks

Department of Homeland Security and, *1:* 144; *2:* 324–25

Office of Homeland Security and, *1:* 100

presidential message after, *1:* 10; *2:* 188, 189 (ill.); *3:* 368

select committees after, *2:* 298–99

Seventeenth Amendment, *1:* lv; *2:* 255–57, 312–13, lv; *3:* lv

Seventh Amendment, *1:* lii; *2:* lii; *3:* 422–23, lii

Seward, William H., *1:* 19

Shays, Daniel, *1:* 33–34, 40; *2:* 232–34, 233 (ill.)

Shays's Rebellion, *1:* 33–35, 40, 41; *2:* 232–34, 233 (ill.)

Sherman Antitrust Act, *2:* 344–45; *3:* 499

Sherman, Roger, *2:* 224, 225 (ill.)

shoestring district, *2:* 302

Shuster, William, *2:* 267

Siegal, Dorothy, *3:* 452 (ill.)

Sierra Club, *3:* 476–77

Sirica, John, *3:* 488

Sixteenth Amendment, *1:* lv; *2:* lv; *3:* lv

overview of, *2:* 253–55

ratification of, *2:* 347, 348–49, 350–51; *3:* 503, 504–5

Sixth Amendment, *1:* li–lii; *2:* li–lii; *3:* li–lii

checks and balances and, *1:* 168–69; *3:* 481

civil liberties and, *1:* 16; *2:* 194; *3:* 375

criminal cases and, *1:* 64–66, 168–69; *3:* 422, 481

judicial power and, *3:* 422

jury trials and, *2:* 355; *3:* 512

Sketches of the Principles of Government, 3: 397–400

slavery

in Constitution, *2:* 205–6, 225–26, 232; *3:* 430

Federal Convention and, *2:* 218–19, 225–26

House of Representatives and, *2:* 226

legislative power and, *2:* 232

representation and, *2:* 225–26

taxation and, *2:* 226

Thirteenth Amendment ends, *2:* 345; *3:* 426–27, 430, 499, 500

Sloop Active, 3: 391

Smith, Adam, *2:* 234–35

Socialist Party, *2:* 275

soldiers, quartering, *1:* 62–63

solicitor general, *1:* 102, 120; *3:* 450

South Carolina, *2:* 228

South Korea, *1:* 166

space exploration, *1:* 125–27

Spanish-American War

declaration of war for, *1:* 54, 80, 149; *2:* 329

writs of habeas corpus and, *2:* 355; *3:* 510

Speaker of the House

committees and, *2:* 295

debate and, *2:* 293

Gingrich, Newt, as, *2:* 272

House majority leader and, *2:* 270–71

legislation and, *2:* 296

overview of, *2:* 269–70

Senate majority leader compared with, *2:* 280

special interest groups, *2:* 283–85, 288, 292, 313

speech. *See* freedom of speech

Speech and Debate Clause, *1:* 131–32; *2:* 309–10, 337; *3:* 493

spending power. *See* appropriations power

Spirit of Laws, 1: 27; *2:* 203–5

spying, *1:* 124

Stalin, Joseph, *1:* 148 (ill.)

standing committees, *2:* 266–67, 290, 291, 297, 299–301

state conventions, *2:* 236, 241–42, 258, 348; *3:* 504

State, Department of

creation of, *1:* 50, 73, 104

foreign relations and, *1:* 56

historic roots of, *1:* 31

overview of, *1:* 104–6

State of the Union address, *2:* 188 (ill.), 313 (ill.); *3:* 368 (ill.)

legislation and, *2:* 289

line item veto and, *2:* 316

overview of, *1:* 9–10, 51–52, 139–40; *2:* 187–88, 319–20; *3:* 367–68

state, secretary of, *1:* 104–6, 108–9

states. *See also* colonies, American

admission of, *1:* 3–4; *2:* 181–82, 236; *3:* 361

under Articles of Confederation, *2:* 217, 235

Bank of the United States and, *2:* 247–49

bicameralism and, *2:* 212–15

Bill of Rights and, *3:* 430

cases concerning, *1:* 14, 15; *2:* 192, 193, 346; *3:* 373, 403–4, 415, 417, 423–24, 501

Constitution and, *2:* 240–42

electoral system and, *1:* 47–48, 66

Eleventh Amendment and, *3:* 423–24

at Federal Convention, *1:* 3, 4; *2:* 181, 182, 197–98, 223–24; *3:* 361, 362

freedom of religion in, *3:* 389

governments of, *1:* 30–31

judicial review and, *3:* 418, 424

judicial systems of, *1:* 13–14; *2:* 191–92; *3:* 371–72, 387–90, 417, 424

line item veto in, *2:* 316

term limits and, *2:* 261

voting rights in, *1:* 70–71; *2:* 256–57

statutory law. *See* legislation

steel seizure case, *1:* 166–67

stenographers, *3:* 450

stenotype, *3:* 450

Stevens, John Paul, *3:* 372 (ill.), 463 (ill.)

Stewart, Potter, *3:* 439 (ill.)

Stimson, Henry L., *1:* 118, 118 (ill.)

Stockman, David, *2:* 300 (ill.)

Story, Joseph, *3:* 398–99, 399 (ill.)

subpoena power, *1:* 65–66, 168–69; *3:* 422, 481, 488–89

Substance Abuse and Mental Health Services Administration, *1:* 100

suffrage, *1:* 70, 71 (ill.); *2:* 256. *See also* voting rights

summary judgment, *3:* 446

Sumners, Hatton W., *1:* 137, 137 (ill.)

superior common law courts, *3:* 384–85

Supremacy Clause, *2:* 340; *3:* 411, 412, 424, 495–96

Supreme Court, *1:* 12 (ill.); *3:* 439 (ill.), 463 (ill.), 465 (ill.). *See also* justices, Supreme Court

appeals to, *3:* 380–81, 407–8, 415, 417–18, 429, 432–33, 435, 440–43, 462–68

appointment to, *1:* 144; *2:* 324, 325, 349, 352–53; *3:* 413, 425, 433, 437, 439, 506

chief justice in, *3:* 417, 462

civil liberties and, *2:* 251–53

clerk of the court of, *3:* 449–50

Congress and, *3:* 425–26

in Constitution, *1:* 12; *2:* 190–91; *3:* 370, 402, 415, 417–18, 462

decision-making by, *1:* 16; *2:* 194, 352; *3:* 375, 439–43, 448, 465–68, 507

election of 2000 and, *3:* 464–65

on equal protection, *2:* 345; *3:* 499–500

Federalist Party and, *3:* 425

First Amendment and, *2:* 243, 244

on gerrymandering, *2:* 302

historic roots of, *3:* 386, 387, 392–93

income tax and, *2:* 254–55, 346–47; *3:* 503

Interstate Commerce Clause and, *2:* 250–51, 251–53

on judicial review, *2:* 342–44; *3:* 498

jurisdiction of, *1:* 15; *2:* 193, 342–44; *3:* 373, 403–5, 424–25, 497–98

law clerks at, *3:* 448

line item veto and, *2:* 316

Necessary and Proper Clause and, *2:* 249

opinions of, *3:* 448, 451–52, 466–68

oral argument in, *3:* 465

overview of, *3:* 380–81

preamble to Constitution and, *3:* 399

on protest, *3:* 408–9

Reconstruction and, *3:* 425–26

on removal power, *1:* 146; *2:* 325–26

reporter of decisions in, *3:* 451–52

Roosevelt, Franklin D., and, *1:* 174–75

Schiavo case and, *3:* 381

on search and seizure, *3:* 420–22

size of, *1:* 16, 174–75; *2:* 194, 351–52; *3:* 375, 417, 425–26, 436–37, 462, 506–7

solicitor general and, *1:* 102

state cases reviewed by, *3:* 418

on state power, *3:* 423

term limits and, *2:* 261

treaties and, *1:* 147; *2:* 327

trials in, *1:* 15; *2:* 193; *3:* 373, 415, 417, 424–25

veto power and, *1:* 135; *2:* 315

work of, *3:* 462–68

writs of certiorari in, *1:* 14; *2:* 192; *3:* 372–73

surveillance, *1:* 120

Sutherland, George, *1:* 174

symbolic speech, *3:* 408–9

Taft, William Howard, *2:* 255; *3:* 442, 442 (ill.)

Taft-Hartley Act, *1:* 166

Takings Clause, *3:* 422

Taney, Roger B., *3:* 500

Tax Court, U.S., *3:* 432, 458

taxation

    under Articles of Confederation, *1:* 31–32, 39–40; *2:* 215, 217, 235; *3:* 395

    commerce and, *2:* 231–32, 249

    Congress and, *2:* 215

    in Constitution, *1:* 2; *2:* 180, 231–32, 235–36, 253–55; *3:* 360

    Federal Convention and, *2:* 231–32, 235–36

    Hamilton, Alexander, on, *2:* 231–32

    on imports, *2:* 253–54

    income tax, *2:* 253–55, 346–47, 350–51; *3:* 503

    Internal Revenue Service and, *1:* 107, 119

    Joint Committee on Taxation and, *2:* 299

    legislative power and, *2:* 231–32, 235–36

    Madison, James, on, *2:* 235

    Sixteenth Amendment and, *2:* 253–55, 347; *3:* 503

    slavery and, *2:* 226

    Tax Court and, *3:* 458

    Washington, D.C., and, *2:* 286

Tenth Amendment, *1:* lii; *2:* 246, lii; *3:* lii

term limits, *2:* 259–61, 272; *3:* 433

territories, *1:* 4; *2:* 182, 236; *3:* 361–63

test cases, *2:* 346–47; *3:* 503

That Politics May Be Reduced to a Science, *2:* 206

Thatcher, Margaret, *1:* 84

Third Amendment, *1:* 62–63, li; *2:* li; *3:* li

third parties, *2:* 267, 275

Thirteenth Amendment, *1:* liii; *2:* liii; *3:* liii

    enforcement of, *3:* 427–28

    as labor amendment, *3:* 466–67

    ratification of, *3:* 426–27, 430

    slavery ended by, *2:* 345; *3:* 499, 500

Thomas, Clarence, *2:* 352–53

Thompson, Jacob, *2:* 187 (ill.)

Thompson, Tommy, *1:* 8 (ill.)

three-fifths compromise, *2:* 226

Thurmond, J. Strom, *1:* 154 (ill.); *2:* 260, 260 (ill.), 294

Tinker, John P., *3:* 408–9

Tinker, Mary Beth, *3:* 408–9

Tinker v. Des Moines Independent Community School District, *3:* 408–9

Tisdale, Elkanah, *2:* 302

torts, *3:* 468

Toucey, Isaac, *2:* 187 (ill.)

trade. *See* commerce

Train, Russell, *1:* 170 (ill.)

Transportation, Department of, *1:* 98, 106

transportation, secretary of, *1:* 106

treason

bills of attainder and, *2:* 205

definition of, *3:* 406

as impeachable offense, *1:* 5, 91, 153; *2:* 182–84, 333, 353–54; *3:* 363, 437, 508

as infamous crime, *1:* 65, 166–67; *3:* 480

Speech and Debate Clause and, *1:* 131–32; *2:* 309–10, 337; *3:* 493

Treasury, Department of the

Bureau of the Budget and, *1:* 72

creation of, *1:* 50, 73, 104

head of, *1:* 106–7; *2:* 229, 247

historic roots of, *1:* 31

work of, *1:* 119; *2:* 229, 247

treasury, secretary of the, *1:* 106–7, 108–9; *2:* 247

treaties. *See also* foreign relations

Antiballistic Missile Treaty, *1:* 57

cancellation of, *1:* 57, 147; *2:* 327

cases concerning, *2:* 346; *3:* 402, 415, 418, 501

checks and balances and, *1:* 11, 146–47; *2:* 190, 327–28; *3:* 369

executive agreements, *1:* 147; *2:* 328

House of Representatives and, *1:* 147; *2:* 327

Moscow Treaty on Strategic Offensive Reductions, *1:* 11, 57; *2:* 190; *3:* 369

president and, *1:* 56–57; *2:* 277

Senate approval of, *1:* 5, 11, 57; *2:* 184, 190, 277; *3:* 363–64, 369

Supreme Court and, *1:* 147; *2:* 327

Treaty of Versailles, *1:* 147; *2:* 327, 328 (ill.)

trials

in American colonies, *3:* 386

bench, *3:* 379, 409, 446–47, 459, 460

in circuit courts, *3:* 417, 428–29

civil cases, *3:* 445–47, 459–60

closing argument, *3:* 457, 459, 460

Constitution on, *3:* 406–7

criminal cases, *3:* 445–47, 456–59

discovery for, *3:* 445–46, 447, 459

evidence at, *3:* 446, 457, 460

in federal district courts, *3:* 379, 416–17, 428–29, 432, 435, 445–47, 455–60

Fifth Amendment and, *1:* 64–65

First Amendment and, *3:* 422

friendly suits, *2:* 346–47; *3:* 503

judgment in, *3:* 445–46, 447

judicial interpretation in, *1:* 15; *2:* 193; *3:* 373–74, 409–11

jury, *2:* 205, 355; *3:* 379, 406, 409, 422, 446–47, 457–59, 460, 510–12

jury selection for, *3:* 457, 460

location of, *3:* 406, 422

magistrate judges and, *3:* 447–48

motions in, *3:* 449, 459

opening statement, *3:* 457, 459, 460

original jurisdiction and, *3:* 403–4

overview of, *1:* 13; *2:* 191; *3:* 371, 406–7, 445–47

phases of, *3:* 445–47

pleadings for, *3:* 384, 445, 459

post-trial motions, *3:* 447

pretrial motions, *3:* 447

public, *1:* 65, 168–69; *2:* 355; *3:* 422, 481, 512

sentencing, *3:* 459

Seventh Amendment and, *3:* 422–23

Sixth Amendment and, *1:* 16, 64–66, 168–69; *2:* 194; *3:* 375, 422, 481

speedy, *1:* 65, 168–69; *2:* 355; *3:* 422, 481, 512

summary judgment before, *3:* 446

in Supreme Court, *1:* 15; *2:* 193; *3:* 373, 415, 417, 424–25

test cases, *2:* 346–47; *3:* 503

verdicts in, *3:* 447, 458–59

tribal assembly, *1:* 21; *2:* 199, 200

Truman, Harry S., *1:* 118 (ill.), 148 (ill.); *3:* 367 (ill.)

Defense, Department of, and, *1:* 50

executive agreements of, *1:* 147; *2:* 328

State of the Union address of, *1:* 9; *2:* 187; *3:* 367

steel seizure case and, *1:* 166–67

as vice president, *1:* 115–18

Trumbull, John, *3:* 431 (ill.)

Twelfth Amendment, *1:* 48, 66–67, 69, 92, lii–liii; *2:* lii–liii; *3:* lii–liii

Twentieth Amendment, *1:* lvi–lvii; *2:* lvi–lvii; *3:* lvi–lvii

Twenty-fifth Amendment, *1:* 93, 96, lviii–lix; *2:* lviii–lix; *3:* lviii–lix

Twenty-first Amendment, *1:* lvii; *2:* 258, lvii; *3:* lvii

Twenty-fourth Amendment, *1:* 70–71, lviii; *2:* 257, lviii; *3:* lviii

Twenty-second Amendment, *1:* 19, 58, 67–68, 91, lvii–lviii; *2:* lvii–lviii; *3:* lvii–lviii

Twenty-seventh Amendment, *1:* lx; *2:* 257–58, lx; *3:* lx

Twenty-sixth Amendment, *1:* 71, lix–lx; *2:* 257, 349, lix–lx; *3:* 505, lix–lx

Twenty-third Amendment, *1:* 68–69, lviii; *2:* 286, lviii; *3:* lviii

Two Treatises of Government, *1:* 26, 49; *2:* 203, 204 (ill.), 205

Tyler, John, *1:* 92, 92 (ill.), 137; *3:* 442, 507 (ill.)

tyranny, *1:* 22–25, 159–60; *2:* 337; *3:* 473, 493

unanimous consent, *2:* 280, 293

unicameralism, *2:* 197, 211–15, 223, 312

Unified Commands, *1:* 98–99

Uniform Code of Military Justice, *3:* 458

United Nations, *1:* 105–6, 147; *2:* 327

United States of America (as litigant), *1:* 14; *2:* 192; *3:* 373, 403, 415, 418

United States Reports, *3:* 451

United States v. Nixon, *1:* 151; *2:* 331; *3:* 488–89

United Steel Workers of America, *1:* 166–67

Uribe, Alvaro, *2:* 294 (ill.)

U.S. attorneys, *1:* 50, 120, 121–22; *3:* 450, 455, 456–57. *See also* attorney general

U.S. Botanic Garden, *2:* 305

U.S. Capitol, *2:* 287 (ill.), 305, 313 (ill.)

U.S. Chamber of Commerce, *1:* 116; *2:* 268

U.S. Department of Agriculture, *1:* 95–98

U.S. Department of Commerce, *1:* 97

U.S. Department of Education, *1:* 99

U.S. Department of Energy, *1:* 99

U.S. Department of Health & Human Services, *1:* 99–100

U.S. Department of Homeland Security, *1:* 100–101

U.S. Department of Housing & Urban Development, *1:* 101–2

U.S. Department of Interior, *1:* 102

U.S. Department of Justice. *See* Justice, Department of

U.S. Department of Labor, *1:* 102–3, 119

U.S. Department of State. *See* State, Department of

U.S. Department of the Treasury. *See* Treasury, Department of the

U.S. Department of Transportation, *1:* 98, 106

U.S. Department of Veterans Affairs, *1:* 107

U.S. Fish and Wildlife Service, *1:* 102

U.S. Geological Survey, *1:* 102

U.S. Term Limits, *2:* 261

U.S. Term Limits v. Thornton, *2:* 261

U.S. trade representative, *1:* 107

Van Devanter, Willis, *1:* 174, 175

Veneman, Ann, *1:* 8 (ill.)

verdicts, *3:* 447, 458–59. *See also* judgment

veterans, *3:* 458

Veterans Affairs, Department of, *1:* 107; *3:* 458

veterans affairs, secretary of, *1:* 107

veto power, *2:* 321 (ill.)

appropriations power and, *1:* 141; *2:* 321

checks and balances and, *1:* 11, 133–39; *2:* 189–90, 222, 314–19; *3:* 369

historic roots of, *1:* 29

legislation and, *1:* 52–54, 72, 114, 133–39; *2:* 314–19

legislative veto, *1:* 138–39, 141, 142–43; *2:* 318–19, 322, 323

line item veto, *1:* 141; *2:* 272, 316–17, 321

override of, *1:* 5, 11, 54, 72, 80, 136–38; *2:* 182, 189–90, 209, 222, 265, 296–97, 316–18; *3:* 363, 369

overview of, *1:* 52–54, 133–36; *2:* 265, 296–97, 314–19

pocket vetoes, *1:* 54, 134–35, 136, 138; *2:* 315, 318

as policy tool, *1:* 71–72, 137

political parties and, *1:* 138; *2:* 318

recommendation power and, *1:* 11; *2:* 189; *3:* 368–69

return vetoes, *1:* 53–54, 134, 136, 138; *2:* 296–97, 314–15, 318

separation of powers and, *2:* 209

Supreme Court and, *1:* 135; *2:* 315

vice president

   advice and consent and, *2:* 352

   in cabinet, *1:* 8, 94, 107, 115; *2:* 186; *3:* 366

   ceremonial duties of, *1:* 118

   day in the life of, *1:* 115–18

   debate by, *2:* 278

   election of, *1:* 58, 66–69, 93–94

   Federal Convention and, *2:* 277

   in foreign relations, *1:* 94, 118

   Founding Fathers and, *2:* 277

   history of, *1:* 21, 93–95; *2:* 277–78

   impeachment trials and, *1:* 152–53, 172; *2:* 332; *3:* 413, 484–85

   legislation and, *1:* 115, 133–34; *2:* 277–78, 295, 296, 314

   in National Security Council, *1:* 108, 115

   office of, *2:* 277

   political parties and, *1:* 93–94

   powers of, *1:* 57–58, 61, 92–95, 115–18

   president and, *1:* 93–95, 104–5

   as president temporarily, *1:* 104–5, 115

   qualifications to be, *1:* 92

   replacement of, *1:* 96

   in Senate, *1:* 58, 61, 92, 115, 133–34, 152–53, 172; *2:* 277–78, 280, 295, 314, 332, 352; *3:* 413, 484–85

   term of, *1:* 37, 58, 66, 92

Vices of the Political System of the United States, 2: 230–31

Vietnam War, *1:* 150 (ill.); *2:* 330 (ill.)

   amnesty after, *1:* 53

   end of, *1:* 116–17

   protest of, *3:* 408–9

   as undeclared, *1:* 55

   War Powers Resolution and, *1:* 149; *2:* 329

Vinson, Frederick M., *1:* 166–67

Virginia, *2:* 241, 243, 244; *3:* 388, 389

Virginia Declaration of Rights, *3:* 389

Virginia Plan, *1:* 47; *2:* 223–24

Volstead Act, *2:* 258

Volstead, Andrew J., *2:* 258

voting rights

   class and, *2:* 226–29, 255–57

   Congress and, *2:* 226–29

   in Constitution, *2:* 226–29

   democracy and, *2:* 226, 255–57

   Federal Convention and, *2:* 226–29

   Fifteenth Amendment and, *2:* 256; *3:* 427

   Fifth Amendment and, *1:* 70

   House of Representatives and, *2:* 208

   Nineteenth Amendment and, *1:* 70; *2:* 257

   property and, *2:* 202, 228, 229, 233, 256

   representation and, *2:* 226–29

   Senate and, *2:* 255–57

   states and, *1:* 70–71; *2:* 256–57

   Twenty-fourth Amendment and, *1:* 70–71; *2:* 257

   Twenty-sixth Amendment and, *1:* 70–71; *2:* 257

   in Washington, D.C., *2:* 286

Walker, Clement, *2:* 209

Walker, Hezekiah, *2:* 304 (ill.)

Wallace, Henry A., *1:* 93, 94 (ill.)

War, Department of, *1:* 31, 50, 73, 97, 104. *See also* Defense, Department of

War of 1812, *1:* 54, 80, 149; *2:* 305, 329

war powers. *See also* commander in chief; military

    appointment power and, *3:* 425

    checks and balances and, *1:* 147–49; *2:* 329–31

    Federal Convention and, *1:* 54–55, 148–49; *2:* 329

    historic roots of, *1:* 21, 22

    separation of powers and, *1:* 22, 54–55, 80–82

    War Powers Resolution and, *1:* 80–82, 149; *2:* 329–31

War Powers Resolution, *1:* 80–82, 149; *2:* 329–31

warrants, search, *1:* 64, 120, 163–64; *3:* 419–22, 478–79. *See also* search and seizure

Warren, Earl, *3:* 439 (ill.)

Warren, James, *2:* 231

Washington, D.C., *2:* 221 (ill.)

    creation of, *2:* 220–21

    government of, *2:* 286–87, 287 (ill.)

    statehood for, *1:* 3–4; *2:* 181–82; *3:* 361

    Twenty-third Amendment and, *1:* 68–69; *2:* 286

Washington, George, *1:* 43 (ill.); *3:* 362 (ill.), 392 (ill.)

    admiralty courts and, *3:* 392

    appropriations power and, *2:* 288–89

    Bank of the United States and, *2:* 247

    cabinet of, *1:* 74 (ill.), 77

    on commerce, *2:* 231

    election of, *1:* 67

    executive departments under, *1:* 31, 104

    executive orders of, *1:* 76

    executive privilege of, *1:* 77

    Federal Convention and, *1:* 42–43

    Necessary and Proper Clause and, *2:* 247

    pardons by, *1:* 52

    on power, *2:* 231

    on separation of powers, *2:* 221–22

    Shays's Rebellion and, *1:* 34–35

    State of the Union address of, *1:* 9; *2:* 187; *3:* 367

    terms of, *1:* 67, 91

    treaties and, *1:* 146; *2:* 327

    vetoes by, *1:* 71

Washington Monument, *2:* 287 (ill.)

Watergate scandal

    executive privilege and, *1:* 78–79, 176; *3:* 487, 488–89

    impeachment threat during, *1:* 91

    pardon power and, *1:* 52, 96

Wayne, James M., *3:* 426

Wealth of Nations, *2:* 234–35

Weinberger, Caspar W., *1:* 119 (ill.), 176 (ill.)

    pardon of, *1:* 153, 176; *3:* 490

    as secretary of health, education, and welfare, *1:* 116

whips, *2:* 273–74, 281

Whiskey Rebellion, *1:* 52

White, Byron R., *3:* 372 (ill.), 439 (ill.), 463 (ill.)

White House, *2:* 221, 277

White House Office, *1:* 75

Whitman, Christine Todd, *1:* 8 (ill.)

Whittemore, James D., *3:* 381

Wickard v. Filburn, *2:* 251

William III, *1:* 24

Wilson, James, *1:* 46

Wilson, Woodrow, *1:* 9 (ill.); *2:* 290 (ill.)

    on Congress, *2:* 290

    on lobbying, *2:* 285

    on the Senate, *2:* 280

    State of the Union address of, *1:* 9; *2:* 187; *3:* 367

Treaty of Versailles and, *1:* 147; *2:* 327

Wilson-Gorman Tariff Act of 1894, *2:* 254

wiretaps, *1:* 120

Wolfson, Louis E., *3:* 511

women, *1:* 70, 84; *2:* 257, 267

World War I

    declarations of war for, *1:* 54–55, 80, 149; *2:* 329

    Treaty of Versailles ending, *1:* 147; *2:* 327

World War II, *1:* 148 (ill.)

    declarations of war for, *1:* 55, 80, 149; *2:* 329

    executive agreements and, *1:* 147; *2:* 328

    National Security Council and, *1:* 108

    writs of habeas corpus and, *2:* 355; *3:* 510

writs of certiorari

    overview of, *3:* 432–33

    petitions for, *1:* 14; *2:* 192; *3:* 372–73, 440, 448, 464

    procedure for, *1:* 14; *2:* 192; *3:* 372–73, 440, 463–64

    votes required for, *1:* 16; *2:* 194; *3:* 375

writs of habeas corpus

    checks and balances and, *1:* 171; *2:* 354–55; *3:* 482–86, 510

    judicial power and, *3:* 409

    legislative power and, *1:* 6; *2:* 184; *3:* 364

    liberty and, *2:* 205

    in *Robertson v. Baldwin, 3:* 466–67

writs of mandamus

    Marbury v. Madison and, *1:* 162–63; *2:* 342–44; *3:* 424–25, 477–78, 497–98

    overview of, *1:* 171–72; *3:* 483

writs of prohibition, *1:* 171–72; *3:* 483

Youngstown Sheet and Tube Co., *1:* 166–67, 167 (ill.)

Zerfas, Herman H., *1:* 116

Zoellick, Robert, *1:* 8 (ill.)

Zylstra, Ival E., *1:* 116